Mobilizing Gay Singapore

In the series *Sexuality Studies,*
edited by Janice Irvine and Regina Kunzel

Also in this series:

Thomas A. Foster, *Sex and the Founding Fathers: The American Quest for a Relatable Past*

Colin R. Johnson, *Just Queer Folks: Gender and Sexuality in Rural America*

Lisa Sigel, *Making Modern Love: Sexual Narratives and Identities in Interwar Britain*

Mobilizing Gay Singapore

Rights and Resistance in an Authoritarian State

Lynette J. Chua

Temple University Press Philadelphia

TEMPLE UNIVERSITY PRESS
Philadelphia, Pennsylvania 19122
www.temple.edu/tempress

Copyright © 2014 by Temple University
All rights reserved
Published 2014

Library of Congress Cataloging-in-Publication Data

Chua, Lynette J., 1977–
 Mobilizing gay Singapore : rights and resistance in an authoritarian state / Lynette J. Chua.
    pages cm. — (Sexuality studies)
 Includes bibliographical references and index.
 ISBN 978-1-4399-1031-3 (cloth : alk. paper) — ISBN 978-1-4399-1033-7 (e-book) 1. Gay rights—Singapore. 2. Gays—Political activity—Singapore. 3. Gay liberation movement—Singapore. I. Title.
 HQ76.8.S55C48 2014
 323.3'264095957—dc23

2013043280

∞ The paper used in this publication meets the requirements of the American National Standard for Information Sciences—Permanence of Paper for Printed Library Materials, ANSI Z39.48-1992

Printed in the United States of America

2 4 6 8 9 7 5 3 1

In loving memory of Catherine L. Brown

Contents

Preface and Acknowledgments	ix
1 Mobilizing Gay Rights under Authoritarianism	1
2 Legal Restrictions, Political Norms, and Being Gay in Singapore	26
3 Timorous Beginnings	45
4 Cyber Organizing	63
5 Transition	79
6 Coming Out	98
7 Mobilizing in the Open	118
8 Pragmatic Resistance, Law, and Social Movements	146
Appendix A: Research Design and Methods	169
Appendix B: Study Respondents: Singapore's Gay Activists	179
Appendix C: Singapore's Gay Movement Organizations and Major Events	186
Notes	187
References	197
Index	211

Preface and Acknowledgments

Living in this country is like drinking bubble tea[1] with a normal straw. You just have to suck extra hard, and finally you get to the pearl! (Stella, gay activist in Singapore)

As this book went to press, gay activists in Singapore waited for the country's highest court to rule on the constitutionality of Section 377A of the Penal Code, the provision that criminalizes sexual conduct between men. The cases of *Tan Eng Hong v. Attorney-General* (2013) and *Lim Meng Suang and Kenneth Chee Mun-Leon v. Attorney-General* (respectively, *Tan Eng Hong* 2013 and *Lim Meng Suang*) mark one of the first attempts to claim gay rights through the judicial branch of the de facto one-party state.[2] But it is by no means the first milestone for Singapore's gay movement. Gay activists' endeavors in Singapore stretch beyond the courtrooms and reach back in time nearly twenty years. The currently pending lawsuits are only one important step in their struggles for justice and equality in a state where law is used to stifle basic civil-political liberties, hamper collective mobilization, and control political dissent. Speaking out in Singapore, especially in the form of collective action, is seen as resistance against the ruling powers, regardless of how that resistance is carried out and what it concerns.

Although law is central to the tactics of Singapore's gay movement, few of its actions have focused on litigation or other forms of public contestation through formal political institutions. In this book, therefore, I provide an expansive view of the movement that examines not only its emergence, development, strategy, and tactics but also the subtle and multiple roles that law and rights play in its social processes. Looking beyond the explicitly political aspects of collective organizing to its social, cultural, communal, and commercial aspects, I encountered a dynamic and tenacious group of people who deftly negotiate the interplay between legal restrictions and constraining political norms by means of "pragmatic resistance"—a strategy that seeks to advance the movement while ensuring that it survives the scrutiny and potential retaliation of authoritarian rulers. Gay activists "push boundaries" at the same time that they "toe the line," adjusting, escalating, or scaling back movement tactics according to changes in formal law and political norms and according to the opportunities that they identify and create from the relationship between law and politics.

Pragmatic resistance is a strategy born out of the creativity and resilience of human agency in the face of adversity. The quotation that opens this Preface and Acknowledgments section vividly captures the spirit of Singapore's gay movement—the realism, humor, and wit of the people who give it life. Stella's refrain is also poignant because she learned it from a veteran activist. Its repetition reflects the endurance of the spirit and wisdom of pragmatic resistance as they are carried forward from one generation of Singapore's activists to the next.

The opportunity to learn and write about this movement and its activists has been an honor and a privilege. Throughout these years, I have been fortunate to receive encouragement, support, and assistance from many people. I owe the deepest gratitude to Kristin Luker, Catherine Albiston, Calvin Morrill, and Kim Voss, who believed in me from the project's earliest conception and roughest drafts. I thank Janet Francendese, the rest of her team at Temple University Press, Janice Irvine, Regina Kunzel, and the anonymous reviewers for giving this project a chance. In addition, I thank Martin Shapiro, Lauren Edelman, David Lieberman, Jonathan Simon, Malcolm Feeley, Sarah Song, Robert Kagan, Marianne Constable, Michael Musheno, and my peers and friends from the years I spent at 2240 Piedmont Avenue, University of California, Berkeley. I am grateful to Simon Chesterman, Tan Cheng Han, Andrew Harding, Prasenjit Duara, Chua Beng Huat, Michael Hor, Stephen Girvin, Victor Ramraj, Kumaralingam Amirthalingam, Joel Lee, Arun Thiruvengadam, Mike Dowdle, Eleanor Wong, and Elaine Ho at the National University of Singapore. I also thank Michael McCann, David Engel, Frank Munger, David Nelken, Mark Sidel, George Chauncey, Anna-

Maria Marshall, Lynn C. Jones, Tom Ginsburg, Amanda Whiting, Tim Hildebrandt, Mark Massoud, Leila Kawar, and Sanjay Ruparelia for taking an interest in my work.

I am indebted to Indulekshimi Rajeswari, Adrian See, and Mohan Gopalan for their excellent organization and compilation of legal and political background information on Singapore (Indulekshimi deserves special mention for putting up with and answering my endless questions via e-mail, instant messaging, and texting) and to Chu Boyang, Carmen Chu, Nicholas Deroose, Koh Xintian, Rachel Leow, Rachel Lin, Sherilyn Teo, Amos Toh, Azimin Saini, Elida Wong, Yeap Laipeng, and Lynette Zheng for their assistance in small but crucial ways that paved the way for smooth and productive fieldwork. As I navigated the bureaucracies of academic institutions, Margo Rodriguez, Rod Watanabe, and Evelyn Wong at Berkeley and the administrative staff in the Faculty of Law at the National University of Singapore patiently rendered invaluable help. I also extend my thanks to my family and friends, especially Catherine, Kim, Ron, and Zahn.

The research for this project was funded in part by the Social Science Research Council and the National Science Foundation's Program in Law and Social Sciences (Award no. SES-0962129). I also received financial support for my work from the National University of Singapore (Start-up Grant WBS No. R-241-000-101-133). In addition, the Fulbright Graduate Study and Research Program, which sponsored the first two years of my doctoral studies at Berkeley, set me on the path to making this book a reality.

Finally, and most importantly, I express my gratitude to my study respondents and informants: Thank you all for offering your time, opening up your hearts, and sharing your stories.

1

Mobilizing Gay Rights under Authoritarianism

> If you're talking about gay men being "attacked" very openly, very visibly, it happened. If you're talking about gay men organizing themselves, it happened. If you're talking about gay men fighting back, it happened. So for all intents and purposes, it was our Stonewall. (Keenan)[1]

May 30, 1993: Beach Road, Singapore

The night for Keenan and his friends started out like any other Sunday night at Rascals, when the disco attracted a regular crowd of gay men. People were dancing, drinking, and enjoying themselves. Suddenly, the music stopped and the lights went up. Out of the corner of his eye, Keenan saw a senior partner at his law firm try to hide himself in the crowd.

"Shut up!" "Police raid." A plainclothes officer in a striped polo T-shirt warned everyone to keep quiet or, he threatened, "I'll knock your heads." He and other officers divided Rascals patrons into those who carried identification documents on them and those who did not. Keenan was carrying his identity card, so he was allowed to leave the club. But his flatmate did not have identification and was detained. Keenan rushed home to fetch his flatmate's card and hurried to the Beach Road police station. There, he found his flatmate huddled together with other detainees taken from Rascals, all made to squat outside the station. Keenan produced his flatmate's identification to the police and had him released. The rest were released in the morning without charges.

Keenan's encounter was common in authoritarian[2] Singapore of the early 1990s. The police frequently raided gay businesses congregated along Beach Road, a popular strip of bars and clubs at the time. What transpired after the raid of May 30, 1993, however, was far from common in the island state and former British colony. Angered by the night's events, Keenan looked into Singapore's legislation. He discovered that the police had no authority to detain a person who did not carry his or her identification card unless they had reasonable belief that the person had committed some wrongdoing, which he did not think was apparent at Rascals. The recent law school graduate decided to write a letter to the police and looked around for signatories. The senior lawyers he approached refused to co-sign the letter. After much effort and persuasion, he finally managed to collect 21 signatures from among Rascals patrons and submitted the letter to the police and the Ministry of Home Affairs, its parent ministry.

The letter cited the relevant statutory provisions that supported Keenan's allegations and went on to say:

> It is particularly disturbing to find Singapore law enforcement officers behaving rudely towards and verbally threatening citizens who have not committed any offences. It would also be in the public interest to clarify the legal powers of police officers (plainclothes) to demand the production of personal particulars in cases where no offences have been committed. (Rascals letter, May 31, 1993)

A month later, the assistant superintendent of the Beach Road police station called Keenan:

> He said, "Look, we've received your letter. What do you want us to do? Basically, what we have done internally was that we have educated our police officers that what they did was not in accordance of [*sic*] the law." They had told [their officers] that they cannot do this in the future. So I said, "Fine. I want your assurance that there will be no more future occurrences." . . . And he gave me that assurance. (Keenan)

A few days later, Keenan received a letter from the Central Police Division Headquarters, signed by its acting commander, explaining that the police had received complaints of overcrowding at Rascals and had suspected some patrons of providing false identification. Then it went on to apologize:

Due to the confusion at the initial stage, our officers had difficulty controlling the large crowd at Rascals. Some of the patrons became unruly and our officers had to raise their voices. We apologise for their lack of tact in dealing with the situation. We will take steps to prevent a recurrence and to caution the officers concerned. (Police reply to Rascals letter, June 29, 1993)

Old timers often hail Rascals as Singapore's Stonewall, crediting the raid for galvanizing a fledging gay movement[3] that was quietly taking shape in the early 1990s in Singapore. Of course, these activists are speaking of Stonewall the myth—that it started everything (D'Emilio 2002)—rather than Stonewall the socially and historically contextualized event. Many of them were mere toddlers and some of them were not even born when the notorious riots happened. The famous New York City incident did not single-handedly launch the movement in the United States that had deep roots in earlier decades (D'Emilio 1998; Armstrong 2002). Nor does their Rascals campaign bear much resemblance to the events that ensued after the police raids in June 1969. In the Stonewall narrative, the name of the famous bar is associated with open confrontation and street riots. In contrast, the absence of open confrontation and the reticence of angry protests on the streets epitomize the Rascals story.

My purpose here is not to debate the differences and similarities between the two incidents but instead to point out that the two events did more than trigger instant and singular reactions to systemic repression. As a result of Stonewall and Rascals, some people decided to organize and mobilize collectively (D'Emilio 2002; Hirshman 2012) and made choices on how to do so.[4] The two incidents are memorable because they represent turning points in gay history. The initial and evolving responses to these events created moments of opportunity that activists seized to advance collective action whose legacy continues unbroken, though sometimes untidy, to this day.

I also want to point out that the collective mobilizations that occurred after these incidents were shaped by the specific historical contexts and sociopolitical conditions that surrounded them. Stonewall occurred at the end of a decade in the United States made up of civil rights protests, black militancy, campus demonstrations, and the rise of the New Left. In Singapore, the Rascals raid occurred at the end of a period of increasing oppression. The ten-year period preceding Rascals started with the ruling party's decision to permit limited space for political debate and dissent—containment—but ended with detentions without trial of young social activists and community organizers accused of plotting a "Marxist conspiracy" against the state.

Because of their different history and sociopolitical context, Keenan and other gay activists in Singapore have developed strategies that suit their environment; the American events may be their inspiration but cannot offer them a blueprint for building a movement. Acting on what they believe best serves their interests, Singapore's activists set an agenda to improve social conditions, to repeal the Penal Code's Section 377A against sexual conduct between men,[5] and to achieve greater legal protection and equality for gays in Singapore. At a more fundamental level, they must also ensure that the movement and its members can *survive* to carry on the struggle, and that means avoiding retaliation from an authoritarian state known to curb basic civil-political liberties that facilitate and protect collective action in the first place.

This is the story that *Mobilizing Gay Singapore: Rights and Resistance in an Authoritarian State* sets out to tell. How did a movement that started out dodging state surveillance and media exposure, in a matter of twenty years, develop into one that holds a 15,000-strong gathering and dares to argue openly for the repeal of Section 377A in Parliament and the courts? This book relies on in-depth interviews with gay activists in Singapore spanning the entire twenty-year period of the movement, observations of movement activities, and analyses of more than two decades of movement documents, government statements, legal documents, and media reports. It tells the story of how a marginalized minority works toward social change in a society where, in contrast to liberal democracies, civil-political rights and democratic processes are limited. The Singaporean state has no tradition of tolerating open confrontation and protest and uses the law to suppress such actions and cultivate cultural reticence. The rule of law prevails in the Singaporean state, but it takes a specific form. At the helm of the state is the People's Action Party (PAP); since independence from the British in 1963, the PAP has used a kind of legal reform to attain economic prosperity, earning Singapore one of the world's top ten Gross Domestic Product per capita and a ranking among the freest economies in the world (Heritage Foundation 2011).[6] However, this same type of rule of law, one of a rule-bound character, is also simultaneously harnessed to quell political differences and engineer social order. The state legitimizes the curtailment of constitutionally guaranteed civil-political liberties, such as speech, assembly, and association, by legislating the restrictions in accordance with existing law; correspondingly, it deploys law to delegitimize dissenting voices through prosecutions and legal sanctions (see also Rajah 2012).

Under such authoritarian conditions, gay activists in Singapore learn to be creative as they find alternative ways to advance their movement while ensuring its survival. Even though they aspire toward legal reform and greater protection of their rights, they often do not deploy strategies and tactics familiar to activists in liberal democracies, especially street demonstrations. The result is a strategy of pragmatic resistance. Strategically and continuously adapted to their circumstances, this is a strategic dance (McCammon et al. 2008) that involves interplay among law[7] and a crucial set of political norms that ostensibly constrain collective mobilization—such as disdain for and rejection of open confrontation, exaltation of "social harmony," desire for legal legitimacy, and above all, efforts to preserve and perpetuate the ruling party's grip on power.

Singapore's gay activists nimbly adjust, escalate, or scale back their tactics as formal law and political norms change and as the relationship between them changes. To survive, activists avoid blatantly breaking the law, directly confronting the state, and being seen as a threat to existing formal structures of power. To advance the movement, they simultaneously push the normative limits, and on the rare occasions when they directly seek legal changes, they appeal to those norms and situate their legal claims in relation to them. Regardless of whether a tactic focuses on community building, directly challenges the state, or responds to movement opponents, all of them contend with the political norms against dissent and collective mobilization. In authoritarian Singapore, to speak out is to mount the first act of resistance, regardless of how it is carried out and what it concerns. That is why the scope of the movement encompasses not only engagement with the state but also the cultural, social, communal, and commercial arenas, all of which have expanded and become more visible and accepted as the movement developed.

With this ground-up, alternative account of collective struggle for gay equality, *Mobilizing Gay Singapore* examines a complex relationship between law and social movements and illuminates the processes of social change outside liberal democracies, especially in societies that are prospering economically but lagging behind in democratic institutions and rights. In particular, the book's central theme of pragmatic resistance advances the study of social movements. It refocuses attention on an interaction-driven and meaning making–centered approach that emphasizes the social and relational nature of human agency (Emirbayer and Mische 1998). As pragmatic resistance shifts along a spectrum of covert-overt forms of action, it shows how activists innovate strategy and tactics to achieve social change under authoritarian conditions. In doing so, it also sheds light on the processes through which activists escalate to grander scales of contention and thus refines social movements' understanding of the relationship between mobilization and repression.

By detailing these mutually constitutive processes of social movements, *Mobilizing Gay Singapore* complicates the meanings of rights and the role of law and advances law and society scholarship at the intersection of social movements and authoritarian contexts. Law matters in ways that extend beyond exercising and claiming rights and mounting legal challenges in the courtroom. Throughout this book, law appears in its formal, or rule-bound, character as restrictions on homosexual conduct and expression and curtailments of civil-political rights. It also assumes cultural forms as a legitimizing source in which obedience to formal law earns cultural legitimacy, whereas disobedience loses it, and as a symbolic resource that inspires and empowers people to believe in their own human worth and dignity.

Consequently, law first matters to the movement as an obvious source of oppression. Legal restrictions prohibit same-sex sexual conduct between men as well as dissent and mobilization. Because oppression does not occur through physical violence, but as discipline (Foucault 1977) and legal regulation or channeling (Earl 2006, 2011), it is less detectable and is in danger of becoming accepted as normal or legitimate. Second, law nevertheless matters as a source and site of contestation. By deploying pragmatic resistance, gay activists mount challenges at and through law. Besides resisting the laws that censor same-sex conduct, they contest the legal restrictions that suppress mobilization. Alternatively, they use law to contend with restrictive political norms against dissent and collective mobilization. By avoiding direct confrontation or threats to existing power structures, activists risk accusations that they acquiesce to law's discipline and control and thus a reification of the existing order. Nonetheless, as this book shows time and time again, gay activists in Singapore are not concerned with challenging law for its sake and do not fret over problems of reification. What they want are equality, justice, and acceptance for gays in Singaporean society. They treat the choices between legality and illegality as merely tactical (Lukács 1920). Therefore, law simply matters to them as a pragmatic concern, not an ideological preoccupation. Ironically, law's power becomes neutered as they reduce legality to being no more than a means to an end and use it scrupulously to seek social change in face of its power and control.

These multiple sites and roles of law reveal the polyvocal and contextual meanings of rights. To gay activists in Singapore, rights are instrumental because they embody the movement's objectives of achieving greater dignity, freedom, and equality. Yet they are circumspect about the efficacy of rights, perceiving them as contradictory to socially constructed political norms that constrain collective mobilization and political dissent. Hence, away from public contention, they quietly draw on the constitutive power of rights to make collective sense of their grievances and motivate supporters and constituents; in open engagement, though informed and motivated by rights, they deploy rights cautiously by leveraging on local political norms to create cultural resonance and legitimacy for their tactics.

What emerges is an unusual politics of gay rights. In contrast to places where rights mobilization is accepted and mainstream, in Singapore, exercising and claiming rights are nonconformist behaviors. Gay activists struggle with the state and their opponents over not only the meanings of equality but also the basic civil-political liberties that enable those challenges, rights that activists in liberal democracies often take for granted in their collective organizing work.

Later in this chapter, I elaborate on the book's central theme of pragmatic resistance and use Rascals as illustration to explain how gay activists in Singapore adapt, deploy, and perpetuate it as a form of strategic adaptation (McCammon et al. 2008). I also show how pragmatic resistance shaped movement development and achieved progress by giving an overview of the key themes that unfold in the chronological analysis in Chapters 3–7. I developed this theoretical approach by relating Singapore's gay movement and its strategy to social movements in other societies, especially gay movements, and law and society studies on the social control of protest, legal mobilization, and the role of rights. Hence, to understand the book's central theme, I first analyze these two bodies of scholarship.

Gay Organizing and Authoritarian Conditions

The development, strategy, and tactics of Singapore's gay movement highlight key themes in social movements literature, as well as areas in which this book makes a new contribution. Analyses of social movements increasingly emphasize interaction among larger sociopolitical conditions and institutions in which movements are embedded, movement organizations and their grassroots, and the subjective meaning making of social movement actors. Among the various approaches, one model known as political process remains dominant. When originally synthesized, the political process accounted for three sets of internal and external factors—political opportunity structures, mobilizing structures or indigenous organizational strength, and cognitive liberation (McAdam 1999)—and examined their interactions. As the model gained dominance, however, the interactive component and the subjective side receded from attention (Buechler 2000; Meyer 2004). Sometimes social actors' interpretation of changes to larger political conditions became conflated with objective treatments of political opportunity shifts (McAdam 1996; Polletta 1999b, 2004). In response to political process, alternative and complementary perspectives arose.[8] Even though these perspectives are numerous and diverse, they all take subjectivity seriously. And, rather than focus on one of the three sets of factors, they emphasize the dynamic relationship among the sociopolitical context at large, movement and movement organizations, and the meaning making of social actors.

Such an approach yields the following implications for understanding the development of gay movements:

First, the waxing and waning and the nature of the strategy and tactics of gay movements often correspond to the liberalization or tightening of sociopolitical conditions. And even though the participation of elites is important, movements are more likely to make progress when they have grassroots support, which often develops in response to sociopolitical changes.

In the United States,[9] the McCarthyism of the 1950s singled out and persecuted gay men as national security threats. The FBI conducted surveillance on gay and lesbian meetings, the police carried out entrapment and bar raids, and the government censored homosexual speech and expression. Against this backdrop, homophile groups such as the Mattachine Society and Daughters of Bilitis were accommodationist, avoided confrontational tactics, and relied on professionals to achieve middle-class respectability for gays. They lacked a mass base and did not focus on building one, choosing to operate away from the public eye (Adam 1995; D'Emilio 1998).[10] By the late 1960s, however, many gays and lesbians had been exposed to the radicalism of the decade and confrontational styles of political action popularized by black militancy, the sexual revolution, and anti-war and student movements (Marotta 1981; Epstein 1999; Valocchi 1999). Would-be gay liberationists seized Stonewall as an opportunity to escalate an existing movement (Hirshman 2012). They harvested the protest culture of the 1960s and an existing New Left constituency as they pursued cultural criticisms and direct action outside of formal political institutions (D'Emilio 1998).

In the politically conservative era of the 1980s, gay activists initially responded to the AIDS crisis with service-oriented organizations. But even with promising signs of treatment, the federal government and medical profession were slow to push efforts forward. As the crisis grew, more and more infected gay men became frustrated and engaged in social action (Wachter 1992). The Supreme Court's 1986 decision to uphold Georgia's anti-sodomy law in *Bowers v. Hardwick* (1986) further sparked nationwide anger and urgency (D. Gould 2009; Bernstein 2002; Chauncey 2004). By

1987, some activists turned to direct action most epitomized by ACT UP (Wachter 1992; Bernstein 2002).

Since the 1980s, the AIDS crisis along with a lesbian baby boom made same-sex couples realize the imperative of securing the benefits of legally recognized relationships. Although the quest for same-sex marriage began as early as the late 1960s–1970s, it did not become a widespread movement goal until people started enduring painful experiences of loss and separation and activists saw encouraging political signals. Marriage seemed to be worth the fight and indeed possible only after the opening up of heterosexual attitudes about homosexuality and marriage, a series of favorable state court decisions, and the Supreme Court's 2003 reversal of *Bowers v. Hardwick* in *Lawrence v. Texas* (Chauncey 2004). These days, as gay activists and the Christian Right shuttle battlegrounds over same-sex marriage among state courts, legislative assemblies, and electoral polls, their uneven developments further highlight the impact of context-specific conditions in which activists mobilize. Movement gains and setbacks have varied across states and local sites, with the Christian Right placing anti-gay referenda on local and state ballots since the late 1980s (see, e.g., Bernstein 2002; Fetner 2008).[11]

The importance of context-specific conditions to a gay movement's development surfaces even more clearly under authoritarian conditions, where gay organizing usually corresponds to the opening up of regimes (Adam, Duyvendak, and Krouwel 1999; Drucker 2000). Gay movements emerged after the fall of South American dictatorships in Argentina (S. Brown 1999), Brazil (Green 2000), and Chile (Mogrovejo 2000). In South Africa, even though gay activists attempted collective organizing during the years of apartheid, the movement took off in parallel to the successful struggle against apartheid oppression (Gevisser 1995; Palmberg 1999; Currier 2012); compared with earlier periods when the movement consisted mainly of the elite white minority, it grew in strength with support from gays in the majority black population (Gevisser 1995). In Russia, with the collapse of the Soviet Union, public spaces for collective organizing became available and gay organizing was one of the mass movements that surged in the first few years that followed (Nemtsev 2008). In Indonesia, after the Suharto regime ended in 1998, activists from a lesbian group drew strength from the democratizing movement and moved from providing support services to a more overt political agenda and direct media engagement (Blackwood 2007).

Second, the emergence, increase, or decrease in the level of gay organizing turns on how activists interpret the sociopolitical conditions that surround them.

Whether "objective" conditions are "political opportunities," that is, openings or closings for activism (Gamson and Meyer 1996), depends on the agency of activists, their organizational resources, and capacities to act (McAdam 1996, 1999). As these vary across individuals and groups (Bernstein 1997, 2003; D'Emilio 2002; Andersen 2006), splits and divisions appear in the American movement. In the early 1970s, after gay liberation, as the United States entered a phase of political conservatism and economic retrenchment, an organized New Right started to emerge while the New Left declined. Although scholars disagree over the exact temporal point, the gay movement generally splintered into various directions after the waning of gay liberation (Valocchi 1999; Seidman 1993; Armstrong 2002). Some activists preferred to pursue gay rights in the form of interest group politics, whereas others, especially lesbian feminists, persisted with radicalism and community building (Vaid 1995; Chauncey 2004).

In an authoritarian environment, the ways in which activists make sense of given conditions and make decisions to act (or not) are crucial to collective organizing as well. Sometimes the situation may seem opportune to an outsider, but activists may perceive it otherwise and choose not to mobilize (Kurzman 1996). The gay movement in South Africa did not take off simply because conditions liberalized with the collapse of apartheid. Rather, activists built on the strength of civil society that emerged and developed among nonwhite communities after the Soweto revolt of 1976 (Palmberg 1999). Even when conditions turn repressive, activists may not necessarily be deterred but may actually escalate their responses (Loveman 1998; Currier 2012) and make use of what may be seen objectively as closings to motivate bolder actions or different tactics (Meyer and Staggenborg 1996; Bernstein 2003). They change their tactics as they make and lose gains (Tilly 1978) and may even innovate if faced with tough constraints (McAdam 1983). Hence, gay activists in Zimbabwe spoke out publicly after state authorities banned their booth from a book fair (Currier 2009). In Poland, despite a repressive right-wing political climate and the mayor's refusal to issue permits, activists chose to push ahead with the Poznan March of Equality in 2005. They saw it as an opportunity to speak out against attacks on democratic freedoms and in favor of minority rights (Gruszczynska 2009).

Third, mobilization strategies that resonate more strongly with a society's emancipation experiences or receive the state's recognition as valid and just are more likely to succeed or to receive widespread support.

In the midst of diverse and untidy developments, certain strategies and tactics tend to outlast others and receive greater support among activists and allies. Usually, these are the ones that generate what social movements scholars call *cultural resonance* (Snow and Benford 1988) because the movement's constituents, supporters, and target audiences are able to relate to and identify with the grievances and claims. Activists draw from "cultural toolkits" (Swidler 1986)—symbols, practices, and ideologies that are common and accepted in their societies—and build their strategies and tactics on the basis of those existing meanings. Hence, in the United States, activists who champion gay rights are able to extend the meaning of civil rights to construct the idea of sexual minorities (Bernstein 1997) who are also entitled to rights (McAdam 1994). For Americans, rights normalize and mainstream an issue (Gamson 1989) and thus bear cultural resonance.[12] While we see radicalism burst into the forefront from time to time, such as gay liberation and ACT UP, the American movement has by and large mainstreamed and sought reformation by seeking access to existing political institutions and focusing on electoral contests, litigation, and lobbying for legal reforms (Vaid 1995), tactics found in a preexisting tactical "repertoire" (Tilly 1978; Werum and Winders 2001). Queer politics and other radical discourses still exist, but do not occupy discursive dominance (Armstrong 2002).

Where conditions are more authoritarian, strategies and tactics also need cultural resonance to prevail. In regimes such as Nicaragua (Thayer 1997), Poland (Graff 2006), and Romania and Czechoslovakia (Long 1999), gay activists formulate their claims on the basis of the prevailing models of emancipation in their societies. In South Africa, as the country transitioned into a post-apartheid era, activists carefully constructed their claims as equality but *not* minority rights. This is because they worried that the latter could become associated with apartheid ideology that gave preferential treatment to minority groups (Hoad 1999; Palmberg 1999).

Further, strategies and tactics are more likely to succeed if the authoritarian state accepts them as valid or legitimate (Adam, Duyvendak, and Krouwel 1999). Thus, in Namibia, where the state is openly hostile to gay rights and organizing, gay activists shun legal tactics to avoid state retaliation (Currier 2009). In China, gay activists and groups also gravitate toward issues that complement government interest and avoid antagonizing the state so that it will continue to tolerate their existence (Spires 2011; Hildebrandt 2013).

However, while most of these studies point out that gay activists in authoritarian states leverage on politically palatable or resonant values, they seldom unpack the interactive processes through which they engage in strategic adaptation. In contrast, I focus on an understudied gay movement[13] and examine from the ground up how its activists interact with an authoritarian state, interpret signals in their broader environment, and decide whether and how to innovate and adjust their tactics. In doing so, I reveal the workings of one key ingredient in their strategy and tactics—law.

Law, Social Control, and Resistance

Singapore's gay movement, like those in the United States and other Western liberal democracies, engages law in an ongoing, constitutive relationship (Barclay, Bernstein, and Marshall 2009). Nevertheless, the ways in which law plays a role in the Singaporean story varies in its empirical nuances and implications. This is because Singapore's gay activists deploy pragmatic resistance, which involves a different relationship between law and social change. In particular, the relationship highlights new ways of thinking about important issues in law and society studies, namely, the meanings of rights and the role of law in relation to social movements.

Contemporary developments in law and society, like those in social movement studies, emphasize subjective meaning making—how social actors experience, understand, and use the law. Such a turn in the scholarship reflects broader shifts in contemporary social theory toward cognition and social construction, which examine how actors draw on cultural schemas to make sense of their social worlds and construct social institutions that shape those worlds (Nielsen 2004; Albiston 2006).[14] With this turn, although law is regarded as helping to shape, influence, and constrain social life and relations, everyday people are also understood to reproduce and reshape the law in their response to it. Hence, scholars try to identify law's power more holistically by examining not only the elite and powerful who effect and implement law from the top down but also the people on whom law is imposed.[15]

Studies on the role of rights in social change are among the law and society studies that reflect these developments. Among them are those that consider the ways in which rights serve as instrumental resources for social movements (see, e.g., Zemans 1983; Rosenberg 2008). Works outside and inside law and society show this to be the case with gay movements. As early as the 1930s, gay activists in American cities brought court challenges against prohibitions on gay bars (Chauncey 1994). From the 1950s onward, activist organizations began to litigate censorship laws, police abuse, antisodomy laws, discrimination, and same-sex marriage (Vaid 1995; Bernstein 2002, 2003; Andersen 2006). Such pursuit raises questions for law and society scholars who doubt the efficacy of rights to bring about social change. Some take what is known as the "myth of rights" perspective and argue that rights are misleading because their articulation and affirmation alone do not produce social change; rights go unrealized, mired in policy making and implementation (Scheingold 2004; Rosenberg 2008). Others find rights to be elitist (Hull 2001; Nielsen 2004) or disempowering because the aggrieved may lack resources to fight legal battles or perceive the process as a type of revictimization (Bumiller 1988), whereas scholars who study international human rights find that they are individualistic and neglect concerns about communities and responsibilities (Merry 2006). Then there are critics who charge that rights are too absolutist and individualistic (Glendon 1991) and queer theorists who find rights to be too conventional and assimilationist to effect any transformative change (Stein and Plummer 1994).

Despite these limitations, gay activists continue to pursue rights, even when courts may no longer be responsive to their claims (Meyer and Boutcher 2007) and litigation has created backlash from their opponents (Rosenberg 2008). One way to understand such tenacity and endearment is to take a more expansive view of both the role of rights and the meaning of social change. Rights can do more than help movements to seek legal reform directly, and social change encompasses more than achieving such an aim. A more expansive view acknowledges that rights *alone* may not be able to achieve social change but also recognizes that they do have something to contribute to social change. Despite being unable to vindicate wrongs completely, rights can be used as cultural symbols that empower and inspire the oppressed to see possibilities for change and bargaining chips that can be used to threaten litigation against unmoving or recalcitrant opponents (Galanter 1974; McCann 1994; Andersen 2006). At the international level, if domestic activists can successfully portray their local grievances as matters of international human rights, they can successfully attract the support of transnational groups and other governments (Bob 2005, 2009). Further, rights may not even need to be mobilized outwardly in a public arena to take effect. They can help individuals to change their identities internally. By learning that they have rights, individuals come to think positively of themselves and reconfigure their relationships with others (Engel and Munger 1996, 2003) or they may start to question social institutions such as gender and work (Albiston 2010). Hence, even if rights are not mobilized to seek legal reform, activists can use rights to reframe grievances so that they or their constituents begin to alter their consciousness and question hegemonic arrangements (Polletta 2000; Barclay, Bernstein, and Marshall 2009).

Such rich studies on the meanings of rights, however, are lacking on authoritarian societies, where states often suppress or withhold rights from certain groups (see, e.g., Currier 2009; Massoud 2011). Activists may not be able to deploy rights-based tactics in the same way that their counterparts do in democratic societies (Johnston 2005; O'Brien and Li 2006). In this book, I detail the processes through which Singapore's gay activists work toward achieving rights for gays and make sense of their grievances in a rights-based language, *even though* they also perceive that rights lack cultural resonance and "don't work" with the government. Hence, this book illuminates further meanings about rights, as made sense by people mobilizing collectively under authoritarian conditions: Rights are multilingual; they are contextual and situational, depending on the social processes involving interactions among formal state institutions and law, the cultural dimensions of law, norms outside of formal law, and social actors. As a result, the book also offers insight into a politics of gay rights under authoritarian conditions: The struggle over the meanings of gay rights goes beyond equality and nondiscrimination on the basis of sexuality; it encompasses the collective organization and speaking out on the grievances of gay people in and of themselves. The exercise of such basic civil-political liberties cannot be taken for granted, and when gay activists resist their prohibitions so that they make known their grievances they take the first step toward the fight for social change.

In unpacking these processes, however, I also explore the role of law beyond the resourcefulness of rights and the vindication of rights by the courts. It is particularly important for a society such as Singapore, where the state champions a type of rule of law, or rule-boundedness.[16] Unlike other postcolonial states that struggle to harness legal power for its economic and social projects (Comaroff and Comaroff 2006), Singapore has used rule-boundedness to push through economic reform and justify the suppression of rights. Repression remains, but it does not manifest in the form of explicit physical violence. To understand how pragmatic resistance is deployed to exercise as well as achieve rights, it is also important to consider the other faces of law—not simply rights—as oppression as well as broader sites of resistance and contestation.

First, a steady line of scholarship elaborates on how laws and legal procedures are used by the state to control dissent and collective action (Earl 2003; Fernandez 2009) and make oppression appear more indirect and acceptable (Kirchheimer 1961; Barkan 1984). For instance, as far back as the early twentieth century, homophobic authorities used the licensing of bars and laws against sodomy to limit the rights of gays to assemble and express themselves in public (Cain 1993; Chauncey 1994; Bernstein 2002). Of course, arrests and prosecutions cost time, money, and physical discomfort (Oberschall 1978; Feeley 1979; Barkan 2006). In the context of social movements, when dragged out over extended periods, these legal processes also sap the material resources and will of activists (Earl 2005). Even short of actual arrest, prosecution, and conviction, the mere existence of legal controls can threaten to discredit a movement that violates them and frighten supporters away (Earl 2005; Barkan 2006). Furthermore, regulation or channeling (Earl 2006) renders repression subtler by allowing room for dissent while obscuring the repressive effects. Over time, the repression becomes less discernible and even legitimate as activists may come to accept the regulations as part of their practices and start to self-regulate (Fernandez 2009).

Second, on the brighter side, social actors can mount resistance against law or by making use of it (Merry 1995). Individuals fight repressive law with covert resistance, such as by working "under the table" while receiving welfare benefits (Gilliom 2001) or occupying physical space in government offices (Sarat 1990). During the early twentieth century in New York, gay men resisted anti-gay policing by communicating with one another in public with their own cultural codes (Chauncey 1994). Although such covert resistance does not openly confront and question the repressive laws, it strives to defy their control and achieve the resister's purpose without the participants getting caught (Ewick and Silbey 1998). Others expose acts of legal repression, such as the arrests of activists, to raise public awareness (Barkan 1977, 1980, 1985), win public support (Kirchheimer 1961; Earl 2005), or attract media attention (Barkan 1980, 2006). Sometimes individuals resist oppression by making use of law (Merry 1995). For instance, they resist existing meanings of other social institutions, such as gender, family, and work, and even influence or reconfigure them by navigating the interactions among these social institutions and law (see, e.g., Albiston 2010). In the context of social movements, gay activists leverage the law to reshape other norms and thus reconstruct understandings of how life should be organized (Barclay, Bernstein, and Marshall 2009).

Most studies, however, do not consider such interactions involving law, other norms in the larger sociopolitical environment, and social actors in relation to gay organizing under authoritarian conditions. In this book, I do so by developing a theoretical framework that is empirically based on an understudied movement. I examine law in both its formal form and cultural aspects and treat the political norms and cultural dimensions of law as being "all over" (Sarat 1990), permeating the larger political context, and interacting with movement organizations and the subjective meaning making of social actors (Emirbayer and Goodwin 1994; Polletta 1999b, 2004). With this framework, on the one hand, I find the ways in which repressive laws act as social control over Singapore's gay movement: Activists shun illegal tactics not only because of formal sanctions but also because law legitimizes power (Thompson 1975) and legal repression therefore sends the message that such tactics can cost them cultural legitimacy; on the other hand, it also uncovers the tactics that gay activists carry out to mount resistance against and through laws—by exploiting the legitimating power of law and the authoritarian state's very nature of rule-boundedness.

Pragmatic Resistance

Bearing in mind the preceding discussions of social movements and law and society, I next turn to the book's central theme of pragmatic resistance. Informed by the study's empirical data, I build this concept from the ground up to reflect the subjectivities of Singapore's gay activists. At the same time, I look to sociological theories on action and culture to help me to develop the concept for *collective* action specifically. The way in which I approach "pragmatic resistance," then, has affinity with American pragmatism (Dewey 1922) and its contemporary sociological renditions (Joas 1997; Frye 2012): Social actors turn to their contextually embedded knowledge and experiences as resources to respond to problems and sometimes creatively adjust them to accommodate emerging exigencies (Emirbayer and Mische 1998). The school of pragmatism helped to shape cultural approaches (e.g., Swidler 1986) that form this book's theoretical roots. They motivate the way in which I situate Singapore's gay movement in relation to that of other societies to elicit an interaction-driven and meaning making–centered approach in social movements analysis. They also influence my engagement with contemporary law and society scholarship that treats law as cultural schemas on which social actors draw to make sense of their worlds, thus reproducing multiple meanings of law and rights in mutually constitutive relations. In Chapter 8, I return to social movements and law and society scholarship to examine the book's contributions.

In the remainder of this chapter, to help readers to navigate the central theme's nuances throughout Chapters 3–7, I elaborate on how Singapore's gay activists strategically adapt pragmatic resistance, deploy its tactics, and perpetuate and sustain it over time to achieve their goals.

> The first thing is a legal system, a good system, so you get the protection of the law . . . so there is more equality and the right of every individual in that way. (Loke)
>
> I believe that everybody should be treated equally and also that we should all really try to get along, not judge people based on certain things that you don't agree with, or you don't really know about. (Yvette)
>
> What I'd like to see is that people can feel good about themselves, or get a sense of well-being. And that also means that there is a certain level [of] acceptance in society. (Chan)

The aspirations of gay activists in Singapore are not much different from those of their counterparts in gay movements elsewhere. They strive for social acceptance and to allow gay people to live full lives, and they want rights and equality for gays. However, as they perceive and read signals from their Singaporean environment, they first strategically adapt (McCammon et al. 2008) away from tactics that could jeopardize the movement's survival. These usually include directly and publicly confronting the state, such as protesting on the streets or demanding rights that seem to pose a threat to existing power structures. Hence, strategic adaptation into pragmatic resistance not only helps the movement to make progress but also ensures its survival. These are the strategy's core characteristics that emerge from the chronological analysis in subsequent chapters.

Most of the time, the tactics of pragmatic resistance aim at immediate gains that change practice and informal policies, not formal laws and regulations. When they do seek legal reform, they also perform pragmatic resistance. The goal is to stay alive and advance with skirmishes rather than court demise by declaring open warfare on grander principles. Although such a nonconfrontational approach may resemble everyday resistance (Scott 1985), the two are different. Pragmatic resistance is a collectively sustained strategy, not an individual and scattered approach. Further, as I show, the strategy adapts, escalates, and becomes less covert over time as and when pragmatic concerns about survival decrease. The collective and coordinated nature of this strategy also distinguishes it from the "rightful resistance" that O'Brien and Li (2006) found among rural Chinese, though they both make use of prevailing cultural conventions to contest power.

The signals that gay activists in Singapore perceive and read include legal restrictions and enforcement, a set of political norms that they interpret to constrain collective action and dissent, as well as shifts in either. The political norms, which I explain further in Chapter 2, concern nonconfrontation, the preservation of social stability as a foundation for economic progress, the maintenance of the ruling party's monopoly, and legal legitimacy. The signals also include responses from the state, ruling party, and opponents to earlier tactics of the movement. Even though the state and the ruling party are authoritarian, they are far from monolithic. Their reactions not only change with time but also can vary across departments and ministries, even from bureaucrat to bureaucrat, and among factions within the party. Consequently, the task of reading signals requires an astute understanding of the internal workings of their government and ruling party, a knowledge that gay activists accumulated with each engagement since the early 1990s.[17]

On the basis of their readings of these signals, gay activists determine whether and how to adapt their tactics. This is an ongoing cycle. With each subsequent tactic, they continue to engage in strategic adaptation, generating and refining a "strategic dance" (McCammon et al. 2008), "tactical dance" (McAdam 1983), "dark dance" (Johnston 2006), or as the activists put it, a "tango" or "complicated ballet." The determinations and actions, however, vary across activists and organizations. That is because they depend on individual agency—how far and how much one is willing to advance the movement at the risk of survival. Therefore, some activists disagree with the decisions of others, believing them to have undertaken a bout of risky business.

Because of the variations in agency, the subsequent chapters show differences and divisions within the movement. Nevertheless, Singapore's gay movement has not experienced deep ideological divides, such as the fissures between radical queer activism and gay rights advocacy or between radical lesbian feminism and the mixed-sex gay liberation movement (Taylor and Whittier 1995). Instead, the movement has steadily developed along the path of pragmatic resistance, the implications of which I discuss at the end of Chapter 7. Generally, its intramovement disagreements (see Chapters 3–7) can be divided into two types: fights over whether and how to respond to a new or changing signal and the objections of lesbian leaders to the male-centeredness of certain organizations. Neither type of disagreement has splintered the movement. Sometimes the factions that disagree with tactical choices or male domination set up new groups or implement their own tactics separately. But these diverse tactics remain characteristic of pragmatic resistance. The phenomenon is consistent with studies finding that factions actually help to sustain movement continuity and perpetuate dominant ideas within the movement. The conflicts force activists to be more self-reflective, reinvigorate their organizations (Schwartz 2002), and continue to mobilize (Reger 2002). Furthermore, as Chapters 3–7 show, gay activists reinforce their belief in the effectiveness of pragmatic resistance with each tactic and its outcomes, particularly the state's reactions; sometimes they interpret the results as prompting a need to refine or change a tactic rather than completely abandon the strategy.

Efforts to reinforce and refine pragmatic resistance and thus perpetuate this movement also draw strength from intramovement relations. Newcomers first encounter the movement either because they are seeking friendship and support or because they have altruistic intentions. Congruent with the literature on social movement networks and recruitment, as newcomers build relationships with people and organizations and participate in movement events, personal ties cultivate their trust in and commitment to the movement (Lofland and Stark 1965; Snow and Machalek 1984; Snow, Zurcher, and

Ekland-Olson 1980; Snow et al. 1986) and their initial motivations transform into a sense of necessity and obligation to "do something about it" for gays and lesbians in Singapore, even in the face of possible state retaliation (Morris 1984; McAdam 1986; della Porta 1988; Loveman 1998). They gain cognitive liberation (McAdam 1999), changing from feeling helpless to believing that they have the ability to alter their conditions (Piven and Cloward 1977). They become politicized as they start to identify or name their personal struggles as collective grievances on the basis of their sexuality and learn to mobilize collectively. The significance of these intramovement relations is further bolstered by the weak presence of participation in other local or overseas activism prior to joining the gay movement. Of the one hundred interviewees, only fifteen were involved in any kind of activism or volunteer social work while overseas, even though two-thirds of them have either worked or lived abroad. Under Singapore's authoritarian conditions, becoming an activist entails overcoming one's fears of becoming publicly identified as a gay activist or getting into trouble with the state. By becoming an activist, therefore, one mounts the first challenge to power that tries to stop dissent and resistance in the first place. It is by crossing the threshold into the gay movement that one begins to engage in strategic adaptation and pragmatic resistance.

Equally as important, by interacting with one another in the movement, activists continuously build new intramovement ties (R. Gould 1991) and perpetuate or reshape existing ones (Payne 1996). They learn from one another how to respond to signals and political norms. Oral, written, and performed narratives about their history expose them to knowledge of pragmatic resistance. Hence, intramovement social relations—friendships, influential leadership, education, and tutelage—help to produce, preserve, and pass on the movement's dominant practices and knowledge (Jasper and Poulsen 1993; Polletta 2002) such that pragmatic resistance is sustained across the movement and through the years. Sometimes seasoned activists offer advice to the less experienced or wield influence over others in making tactical choices. While each activist has his or her own interpretations of political signals, tactical choices, and outcomes, these are also influenced by intramovement relationships. Those who grow frustrated, cannot or will not assimilate into pragmatic resistance, or simply lose interest in the movement drop out and leave the movement.

Pushing Boundaries and Toeing the Line

The processes of pragmatic resistance, thus, involve interplay among gay activists within the movement and with law, political norms, the state, and other parties involved. In activists' own words, the strategy strives for balance between "pushing boundaries" and "toeing the line"—that is, advancement and survival. *Boundary pushing* means expanding the limits of political norms constraining collective action or changes in practices and policies, even law and rights, concerning homosexuality. *Toeing the line* means adhering to these limits to avoid actions that can lead to sanctions and cost the movement legitimacy. Toeing the line too much will achieve little progress, whereas pushing boundaries too aggressively may provoke retaliation.

Although the movement has escalated and emboldened after optimistic readings of signals, its array of tactics belongs to a core repertoire that helps activists to toe the line while pushing boundaries. In Chapters 3–7, readers will repeatedly encounter these tactics, which I analyze in relation to specific events. Below I explain each of these tactical moves and refer back to Rascals for illustration.

Avoid Direct Confrontation with the State

> No hitting the police with heels, no, but we fought back using methods that were acceptable in Singapore. (Keenan)

Keenan's response to the Rascals raid—writing a letter to the police and its parent ministry—highlights the tactic of nonconfrontation. He believed that a Stonewall-like uprising or street demonstrations in general would contradict the political norm of nonconfrontation and would "just be hitting your head against a brick wall" without changing the circumstances that angered him. In addition, this tactic adheres to the norm of maintaining the ruling party's authority. The party not only wants to be in charge; it demands to be seen as in charge. Confrontation calls its power into question and causes its leaders to lose face.

Play to the Preservation of Social Stability

Keenan did not ask for any laws to be changed, but when gay activists in Singapore call for legal reform, they commonly frame their goals in terms of preservation of social stability. They emphasize how the gay movement enhances social harmony by supporting equality and acceptance for all. Sometimes they associate the movement with economic development by arguing that an equal and open-minded society would retain and attract the best talent.[18] Oftentimes they also pair this tactic with nonconfrontation to assure the ruling party that they are not challenging its political power. When dealing with the Christian Right opposition, they turn around to show how its intolerance conversely jeopardizes social harmony by advocating division and hate.

Focus on Specific Actions or Immediate Concerns
Keenan composed the Rascals letter tightly around the police's conduct and legal powers and did not once allude to rights or civil liberties. This is another trait of pragmatic resistance tactics: They usually take on battles aimed at improving specific conditions for gays in Singapore, but do not wage war on the grounds of greater rights and democracy. In the rare instances that they fight on more general terms, it is because they interpret signals to have indicated a safe opening to do so and perhaps even a chance of success.

Leverage Legal Legitimacy
By pointing out that the police had acted outside their legal authority, Keenan appealed to the rule-bound character of the state and ruling party and the political norm that respects legal legitimacy. In Singapore, illegal actions not only attract legal sanctions but also lose legitimacy. Leveraging legal legitimacy takes several forms throughout the movement. Keenan's approach was to make use of legal restrictions or procedures. In other cases, activists get around legal restrictions to bring their actions outside the ambit of prohibitive laws and thus avoid transgression. Alternatively, they obey the law literally without allowing it to achieve the intended purpose in spirit. All of these tactics keep state authorities at bay and enable activists to carry out their activities or alter an external party's conduct with their legitimacy intact.

Appeal to International Legitimacy
Keenan's account also stressed that "the police are not known to break laws," a point that hints at the international image that the PAP seeks to project for Singapore—one of rule of law (at least the rule-bound type). However, seldom do these tactics use transnational movement networks to pressure their home government (Keck and Sikkink 1998) or openly align with international human rights activists. Echoing what scholars have argued elsewhere that engaging transnational movements can lead to backlash and state retaliation (Essig 1999; Hoad 1999; Blackwood 2007; Massad 2007), Singapore's gay activists avoid being seen as having foreign influence. When they do seek out external pressure to leverage the concern with international legitimacy, they act subtly or indirectly to avoid outright confrontation. Their international connections are usually informal and based on personal communication and connections. The most common tactic used to tap the

influence of transnational activism is to mediate and translate (Merry 2006) the symbols and imagery of an urbanized, Western gay identity, such as the rainbow symbol and the color pink (Altman 2001).

Ultimately, what remains paramount for the balance between pushing boundaries and toeing the line is the preservation of the ruling party's hegemony. Chapters 3–7 highlight instances in which the state and the ruling party willingly sacrifice a certain degree of international legitimacy for what they believe is necessary to preserve domestic hegemony. To gay activists, this conversely means that the state tolerates some rule bending on their part, even contraventions, as long as their movement overall does not threaten the appearance of their hegemonic control (Scott 1990). Hence, as they deploy the tactics of pragmatic resistance described earlier, they also take advantage of this contradiction and seek out or create opportunities to advance the movement.

Making Changes Incrementally

As the story of their movement unfolds through my chronological analysis in Chapters 3–7, from its timorous beginnings to coming out, three themes of change become gradually pronounced over the course of twenty years: the movement's coming out, tactical escalation and movement expansion and diversification, and the opening up of political and media spaces. Together, the three themes highlight how pragmatic resistance shapes Singapore's gay movement and produces change incrementally.

Coming Out as a Movement
By the mid-2000s, gay organizing in Singapore had come out openly as a movement. This was not previously the case. As discussed in "Timorous Beginnings" (Chapter 3), the movement stayed in hiding. Gay activists of the early 1990s feared becoming exposed to authorities as gay activists, or even activists, for that matter. After a few scares and setbacks, they shifted their tactics, as examined in "Cyber Organizing" (Chapter 4), and migrated quietly onto the Internet for a few years. After they did not feel the sting of state retaliation, they reemerged in the early 2000s to test boundaries, as discussed in "Transition" (Chapter 5). Around 2005, they shifted again and entered the contemporary stage, explored in "Coming Out" (Chapter 6) and "Mobilizing in the Open" (Chapter 7). State surveillance persists, but activists' fears have largely subsided. They no longer shun publicity, but even pursue it and openly identify themselves as a people who collectively mobilize over shared grievances.

Gradual changes take place because the movement successfully survives by way of pragmatic resistance and activists thus accumulate opportunities to sustain interactions with the state. The ongoing relationship hones their abilities to read political signals and learn from past encounters so that they can better identify where the political boundaries lie and how they can be pushed. They become more confident and grow less afraid of the state's reactions, believing that it has come to perceive them as less of a threat. The reduction in fear reflects a clear generational divide. Activists who joined the movement in the twenty-first century arrived with fewer anxieties and little concern for state retaliation. In contrast, old-timers recall their early trepidations; they had to *learn* to become less afraid. Only with time and experience did their fears lessen.

Escalation, Diversification, and Expansion

Increased confidence emboldens gay activists to escalate their tactics. Even though they still toe the line—and thus stay true to pragmatic resistance—they increasingly push boundaries with intensity and boldness. The movement's first decade largely avoided open advocacy. As it moved into transition, however, some activists interpreted political signals to have become less hostile and attempted the first few direct engagements with the state, state-controlled media, and Singaporean society at large. Gradually, activists worry less about *whether* their movement can survive and become more creative and adventurous about *how* to advance it. The pattern of tactical escalation becomes most evident when readers arrive at its coming out, where they read about an annual pride festival, the Repeal 377A petition campaign, annual Pink Dot rallies, and the unprecedented constitutional challenge against Section 377A in open court.

As tactics escalate, the movement's range of work and activists diversifies, its number of organizations expands, and support for it broadens and strengthens. During its timorous beginnings and the period of cyber organizing, movement activities focused inward on community building and services. The movement consisted of a few groups and a handful of leaders. It also lacked a grassroots community of gays and lesbians and a broader ally base made up of non-gays. The situation changed from the transition period onward. Non-gays begin joining the movement. Indeed, some readers may want the movement to address the interests of women, the working classes, and racial and religious minorities among its constituents more fully. But Chapters 3–7 also show how the injection of new blood brought new organizations and a broader array of activities spanning community support and services, increasing social awareness, media advocacy, and direct state engagement (see

Table 7.1). As the movement comes out into the open, a grassroots base of gays and lesbians and support from non-gay allies also emerge, a phenomenon most visible during the petition campaign and Pink Dot rallies.

Opening Up of Political and Media Spaces

Gay activists' ongoing interactions with the state and the PAP also enable them to understand the movement and modify perceptions of it as a threat to the ruling party's political stronghold. Although some government ministries such as education and defense remain unfriendly, gay activists sense a gradual shift away from condemnation of homosexuality to a more moderate stance framed as "balancing of interests" among various factions of society. At press time, Section 377A remains, but at least key officials and PAP leaders have openly acknowledged in parliamentary debates and local media that gays and lesbians have a place in Singaporean society (though qualifying that their interests cannot trump those of others who disagree).

Regular police raids and entrapment have also largely ceased. Instead of stonewalling gay activists, as they did in the 1990s, bureaucrats and politicians recognize gays as a visible group and engage in ongoing conversations with activists. The state-controlled media are also more willing to feature the viewpoints of activists. Further, the Christian Right opposition started coming out with attacks and mass campaigns in the mid-2000s. Some activists take these responses to be ironic indications of their movement's growth and see them as evidence of shifting state and societal attitudes toward homosexuality and signs of progress that threaten the opposition and compel them to react.

These three themes—coming out; tactical escalation, diversification, and expansion; and the opening up of political and media spaces—demonstrate how pragmatic resistance enables Singapore's gay movement to promote a sense of efficacy; cultivate the skills, courage, and tenacity needed to mobilize collectively under authoritarianism; and expand "free spaces" (Polletta 1999a) to build collective identities, strengthen grassroots, and amass ally support. But they also reveal what is *lacking*—formal legal changes.[19] How then do we make sense of pragmatic resistance? I discuss its implications for the movement at the end of my chronological analysis. After that, I return to the book's theoretical motivations in "Pragmatic Resistance, Law, and Social Movements" (Chapter 8) to elucidate its contributions to the study of social movements, law and society's understanding of rights, and the role of law and articulate a politics of gay rights under authoritarian conditions. Contemporary research on China suggests that social actors who seek changes from authoritarian states may not wish to rearrange the entire political order (Tsai 2007), may avoid any democratic claim making to ensure the state's tolerance of their existence (Spires 2011), or may obtain incremental gains that end up leaving the top leadership untouched (Stern 2013). By extending and refining the existing understanding of the relationship between law and social movements, *Mobilizing Gay Singapore*'s ground-up approach to an understudied movement further illuminates the processes of social change in authoritarian contexts.

I organize the rest of this book as follows: in "Legal Restrictions, Political Norms, and Being Gay in Singapore" (Chapter 2), I provide background on the country, especially its laws and political norms for mobilization, and give an account of the sociolegal conditions for gays and lesbians in Singapore. In "Timorous Beginnings," "Cyber Organizing," "Transition," "Coming Out," and "Mobilizing in the Open" (Chapters 3–7), I analyze the movement chronologically to explicate the strategy and tactics of pragmatic resistance. These are also the chapters that appeal to readers who are most interested in a narrative about the movement.

Throughout the book, I use pseudonyms for respondents, movement organizations, and venues to protect confidentiality. The exceptions are people identified as public figures in major public events and respondents who insisted on the disclosure of their identities (and therefore waived confidentiality). To honor these requests, I indicate their real names in Appendix B. In choosing pseudonyms, to preserve the nature of their original names, I replaced Western names with other Western names and Muslim, South Asian, and Chinese names with the like.

As readers move through Chapters 3–7 sequentially, the three themes of coming out; tactical escalation, movement expansion, and diversification; and the opening up of political and media spaces unfold and become increasingly evident. Alongside these achievements, I point out potential issues with pragmatic resistance at the end of the chronological analysis in Chapter 7. In Chapter 8, "Pragmatic Resistance, Law, and Social Movements," I conclude by elaborating on the book's theoretical contributions, particularly the significance of pragmatic resistance to the study of social movements and sociological understandings of law and rights.

2

Legal Restrictions, Political Norms, and Being Gay in Singapore

Singapore's sociopolitical background brings out important elements in the social processes of pragmatic resistance. The laws, regulations, and political norms are signals that gay activists consider when mobilizing and implementing pragmatic resistance and are intricately linked to a PAP-centric historical narrative. They revolve around maintaining political hegemony through suppressing confrontation, quelling dissent in the name of social stability and economic progress, and using the law to achieve these aims. Understanding the connections of these laws, regulations, and political norms to this narrative has implications for evaluating pragmatic resistance and the roles of law and rights examined in Chapters 7 and 8.

The conditions for gays and lesbians in Singapore, discussed in the second part of this chapter, motivate gay activists to join the movement. These legal and social conditions are diverse and affect each of them differently, thus influencing the ways that they carry out pragmatic resistance. Subsequent chapters elaborate on these tactical choices and discuss gay life and culture where they intersect with the movement's development.

Singapore is a Southeast Asian city-state with a population of approximately five million. Its main island, measuring about 274 square miles at low tide, sits on the southern tip of the Malayan Peninsular and the Straits of Malacca, a major thoroughfare that connects the Indian and Pacific oceans. When the British East India Company first set up a trading post here in 1819, it was

Figure 2.1. Geographical location of Singapore. *(Map by Lee Li Kheng.)*

a sleepy fishing village controlled by a Malay sultanate. Under British rule from 1826 to 1963,[1] the island transformed into the center of the colonial empire's trade in Southeast Asia (see Figure 2.1).

Singapore attained self-governance from the British in 1959. After gaining full independence in 1963, it joined former British territories on the Malayan Peninsula and Sabah and Sarawak on Borneo to form the Federation of Malaysia. Soon after, the ruling party governing Singapore, the PAP, became embroiled in political strife with the United Malays National Organization that controlled the federal government. Whereas the PAP was Chinese-dominated in a predominantly ethnic Chinese state, the United Malays National Organization was controlled by Malays, who had political and popular majority in the rest of the Federation. The latter regarded the PAP as a threat to the continuation of Malay political dominance in the Federation and allegedly incited Malays to attack ethnic Chinese in Singapore, escalating into racial riots in 1964 (Leifer 1964). Racial and political tensions led to Singapore's departure from the Federation in 1965 (Hill and Lian 1995), leaving the PAP to manage an island nation cut off from its peninsular hinterland and without a self-sufficient supply of fresh water (Lee 1998).

The race riots of 1964 were among several racially or religious motivated riots in the years surrounding the independent republic's conception, and they left a strong imprint on its politics.[2] Today the country remains multiracial and multireligious, with about 74 percent ethnic Chinese, followed by 13 percent Malays, 9 percent Indians, and a mix of other races. About 44 percent of residents are Buddhist or Daoist, 18 percent are Christian, 15 percent are Muslim, and 5 percent are Hindu, and together they make up the most popular religious affiliations (Census of Population 2010). Even though racially or religiously motivated riots have not broken out in the past four decades, the fear of returning to the social unrest of the 1950s and 1960s, though unlikely and perhaps irrational to some, continue to influence the PAP government's rhetoric and lawmaking as well as Singapore's political norms.

Even before formal independence, the PAP demonstrated that preserving its political dominance was paramount. During the 1950s, at the height of the Malayan Emergency that the British declared against communist insurgents on the Malayan Peninsula, the PAP—then in opposition—protested the government's efforts to quash strikes and protests advocating for better labor conditions in Singapore. But by the early 1960s, in the transition to formal independence, the PAP acquiesced to the use of the Internal Security Act (ISA)—legislation carried over from British colonial rule—to detain leftist parliamentarians without trial and continued its use after independence. By the late 1960s, with the PAP purged of its leftist members and consolidating its power, any inkling of a mass labor movement faded way, as the PAP reshaped and coopted trade unions and leaders into its vision and plans for industrialization (Mauzy and Milne 2002).

Despite the violent riots, the republic's founding history lacked social upheavals of another kind—peaceful, popular rights-based movements. Its self-governance and independence were secured through negotiations between the British and local elites, many of whom were educated in England.

Although women did rally together in the 1960s to push for laws banning polygamous marriages, the PAP's political maneuvers soon absorbed any momentum toward a women's movement. To wangle women's support away from their communist opponents, the PAP staged a pro-woman platform in exchange for women's votes[3] and passed the Women's Charter after coming into power (G. Heng 1997).[4] By the early years of Singapore's independence, the PAP had achieved political monopoly.

> I think part of the deal for us to become economically viable, [with] all this chaos back then, we gave up freedom of speech, expression and assembly because we had a government that concentrated on building Singapore. Yes. And at the end of the day, it still prevails. (Ricky)

The PAP constantly reminds Singaporeans of their nation's tumultuous conception and touts social harmony as essential to economic survival, framing the two together as paramount to the nation's security. To achieve its economic agenda of transforming the postcolonial state into an attractive international financial and trade center, the PAP government aggressively deploys its particular brand of rule of law, which is adherence to rules and procedures rather than the protection and vindication of rights and equality (Rajah 2012). In fact, Ricky and many other gay activists describe the PAP as trading off civil-political rights for economic prosperity and social stability, a bargain that remains to this day. Within five decades, the island transformed into a nation with the world's sixth highest gross domestic product (Central Intelligence Agency 2010), one of the freest economies (Heritage Foundation 2011),[5] and one of the busiest seaports. Meanwhile, as part of the trade-off, the PAP government deploys the same brand of rule of law to secure legitimacy domestically and internationally through the power of law. It thus bases its return to power on being reelected by the populace at every legally mandated election, but to ensure its victorious return and political monopoly, it imposes legal restrictions to curb civil-political liberties and political access provided by its Westminster-style Constitution and in some instances retain, or even enhance, the restrictions already put in place by former British colonial masters. Those who transgress these restrictions are delegitimized through the legal process.[6]

This background informs contemporary laws and political norms in Singapore. Next I discuss those that limit collective mobilization. In both formal and informal instances, the barriers reflect the socially constructed, PAP-centric narrative of political turmoil and economic imperatives.

Formal Barriers to Collective Mobilization

Several formal barriers to civil-political liberties and democratic processes affect collective mobilization. They are among the signals that gay activists interpret in the processes of strategic adaptation.

Association and Assembly

The formation of "societies" of ten or more persons is illegal without approval under the Societies Act.[7] Approval for groups organizing around issues of religion, gender, sexual orientation, or politics is subject to the discretion of the Registrar of Societies—whether he or she believes that the group could prejudice "public peace, welfare or good order" or "national interest." A gay movement organization has been denied registration twice on such grounds. The stringent rules also constrain local groups from openly associating with international non-governmental organizations (NGOs), especially in formal funding relationships, because they could lead to accusations of coming under the influence of foreign organizations that plot to interfere in domestic politics.

Public assemblies similarly face severe legal obstacles. According to the Public Order Act, public assembles include demonstrations by a single individual, and the police may issue orders to disperse even a single demonstrator; permits are subject to considerations such as whether they may cause "enmity, hatred, ill-will or hostility between different groups in Singapore." Although permits are also required for protest activities in liberal democracies, approval in Singapore is stringent and typically denied to those protesting the government.[8]

Speech and Press

The freedom to speak in public, especially about local politics, race, and religion, is similarly subject to stringent conditions and administrative discretion. The Sedition Act prohibits speech that has a "tendency . . . to excite disaffection against the Government" or "the administration of justice in Singapore" or "promote feelings of ill-will and hostility between different races or classes of the population of Singapore." The Maintenance of Religious Harmony Act restricts members of religious groups, especially leaders, from using religious activities as a "guise" to "promote a political cause" or carry out "subversive activities," and the Legal Profession Act bans the Law Society from commenting publicly on any legislation unless asked by the government to do so.

The local media are controlled through a licensing system and state approval of their management appointees under the Broadcasting Act and the Newspaper and Printing Presses Act. These legal controls enable the state to enforce local media's role as one of "nation building" rather than watchdog (Bokhorst-Heng 2002).[9] In addition, their content is censored, especially on issues of politics, religion, and sexuality. Foreign newspapers are checked using license conditions that restrict circulation volume and prohibit their contents from "interfering" with Singaporean politics. Contempt of court laws extend to critical speech about the courts and judges uttered outside the immediate setting of the courtroom, to which such contempt laws are usually confined in other jurisdictions, and PAP leaders are known to win defamation lawsuits against foreign publications that write about Singapore or their leadership in ways they consider negative.

Life and Liberty

After suppressing early communist rivals with the ISA, the PAP continues to deploy the draconian law on grounds of national security. During the 1960s–1970s, it detained journalists and editors from Chinese- and Malay-language media organizations, ostensibly because of their affiliations with groups such as opposition parties and trade unions (George 2012).[10] In the late 1980s, it used the ISA against the solicitor-general, Francis Seow, who was accused of receiving foreign funds for his political campaign. It also detained a group of young social activists and community organizers who advocated for migrant workers' rights. Even though the ISA's original intention was to suppress communist insurgency, it has since been applied to other situations, most notably against Jemaah Islamiyah members who were known to have links to Al Qaeda and were suspected of plotting terrorist acts in Singapore in the 2000s.

Political Access and Representation

Ever since independence was achieved, the PAP has maintained hegemonic control over political access and representation and dominated Singapore's unicameral Parliament with at least 80 percent of the seats.[11] Singapore's Constitution does not provide for popular referendums, except to determine Singapore's sovereignty, so all it takes is for a two-thirds majority vote in Parliament to amend the Constitution. With a dominant parliamentary majority, the PAP thus has amended constitutional provisions to convert single-member constituencies—one vote for one member of Parliament

(MP)—into group representation constituencies, one vote for several MPs of the same party. To contest in a group representation constituency, a political party must field a required number of candidates, including a designated racial minority. The winning "team" is thus elected as a unit, creating a high threshold for political turnover. In addition, PAP leaders are famous for suing political opponents for defamation and winning huge damages that result in their opponents' bankruptcy and disqualification from holding political office in Parliament.

Access to Courts and Judicial Review

> I'm not sure. I don't know the legal process. . . . Partly I don't know enough. Partly it's never—I've never heard any success stories. (Nina)

> I think that [the courts] have interpreted some laws actually not in favor of the government. . . . [T]he very next day, the [attorney general] will draft an amendment. . . . [I]t's very easy for the government to change things because we don't have parliamentary opposition to check and balance. (Keenan)

These responses on rights litigation are typical and common. Singapore's judiciary lacks a record of upholding constitutional liberties over state interests, such as "public order" or "national security," so gay activists have few courtroom victories from which to learn and find inspiration.[12] Singapore's Constitution, including the provisions on fundamental liberties, can be amended by two-thirds of votes in Parliament, which is dominated by the PAP. In one rare instance, when the court's opinion favored constitutional liberties over executive power, Parliament swiftly passed constitutional and legislative amendments to overrule it and freeze the law as it stood prior to the case.[13] These signals have come to inform and reinforce views that Parliament and the executive do not take well to what they perceive to be judicial activism, especially if it vindicates constitutional rights by limiting state power. They have also led gay activists to doubt the efficacy of rights litigation. When speaking about their activist work, few mentioned rights litigation on their own accord. For the first two decades, the gay movement did not attempt rights litigation to challenge either the constitutionality of Section 377A or the administrative decisions that impinged on their civil-political liberties, such as those on the registration of societies and the licensing of speech.

In August 2012, Singapore's Court of Appeal declared that a gay man has legal standing to challenge the constitutionality of Section 377A of the Penal Code without having first to be prosecuted under it. This court decision on procedure has given some hope and encouragement to gay activists that legal change through the courts may at long last seem viable, a development considered in Chapter 7, "Mobilizing in the Open." However, a long road lies ahead as activists initiate substantive challenges against the law on constitutional grounds. Generally, outside the challenge of Section 377A's constitutionality, gay activists, regardless of their generation, age, organizational affiliation, gender, and other demographic differences, still perceive the courts' position on rights to be conservative.

Political Norms Affecting Collective Organizing

In addition to the formal restrictions on civil-political liberties and access to formal institutions, the following set of political norms affects gay organizing in Singapore. They are also signals that gay activists heed when engaging in strategic adaptation. Having considered the preceding background, they may seem familiar and perhaps unsurprising. Indeed, these unofficial norms are socially constructed by gay activists on the basis of their interpretation of other signals that include formal restrictions on civil-political liberties, the lack of judicial decisions that uphold these liberties, the barriers to political access and representation, and government statements and political speeches. Taken together, these norms point toward a central concern—the preservation of the status quo. If any of the norms conflict with one another, the resolution that best protects PAP monopoly usually prevails.[14]

Nonconfrontation

> In this country, when you confront, you're actually shaming and shaming is not a tactic that works. (Stella)

Nonconfrontation refers to activists' perception of the state and the PAP's perception of their actions (bearing in mind their conflation of *government* or *state* with the ruling party). To be confrontational means to oppose PAP rule, a perception that reflects the PAP's elitist conception of the state-society relationship as one between superiors and subordinates. It connotes openly embarrassing one's superior and thus going out of line. In essence, it boils down to shaming: the idea that a subordinate ought not to be publicly accusing one's superiors of wrongdoing and telling the latter what to do.

The most obvious act of confrontation is street protests, reflective of the PAP government's fear of social chaos and also linked to the norm of maintaining social stability, to which I next turn. More broadly, exercising or claiming rights could also be seen as an affront to authority. Therefore, rights litigation that claims a violation of rights by the state could be construed as confrontational. Later in the book, however, I consider how some activists surprisingly drew from signals at the time to find hope in litigating the constitutionality of Section 377A and examine why they perceive the case ultimately to conform to this norm.

Preservation of Social Stability

The avoidance of confrontation is presumed to maintain social stability. By *social stability*, what gay activists, the state, and the PAP really mean is the absence of patent antagonism or ill sentiments publicly expressed against different social groups, especially racial and religious groups. The PAP essentializes race and religion; it treats people as being culturally different on the basis of perceived racial or religious traits. Yet, it wants them to coexist in harmony while maintaining essentialized differences.[15] For gay activists, this political norm serves as a caution against appearing to attribute homophobia to essentialized racial traits or attacking the religious views of those who use religion to justify homophobia.

With social stability comes the presumption that Singapore's economic engine can run smoothly, without disruption brought about by protests and riots that Singaporeans learn from the PAP-centric historical narrative and witness in developing nations. The PAP portrays social stability leading to economic progress as paramount because it relies on economic performance to return legitimately to office at every election. To revisit Ricky's statement, that is why antagonistic exercises of rights, such as protests, are suppressed: Basic civil-political liberties are seen as trade-offs for engineering this particular vision of social stability and its fruits of economic progress.

Such a common interpretation by Ricky and other gay activists also appears in official statements by PAP leaders and the government.

> People on both sides hold strong views [about homosexuality]. . . . [I]nstead of forging a consensus, we will divide and polarise our society. When it comes to issues like the economy, technology, education . . . when necessary on such issues, we will move even if the issue is unpopular or controversial. (Singapore Parliamentary Debates, Prime Minister Lee Hsien Loong, October 23, 2007)

Note the statement's contrasting positions between social and economic issues. The contrast brings out Ricky's interpretation in a different way. The PAP will not press forward on social issues when it perceives public opinions to be strongly divided because it fears destabilizing social harmony and potentially costing the party electorate support. However, if the PAP sees an issue as carrying significant economic weight, such as whether to allow casinos—though also linked to social concerns—it will impose a controversial decision despite divided public opinion. That is because it believes that long-term economic gains will and should prevail over immediate social discontent. These findings also explain why some activists consider the norm of social stability antithetic to civil-political rights specifically and not to socioeconomic rights, such as health care and education, which can be seen as more directly beneficial to economic progress.

Coveting Legal Legitimacy

Since the PAP's early use of the ISA against its political threats, it has adopted a common practice of using legal means instead of explicit physical violence to suppress and control dissent. Ruling with the power of law rather than the might of the sword, the PAP exacts social control and violence (B. Moore 1966) far more clinically and subtly. With the use of law as a tool of oppression, the PAP correspondingly perpetuates a political norm of coveting legal legitimacy to which gay activists and Singaporean society at large respond.

The norm operates at two levels. The first is its rule-bound nature—what the PAP touts as rule of law—that concerns the securing and conferring of cultural legitimacy through legal abidance; transgressions erode good repute and credibility, regardless of one's moral or ethical grounds. Therefore, the PAP secures power through elections according to formal laws and procedures, ensures its ability to return to power by controlling political discourse with restrictions passed in accordance with the law,[16] and proves itself worthy of power by using the law to manufacture a stable society that is perceived as conducive to economic growth. Its civil servants and bureaucrats also have been inculcated and trained to uphold their notion of rule of law. Due to the same consideration, gay activists do not protest on the streets without permits (which they believe would be denied). Becoming outlaws delegitimizes one's cause, a familiar sight among the PAP's political opponents who have been prosecuted for illegal protests or have been sued by PAP leaders for defamation and lost.

On another level, the norm relates to the state's concern with Singapore's international image as a nation of rule of law with some extent of liberties. Gay activists understand that the PAP certainly does not want Singapore to be lumped together with the extremes of North Korea because it sees a need to be regarded as legitimate by Western democracies with which Singapore builds economic ties. However, the activists are also circumspect. This international consideration of the norm has limited influence. Ultimately, the norms of nonconfrontation, social stability linked to economic progress, and the upholding of legal legitimacy point to the imperative of maintaining the ruling party's power.

Perpetuation of the Ruling Party

The state and the core PAP leadership come across to gay activists as fundamentally concerned with the preservation of the party's political power and continuation of the existing political order. This norm can be interpreted in multiple, coexisting ways. According to the more straightforward interpretation, to maintain its monopoly, the ruling party believes that it needs to be seen as being in control. Hence, it avoids being seen as bowing to grassroots demands (though dialogue with various social groups may take place behind closed doors) and thus appearing weak or unstable, a common concern among authoritarian rulers (Boudreau 2005). For the same reason, it does not like to accede to international pressure, at least openly or directly.

According to a less obvious interpretation, the party ironically and perhaps self-contradictorily needs to sustain domestic support to perpetuate its hegemony. The prime minister's contrasting position between economic and social issues illustrates this point. Gay activists know that the state has no qualms about forcefully implementing plans construed as economic, which, like the unpopular legalization of casinos, may also have moral dimensions leading to social implications. That is because the economic benefits are seen to sustain the PAP's monopoly in the long run. Although the state privileges heteronormativity, it weighs homosexuality as a morally problematic issue only if the party's monopoly is perceived to be at stake. That includes not only favoring a majority whom it presumes to be and constructs as conservative but also shaping society in a heteronormative way that it believes to best serve economic progress.

This complex norm thus explains why the state and the PAP sometimes sacrifice international legitimacy when upholding that norm interferes with the imperative of perpetuating the ruling party's power. In particular, where civil-political rights are concerned, the Singaporean state remains reluctant to change at the pace of international human rights discourse or under the ostensible pressure of transnational advocacy and foreign governments. Party and state are unabashed about defending themselves against allegations of rights violations and frequently publish rebuttals to international human rights reports. The retention of Section 377A of the Penal Code is another example. Some PAP leaders are actually sympathetic about its injustice and recognize that its retention compromises Singapore's international legitimacy. Yet, they refuse to abolish it out of a perception that repeal may create discord and jeopardize its monopoly during elections.[17]

Legal and Social Conditions for Gays and Lesbians in Singapore

The formal legal conditions for gays and lesbians in Singapore are unwelcoming. Although the law that criminalizes same-sex sexual conduct originates from its British colonial past and targets conduct rather than sexuality, it aligns with the postcolonial state's heteronormative policies, which are also motivated by the PAP-centric historical narrative. The PAP seeks to inculcate in its people the thought of Singapore as a small country that is poor in natural resources and must therefore rely on its human resources; hence, it insists, the nuclear family made up of an opposite-sex couple and children forms its basic social unit and economic building block.[18] Given the state's heteronormative policies and formal legal conditions, to live as an openly gay person in Singapore is an act of resistance. But outside formal law, the social conditions are more diverse and vary among individual persons and contexts. In this section, I provide an overview of both the legal and social conditions.

Legalized Suppression of Homosexuality

Section 377A of the Penal Code criminalizes "gross indecency" between men, a provision vague enough to encompass conduct ranging from displays of public affection to private, consensual sexual intercourse. There is no similar provision against women, but same-sex relations either between men or between women do not receive any legal recognition. Before the Penal Code amendments of 2007, Section 377A existed alongside Section 377, which penalized "carnal intercourse against the order of nature" between opposite sexes and between men. Both provisions, however, have seldom been applied in private, consensual situations, and most are typically used in nonconsensual situations or cases involving minors.[19] When the police used to entrap gay men at cruising grounds, they usually prosecuted on the grounds of Section 354, which refers to the assault or use of criminal force with the intent to "outrage modesty" (of the undercover officer). If convicted under Section 354, one faces up to two years of imprisonment, a fine, or caning, or any two of such punishments.

Besides criminalization, gays and lesbians lack legal protection from discrimination on the basis of sexuality. Singapore's Constitution does provide for a general clause on equality in Article 12(1) and specifically on the bases of race, religion, descent, and place of birth in Article 12(2). In addition, Article 152(1) of the Constitution provides that the government has the "responsibility . . . constantly to care for the interests of the racial and religious minorities" of the country. However, such constitutional pronouncements lack the backing of anti-discrimination legislation that provides concrete legal measures for the redress of grievances. Furthermore, sexuality is not a specified category that receives even formal recognition in the Constitution.

The lack of legal recognition of same-sex relations affects gays and lesbians' access to government benefits and services. For example, it limits their housing options in land-scarce Singapore. The government's Housing Development Board (HDB) develops housing estates and sells individual flat units to citizens directly at rates deemed affordable to the population. Such public housing is the residential norm in Singapore. More than 80 percent of its population lives in HDB flats, and about 95 percent of these people own their flats (on a ninety-nine-year lease). To buy directly from the HDB, however, one has to be a Singaporean citizen or permanent resident who is at least twenty-one years old and plans to form a "nuclear" family within that flat, such as with one's parents, a sibling, or a marital partner of the opposite sex. Same-sex couples do not enjoy these options. One alternative for them would be to purchase resale HDB flats as co-owning "singles" in the open market—that is, not directly from the HDB—after they reach thirty-five years old. The other choice would be to buy privately developed property, which is at least twice the price of HDB property. Therefore, only a minority of the population can afford this option.[20] Such legal presumption and privileging of heterosexual relationships also deprives gay and lesbian couples of equal rights and benefits in the areas of taxation, inheritance, adoption and parenting, health care access, government-subsidized financing, immigration and travel, and protection from domestic violence.

Singapore's military service imposes what is commonly known as the "302 policy" on its national service personnel: Adult male citizens and second-generation permanent residents are required by law to serve full time for two years. According to gay activists who have participated in national service, people classified as "302" are officially known to the military as *gay* or *transgender;* the classification is believed to stay on their dossiers, which are transferred to the government agencies where they work if they continue with government service professionally. Once they officially declare themselves to be gay or transgender, they are asked to undergo medical evaluation.[21] On the basis of their 302 status, gay men have been exempt from staying in camp overnight and from certain types of training duties, especially infantry. Instead, they were often assigned noncombat or desk duties. As for professional military personnel, male activists who had been career officers report having been followed, interrogated, and asked to sign documents declaring that they were not "practicing homosexual[s]" or risk being relegated to dead-end positions.[22]

Singaporean media are banned from carrying content that "promotes," "justifies" or "glamorises" "lifestyles such as homosexuality, lesbianism, bisexualism, transsexualism [and] transvestism" (see, e.g., the Free-to-Air Television Programme Code). This is a licensing condition imposed on subscription television, free-to-air television, and film distributors and found in the programming codes of state licenses issued to these media companies. Aside from the offensiveness of the term *lifestyle,* the word *promote* is problematic. When the content simply depicts gay people leading lives as other, straight people would in the same society, the question becomes whether this depiction amounts to "promotion." For instance, a local television station was fined for airing a segment of an interview with actor Anne Heche, who talked about her romantic relationship with Ellen DeGeneres; another station chose to censor the Academy Awards acceptance speech by Dustin Lance Black, the screenwriter for the movie *Milk,* about the life of gay rights activist Harvey Milk. The local cable television provider was fined for broadcasting after midnight pixilated footage of lesbian sex and bondage from a reality television show as well as for showing two fully clothed women kissing in a music video. Even when films depicting gay and lesbian lives—without explicit sex scenes—are allowed to be screened in local theaters, they usually come with age restrictions or zoning rules that limit the screenings to downtown theaters located away from residential hubs.[23]

Social Conditions for Gays and Lesbians

> I've been to Australia, and I've had people hurling bottles at me because I was holding hands with my girlfriend. . . . [Singapore] is quite safe actually. At least I don't feel like I'll be hauled up from the streets and pinned to a fence. (Mabel)

I don't think they would beat us up. We've done it before, held our hands and walked around the streets and they've given us funny looks, but we're okay with that. (Percy)

Despite legalized discrimination and the lack of legal protection, there appears to be lack of fear of physical violence, a sentiment that reflects a general sense of physical safety in Singapore. Although people interviewed for this book feel that holding hands with a partner in public may attract quizzical or uncomfortable stares, they believe that gay bashing is unlikely. Women did recall stories about lesbians who were raped about twenty years ago, one male informant said he was assaulted and heard of similar stories, and both men and women reported bullying incidents in schools. Nevertheless, informants commonly stressed that they would feel physically safer if they were to take a wrong turn down a street in Singapore than they would in certain areas of the United States and Australia.

Beyond physical violence and the lack of legal protection, however, being open about one's sexuality carries different stakes for different people. Surveys by the government, local media, and research institutions paint an ambiguous picture of social acceptance of homosexuality in Singapore. For example, a government-sponsored study in 2002 showed that 85 percent of its 1,481 respondents found homosexuality unacceptable (Chen 2013). According to a 2007 newspaper poll of 284 people twelve to twenty-five years old, only 30 percent objected to homosexuality (Wong 2007). However, a more rigorous survey by a local university found that 68.6 percent of its randomly selected respondents expressed negative views toward "homosexuals" (Detenber et al. 2007). Understanding the various factors influencing social acceptance falls outside the scope of this book, but certain patterns appear consistently among activists who speak from their own personal journeys or involvement in the gay community. For one, the experiences of being openly gay in Singapore are diverse.[24] Generally, they range from depressing and suicidal to living life to the fullest and depend on one's family, religious ties, and social and professional relationships.

At work, gays and lesbians in Singapore find a spectrum of environments. Despite a prime ministerial announcement in 2003 that the Singaporean government does not discriminate against gays in civil service, no concrete anti-discrimination law exists. It all depends on the individual persons and their workplaces. Some people hide their sexuality for fear of harassment, blackmail, or employment discrimination. The arts and entertainment industry is known to be friendly. In corporate settings, the environment is unsurprisingly more conservative, though one may have immediate supervisors and colleagues who are not the least bothered or are even supportive, or work for multinational corporations that have nondiscrimination policies. Some activists and their gay friends who are employed at government agencies and the local press feel comfortable making their sexuality known at work and believe that their sexuality is not held against them.

Two of the most gay-unfriendly government agencies are the education and defense ministries. Yet, the consequences differ across individuals and from one specific office to the next under these ministries. In 2007, Otto Fong became the first public school teacher in Singapore to announce publicly that he was gay. Fong posted an online message that spread fast and furiously over the weekend. All of the local newspapers carried the story. On Monday morning, when Fong went to school and attended the weekly flag ceremony, to his great surprise, the head prefect came up to him and shook his hand. His students smiled at him, he smiled back, and nothing more was said. The reaction from the school and ministry, however, was unclear. Fong had come out at a time when his teaching contract was about to expire in a matter of months at the end of the calendar year, and he had no intention of renewing it. The situation therefore provided a convenient "out" for the ministry and school. They let Fong serve out the remaining months of his contract, and so it remains uncertain how they would have responded had he intended to continue teaching. Some other interviewees and informants have described situations in which people were demoted or censured under circumstances that raise suspicion that homophobia was a motivating factor. However, other teachers among the activists in this study are also known to students and colleagues to be gay and do not believe that they have suffered for it.

Among career military officers, individual experiences also vary. Some are government scholars, people whom the government handpicked for university scholarships. These are the respondents who reported surveillance and being asked to sign declarations that they were not "practicing homosexual[s]." Perhaps one could argue that they were groomed for leadership positions and were therefore placed under stricter state scrutiny. But this cannot be ascertained definitively because the ministry is notoriously opaque about its policies and practices. One activist, Robbie, was a career officer but not a government scholar. After having kept quiet on previous checks, he decided to disclose that he was gay during a routine security clearance. He was ordered to write down the names of places he frequented socially and people he knew. Subsequently, he was blocked from the highest level of security clearance, which he had obtained before; however, Robbie is uncertain whether that was due to his coming out or due to the fact that he had already told his superiors that he did not intend to renew his contract. After his peer colleagues found out what he had done, they reached out to him and expressed concern. His immediate supervisor clearly did not understand much about homosexuality, but he showed kind intentions in trying to grapple with what it meant. During Robbie's remaining months with the ministry, he was still informally allowed to work on issues that his clearance level would have forbidden. According to Robbie, "They just closed one eye."

At home and with friends, gays and lesbians who disclose their sexuality sometimes make straightforward pronouncements in ways that can be described as *coming out*. Others are subtler. There are gay activists who talk about how they or their gay friends integrate themselves and their partners into the family landscape. The reactions they receive from families differ. Some families quickly, if not immediately, accept them. In numerous other accounts, parents reacted poorly, but eventually came around and began to invite the couples to attend family events and to participate in family portraits. The acceptance is often not uttered verbally but conveyed through actions. The mother of one interviewee, Rahim, was at first upset to find out that he was gay, especially since Rahim's brother was also gay. Months later, Rahim broke up with his boyfriend and came home one night sick from drinking. His mother could tell what had happened, went into his room, and simply put her arm around him. In some accounts, a lover would spend the night and the initially resistant mother would make breakfast for them the next morning.[25]

The myriad of family reactions intersects issues of class, education, race, and religion. In postcolonial Singapore, those who are Christian are often English-speaking, although some churches do use Mandarin Chinese. Further, a faction of political or economic elites is made up of English-speaking, Chinese Christians, whereas Chinese-speaking Chinese tend to be more closely associated with the Asian religions of Buddhism and Daoism and the lower classes.[26]

> The biggest problems are those who have Christian parents, educated Christian parents. Those who have parents who are just hawkers[27] ... don't care. My parents are not well educated—they don't care as long as I'm a good girl, as long as I become a decent human being. But if you have the golf membership, you have this, you have to look good in society, you have Christian friends, you have those soirées, and all the people that you meet—gosh, you're queer! How did that

happen? From my personal observations, they tend to get the short end of the stick. (Mabel)

In the days when I was running the support groups, I could almost put people on a scale. All right, the ones who have the hardest time are the Chinese—this is for males, of course—the Chinese boys from Christian families, the ones with the hardest time. The ones with the easiest times are the Chinese boys from Chinese-speaking families. (Trey)

In between the two ends of his scale, Trey places Indian Hindus and Muslims. Among the activists in this book, while Indian Hindus or Muslims also struggle with their sexuality and the consequences of living openly, they seldom emphasize a pressing need to reconcile faith and sexuality compared with their Christian counterparts, especially of the Anglican and Evangelical traditions. Gays and lesbians report experiencing or knowing of others who faced pressure by right-wing churches to undergo "reparative therapy"—"treatments" that include social reconditioning and spiritual training to try to "convert" gays and lesbians to heterosexuality and have been discredited by medical and psychiatric bodies in other countries.

These activists' accounts and perceptions may seem to align with the PAP's essentialized racial and religious differences. However, as my movement analysis in the next five chapters shows, gay activists transcend this static, uncritical ideology. Through community building and social support services, gay activists help people such as those described by Trey and Mabel to overcome homophobia and oppression inflicted by certain racially or religiously affiliated groups. Moreover, these activists do not emphasize racial or religious differences among themselves,[28] though some of their groups organize around particular religions with the aim of carrying out community building and service work.

This aspect of the movement is reflected in Kang's personal journey. Kang comes from an English-speaking, Chinese Christian family and is one of the earliest members of a pioneer movement organization, which is discussed in Chapter 3. When Kang told his parents that he was gay, they got upset and insisted that he seek help from a "reparative therapy" program affiliated with their church, an account that corroborates Mabel's and Trey's observations. Kang refused. He struggled with his own sexuality and soured family relations and found a home in the movement. Eventually, he went on to lead his life as an openly gay man and settled into a long-term relationship.

Although Kang's parents still say, "We can't condone what you're doing," they have changed enough to meet his partner and attend their wedding ceremony overseas. Like Kang's parents, change in Singapore may take trials and tribulations, but it is possible. The varied responses toward gays and lesbians working in national defense, public education, and other areas of civil service, ranging from bigotry to tolerance and some acceptance, reflect a larger environment that is shifting and diverse in values and attitudes. On one hand, oppressive laws and regulations remain on the books; on the other hand, the state's position on homosexuality has moved from condemnation to one of balancing of interests, openly acknowledging gay people, but qualifying that their interests cannot trump the majority whom it believes still opposes homosexuality. The political norms surrounding collective mobilization still pose constraints, but this does not mean that the Singaporean state never bows to grassroots or international pressure. It depends on how pressure is applied and demands are made.

The key is strategic adaptation: how gay activists read signals, take action, and interact with the state, the PAP, and other social actors and how they mutually react and respond to one another. This is the central theme of pragmatic resistance that threads through my analysis of the movement in the next five chapters. I draw attention to how gay activists interpret signals that include the formal barriers to collective mobilization and political norms explored in this chapter and to how they adapt in response to the shifts and changes in signals over time. In the process, I show how activists toe the line as they push the boundaries of these political norms and eventually even contest Section 377A of the Penal Code. In the analysis, I also highlight how the criminalization of same-sex sexual conduct and other legal and social conditions affecting gays and lesbians in Singapore motivate activists to join the movement and persevere in their struggles.

3

Timorous Beginnings

Starting with this chapter, I analyze the development of Singapore's gay movement from its emergence in the early 1990s. I structure the analysis chronologically to show how gay activists respond to ever-shifting signals, engage in strategic adaptation of pragmatic resistance, which is the central theme of this book, and deploy tactics that heed both movement advancement and survival. In the process, the chronological analysis brings out the three patterns of change highlighted in Chapter 1—the movement's coming out; tactical escalation, expansion, and diversification; and the opening up of political and media spaces. As activists strategically adapt pragmatic resistance over time, the three themes become more evident.

This chapter shows how the nascent movement reflected the three patterns from the start. At a time of shifting political terrain in the early 1990s, the movement emerged but stayed hidden from public view, focusing inward on community building and support services. Pioneering gay activists attempted to scale up tactics in response to encouraging signs, but they did so with limited support from grassroots and allies. Faced with external threats from the state and media, they adjusted tactics to fight for the movement's survival.

As Singapore's economy grew and the nation gradually prospered, a wealthier and better-educated middle class emerged. They began to question the PAP's dominance and demand greater accountability. Starting with a by-election in 1981, the PAP began to lose parliamentary seats. No longer did it sweep elections the way it had since 1968. In the 1984 general elections, the PAP went on to lose two of eighty-two seats. Although the party still commanded a clear majority, it attributed its decline partly to the alienation of the middle class (Lyons 2004).

To remedy the situation, the party turned to law once again so that it could allow more political opposition and participation while simultaneously containing it. For example, the PAP-led Parliament amended the constitution and passed new legislation to create two new categories of members of Parliament—non-constituency members of Parliament (NCMPs), who are members of opposition parties and "top losers" in the elections with a certain percentage of votes, and nominated members of Parliament (NMPs), who are appointed by the state to provide "responsible criticism" while being "apolitical" (Thio L. 2004). NCMPs and NMPs have limited power and may not vote on constitutional amendments, supply and money bills, or votes of "no confidence."

The PAP administration also permitted the emergence of a civil society and allowed civil society groups to hold limited debate and express dissent. Among the first of these groups to appear in the 1980s were AWARE, Singapore's first postindependence women's organization (Association of Women for Action and Research), and an HIV/AIDS group after the first two cases of HIV infection were reported in 1985. A flurry of activities sprang up on local university campuses too. Viraj and Quentin recall the excitement of politicized campus organizations and Catholic groups that promoted liberation theology and social justice issues. Local theater companies began to stage socially conscious plays that touched on civil-political liberties and human rights.

Unfortunately, the bloom was brief. To borrow the words of gay activists today, perhaps the boundaries of political norms in the 1980s were pushed too hard. The political intrigue of this era is far too complicated and lies outside the scope of this book, but hints of optimism wilted away as the 1980s bowed out with state acts of repression. One of the two most infamous cases involved the solicitor-general, Francis Seow. After becoming the president of the Law Society in 1986, Seow advocated for the professional body to critique legislation. In the days leading up to the 1988 general elections, he was accused of receiving campaign funds from the United States for his bid as an opposition politician and was detained without trial under the ISA for seventy-two days. Eventually charged with tax evasion, Seow fled to the United States, where he remains in exile.[1] In 1987, the government unleashed the ISA on twenty-odd men and women affiliated with liberal Catholic groups. It alleged that these social workers and volunteers, who advocated for better employment conditions for migrant workers, had ties to foreign communists and plotted a "Marxist conspiracy" to overthrow the state.[2] The crackdown left imprints on pioneering gay activists who were involved with liberal Catholic groups. Quentin, Keenan, and Viraj, for example, know people and their families who were directly affected by the detentions.

After the alleged Marxist conspiracy, Parliament enacted a new statute, the Maintenance of Religious Harmony Act. The new law prohibited members of religious groups, especially leaders, from using their religious activities as a "guise" to "promote a political cause" or carry out "subversive activities." The demise of liberal Christianity also created a spiritual vacuum that was later filled by more conservative Christian churches, fueling the rise of right-wing fundamentalism.[3] These developments returned to influence the gay movement and its strategy and tactics as people from anti-gay Christian churches crossed paths with the movement in the 1990s and the churches' condemnation of homosexuality erupted into an organized opposition in the mid-2000s.

First Openings

Despite ending in government repression, the 1980s left behind awakenings of political consciousness, seeds for collective organizing, early signs of gay life and culture, and cracks and openings for social change. At the end of the decade, Singapore's first prime minister, Lee Kuan Yew, stepped down, and his successor, Goh Chok Tong, spoke of making a "kinder and gentler Singapore." Amid the confluence of warning signs and optimistic first openings, Singapore's gay movement was born.

Before the 1980s, gay life and gay culture in Singapore were largely absent from memory. Scanty accounts recall a gay bar called Le Bistro in the late 1960s and the addition of Treetops and Pebble Bar in the 1970s.[4] Accounts of lesbian life are even fewer, and they usually focus on isolation and loneliness.[5] At most, there were a few places where gays and lesbians could socialize clandestinely. No community or visible gay culture existed, fear of detection and sanction loomed, and no one imagined the possibility of collective action. Such are the stories that old-timers tell. Oliver recalls reading magazine reports about gay liberation in the United States, but he and his gay friends could not fathom gay liberation for themselves.

> We never felt like we should get together a movement. It just wasn't on our intellectual horizon . . . because of fear. . . . It's also . . . you assess and say, "I'm not going to get anywhere with this," and so I

call it "imagination of the possible." And the seventies in Singapore, the imagination of the possible didn't include some sort of gay movement. (Oliver)

In the 1980s, signs of visible gay life began to sprout. More reliable accounts and records of gay and lesbian bars point to a disco, Niche, which opened in 1983 and allowed same-sex dancing. Cruising grounds for gay men seemed to increase in number, including the ones still popularly remembered—Ang Siang Hill, Tanjung Rhu-Fort Road, Bedok Stadium, and Hong Lim Park. Those who cruised ran the risk of arrest, whereas visits to gay bars could coincide unluckily with police raids.

For women, the social scene of the 1980s was sparser. It consisted mainly of "ladies' night" once a week, and even that was an uncommon sight for some of them. One had to be part of the grapevine. Popular clubs in town often had a table or two where lesbians in the know got together for drinks. Women's interactions more frequently took place among friends at private parties and events, so only people who knew one another met and socialized. One woman ran a lesbian feminist newsletter and social group in Singapore, but left for the United States shortly after the alleged Marxist conspiracy implicated one of her collaborators in the arts circle.

Theater nevertheless showed encouraging signs, with the introduction of local gay plays prompted by the boom of the 1980s.[6] When Singaporean playwrights Chay Yew and Eleanor Wong received commissions from the Ministry of Community Development to write plays that raised awareness of HIV/AIDS, they delivered *Ten Little Indians* and *Jackson on a Jaunt*, respectively, both with gay male characters in sympathetic and central roles. The government withdrew its support, deeming the plays to have portrayed homosexuality in a nonnegative or "normal" way, in contradiction of censorship rules.[7] Around the same time, however, another theater company managed to stage *Rigor Mortis*. The play, which is about three friends living together, could be considered the first local gay play ever to be performed on Singaporean stage, but it did not explicitly refer to words such as *gay* or *homosexuality*.

The theater boom offered one pathway to gay activism. Keenan went to law school with gay classmates who went on to set up theater companies or become playwrights, eventually producing and staging some of the most important gay plays in Singapore. These local companies and drama circles later changed the political consciousness of future activists who first joined the theater and connected them to the gay movement. The local theater scene continues to intersect with the movement through interactions and overlaps among the people who work in both fields. Along with other artistic outlets, such as literature and film, it endures as a platform for gay political expression.[8]

Civil society groups that cropped up in reaction to the state-permitted dissent opened another pathway to the movement. Granted, neither AWARE, the women's group, nor the HIV/AIDS group openly associates itself with gay equality, perhaps out of pragmatic resistance on their part. The HIV/AIDS group receives most of its funding from the government to target gay men as well as other social groups; hence, it does not want to be seen as championing gay rights, a position that the state could consider too confrontational. For AWARE, because it is fighting an uphill battle in a deeply patriarchal, heteronormative state, many of its leaders fear that supporting homosexuality would simply create further risk and obstacles. The distancing is also ideological: Much to the frustration of lesbian activists, key AWARE leaders claim to work on "issues," not identities, meaning that they do not make claims based on identity categories, such as "lesbian," racial or religious groups, or certain classes, but frame grievances in terms of matters such as "sexual harassment" or "body image." In Chapter 7, "Mobilizing in the Open," I analyze how AWARE's ambivalence toward homosexuality and gay rights was tested in 2009, when lesbian activists helped AWARE to oust a group of right-wing Christians who alleged that the women's organization was promoting a "homosexual agenda."[9]

Nevertheless, both AWARE and the HIV/AIDS organization have provided contact points for gay activists to enter the movement, right from the start. Gay activists often observe that the two groups are overwhelmingly made up of gay men and lesbians who keep their sexuality undisclosed. Because both groups have government sanction, they offer at least some kind of safety cloak under which gay men and lesbians can come together and find social support.

The first identifiably gay organization was the Coalition. Although nobody reports the same details about how the group began, the exact composition of the founding group, or even when the members first met, certain patterns appear clearly and consistently in the narratives and records. Everybody remembers the buzz of politicization, organizing, and rights talk. They all describe a growing need to "do something" to improve the sociopolitical and legal conditions of gays in Singapore, and they usually remember the involvement of food. For Quentin, it started during a dinner conversation when a social worker recounted a caller on the hotline who asked about gay issues.

That provided the catalyst to discuss this issue for the first time out at social gatherings. . . . And it was just very informal talking about this, and I thought that perhaps it might not be a bad idea then to sort of further verbalize our thoughts and call a couple of meetings, if it was even called a meeting. We went to people's houses for tea. (Quentin)

Quentin, like Viraj and Keenan, was involved in the social justice programs of liberal Catholic groups in the 1980s and absorbed ideals about putting his faith into practice. In the early 1990s, Viraj attended graduate school at a local university, where he worked on a student journal. Through the journal, he came into contact with Mitchell, who found out about the group from Quentin. Mitchell had returned to Singapore from an Australian university to spend his summer vacation. Newly exposed to gay politics in his college courses, he was eager to apply what he had learned.

One connection led to another and brought the Coalition's founding members together by December 1992. They talked about gay consciousness and shared stories about their sexuality. The meetings continued to take place in 1993, and a few more members joined. Some had attended HIV/AIDS awareness events run by the HIV/AIDS organization, where they heard of a group of "like-minded people." Oliver heard similar talk from an artist friend and went to one of the tea sessions at someone's home. By the time Li-Ling, another artist, heard about it and brought along her good friend Si-Yuan, these get-togethers had moved to the cafe at the Fringe Center, a new arts company formed to support local, non-mainstream artistic expressions. Si-Yuan confidently remembers that the cafe served "very good" *char siew rice* (barbecued pork rice).

First Escalation of Tactics

Although they had been meeting since 1992, the Coalition remained a group of friends and acquaintances talking among themselves. Their number stayed small, anywhere from five to fifteen at a given time. Through the lenses of pragmatic resistance, their tactic carefully toed the line. While their meetings and the content of their dialogues challenged norms about politics and heteronormativity, they stayed out of public view and avoided engaging the state directly and certainly did not confront it.

Then Rascals happened and led to the Coalition's escalation of tactics. Detailed in Chapter 1, it was the first direct engagement with the state in an era of frequent police raids on gay bars. Word spread quickly about the police letter apologizing for the officers' "lack of tact" and the verbal assurance that the police would cease the legally questionable practices of detaining persons without their identity cards. Founders of the Coalition noticed the whitewashing by the police, but the fact that they replied with an apology and claimed that they had conducted an internal investigation was groundbreaking for them. It gave them hope that change was possible and galvanized the Coalition, which seemed to talk, in Oliver's words, "endlessly about coming out" up to that point.

> [The Rascals campaign] really took action, they organized the letter, they talked to the police, and so I could feel that the gay ground was bubbling and wanting to do something . . . feeling indignant. . . . "We won't take this anymore." (Oliver)

Oliver and others in the Coalition seized on the optimism of Rascals to organize bigger gatherings to spread word about the incident and bring people together. With Keenan's help, they printed a booklet titled *Guide to Your Legal Rights*. It set out, step by step, what to do during a police encounter—how to react if the police asked for identification, what the police could and could not legally do, the circumstances under which one could be arrested without warrant, one's rights if arrested, and legal options when charged in court.

Consequently, after June 1993, the Coalition transformed from cozy tea sessions and mealtime conversations into monthly Sunday forums. The Fringe Center management, out of friendship with the Coalition leadership, let the group use one of their performance studios. The Sunday forums provided a platform to vocalize shared grievances, helping to strengthen a sense of community. When Mitchell completed his studies in Australia and returned in April 1994, the Sunday forums were well established. It had a regular attendance of thirty to fifty, with occasional spikes of up to two hundred, depending on the weekly topics, which ranged from legal and political concerns to beauty and health care.

Meanwhile, the Coalition's newsletter regularized with monthly editions. Si-Yuan and another member often snuck into a fellow member's workplace late at night to photocopy the newsletter. The newsletter included updates about meetings, commentaries by members, and reviews on gay media content as well as reprinted gay news from other countries.

Compared with the earlier get-togethers, the Coalition's tactics *after* Rascals pushed boundaries a little more. The initial forum about Rascals and bar raids exposed state repression, an act of shaming the authoritarian state.

The legal rights booklet empowered people to think in terms of rights and an oppositional relationship with state agents. The Sunday forums enabled gays and lesbians to speak out and build contentious political identities. Although they were held in a private space, they contested the spirit behind laws that curtail basic civil-political liberties of association, assembly, and speech. So did the newsletters, which were published and distributed without the required licenses. Nonetheless, these actions simultaneously stayed within bounds. The Coalition did not openly confront the state with demands for greater rights and did not shame it in public; their exposure of state repression, rights discourse, forums, and newsletters were inward in target, aimed at a particular group of people.

First Expansion and Diversification

As the Sunday forums thrived between 1994 and 1996, the Coalition generated opportunities for newcomers to interact with the organization and a larger collective. These interactions led to the movement's first expansion and diversification. Newcomers came into contact for the first time with people who imagined themselves as bearing legitimate legal and political claims based on their sexuality and had the desire and courage to change existing circumstances. Some of them later came to play influential roles in the Coalition or other movement organizations. Through these interactions, they discovered other needs and issues that the Coalition did not or could not address and began to spin off new groups from the Coalition's base. For example, Trey became the Coalition's most prominent leader and formed peer support groups for gay men. Kang, whose parents pressured him to undergo a Christian "reparative therapy" program, cofounded the Harbor as an outlet for gay Christians to discuss homosexuality and faith.

Two women, Cheryl and Gillian, spun off a lesbian group.

> From [the Coalition] we realized that there're too many guys, and I think the girls needed a girls' group. . . . That's how [Cheryl] and I rounded up about five or six of our friends to set up [Argot]. (Gillian)

Lesbian interviewees and informants provide conflicting accounts as to whether "Argot" was simply another name for the "women's wing," which first reported its gathering in the Coalition's August 1994 newsletter. After July 1995, the "women's wing" vanished from the newsletters, while reports referring to Argot, aimed at creating social ties and identity building among lesbians, began to appear.

However, both the Coalition's men and women consistently remember the presence of three lesbians, Li-Ling, Cheryl, and Gillian, the few lesbian activists from the Coalition's founding years. The Coalition's forums, though open to all, were too gay men-centric to sustain the interest of women who decided to give the Sunday event a chance. They usually showed up for a few meetings, quickly lost interest in the topics and audience, and disappeared. Of course, the social scene and private gatherings still existed, but few lesbians took leadership roles in the movement in the early 1990s. To contemporary lesbian activists, the older generation not only was more fearful of living openly but also distrusted men. Hence, the few lesbian leaders in those days were those willing to coexist with the Coalition's male leadership; men and women did not always coorganize events, but they did support one another. Quentin used to arrange his schedule to be away from his house and let Li-Ling or other lesbian leaders host gatherings there. More lesbians would take up gay activism in later years, but they would continue the pattern of pragmatic resistance rather than break away into radical factions, as happened in the United States. Thus, the increased number of women contributed to the expanded use of pragmatic resistance by diversifying the movement's tactics, services, and organizational types.

Mixed Signals

Despite the first openings for the movement, followed by its first escalation, expansion, and diversification, the early 1990s proved to be a hostile time to be gay in Singapore. The police frequently raided gay businesses and entrapped gay men at popular cruising grounds. HIV/AIDS and gay activists believe that police persecution intensified after the first case of an HIV/AIDS-related death was reported in Singapore in 1987[10] and the government identified gay men as a high-risk group. Even lesbian bars were affected. A nightclub that hosted a monthly all-women's party was forced to shut down. It did not help that a local newspaper had portrayed the parties as violent events in which women fought over each other. Compelled by such negative portrayals and suppression of the little social space that lesbians had, Gillian—who used to frequent the club—later started women-only commercial parties and nightspots. Others in later years of the movement reacted to the lack of lesbian social spaces differently, by offering alternative, alcohol-free events.

In November 1993, the police carried out the most infamous entrapment operations of gay men. They arrested twelve men along Fort Road in the Tanjung Rhu district, a popular cruising ground, and local newspapers published the names, personal details, and photographs of those who were arrested. To this day, that operation remains *the* incident to which activists refer as "the Tanjung Rhu arrests." The story is told and retold in gay activists' oral history, from one generation to the next, and memorialized and reinterpreted in plays and films that influence future generations of activists.[11]

Around this time, Viraj, together with Keenan and a few others within the Coalition and the local arts scene, toyed with the idea of submitting a "position paper" to the government about the decriminalization of same-sex sexual conduct. Before they took any formal action, though, they sent out feelers through someone who had access to the PAP leadership. The rebuke was harsh. They were told that if they were to go public with such a demand the government would "come down very strongly on us."

Yet, as is usually the case with Singapore, silver linings appear amid looming clouds. Despite the controversy and scares, several gay plays made history in this period. The first Chinese-language gay play, Otto Fong's *Another Tribe,* was staged in 1991. The first two plays ever to feature a lesbian protagonist, Eleanor Wong's *Mergers and Acquisitions* and the sequel *Wills and Secessions* (Wong was a corporate lawyer), debuted in 1993 and 1995, respectively. The censorship review committee (1992) had just reaffirmed that "materials encouraging homosexuality" should continue to be banned. However, theater sometimes squeaks through because censors can be persuaded to give more leeway to its small and niche audience reach. It is often regarded as having limited impact with ideas that may otherwise openly challenge the existing political order.[12]

Out of police entrapments peeked another silver lining. One man who was arrested in a September 1993 operation, Tan Boon Hock, pleaded guilty to the charge under Section 354 of the Penal Code, but appealed against the harsh sentence of four months' imprisonment and three strokes of the cane. On appeal, Chief Justice Yong, known to be tough on crime, unexpectedly substituted the original sentence with a S$2,000 fine (approximately US$1,400). He ridiculed police entrapment, saying that he was "bemused" by the charge. Undercover police in entrapment cases usually enticed gay men to initiate physical contact and then arrested them for "outrage of modesty" under Section 354. The provision impliedly requires force or nonconsent, but since the undercover police, by the very nature of entrapment, would have communicated consent to the physical contact, the Chief Justice thought that the charge did not make any sense. The appellant did not contest the question of consent and had already pleaded guilty, so this particular remark was not pertinent to his appeal—that is, it was not the *ratio decidendi* of the chief justice's decision. While both men and women recall incidents of police intrusion on gay businesses, often associated with illegal drug use, they consistently point out in their interviews that entrapment has ceased since 1994. This observation concurs with the absence of court judgments and the decline in media reports since the mid-1990s.[13] Even though *Tan Boon Hock* (1994) was neither activist-initiated nor a case of rights litigation, it represents an instance of how the Singaporean legalistic approach to the rule of law aided the movement and might have inadvertently helped to alter legal conditions for gays.

Rising Fear

Faced with mixed signals, the movement's pioneers remained wary while taking heart in the few glimmers of hope. They crept along, harboring excitement and optimism mixed with a strong dose of fear. Perhaps the fear of surveillance first grew out of paranoia, but it increased with the harsh realization that they were indeed under surveillance.

> There was always a mixture of exhilaration, of euphoria. . . . But it was also always colored by nervousness. Every month as the meeting approaches, you're bound to hear some story. "Hey, I heard this month the police are coming." (Oliver)

As the Sunday forums blossomed, the Coalition's leaders started hearing rumors from friends and acquaintances who claimed to have insider information. Then the evidence became more concrete. At one Sunday forum, a man identified himself to the Coalition's leaders as belonging to the Internal Security Department. When two Coalition leaders met with him, he disclosed that he had been asked at the last minute to monitor their events, without any prior briefing that it was a gay organization. Even more strangely, he suggested that the Coalition relocate to a neighboring country for precautionary reasons. The man appeared nervous, and the two activists found no reason for him to disclose his actions at the risk of breaching security rules. The two theorized that possibly this officer had fallen prey to a cruel prank of his colleagues, who might have suspected that he was gay. But whatever his true motivations were, the Coalition sensed the first hints of danger associated with violating laws restricting association.

> The police were watching them. They'll take down their car plate number if it's parked outside [the Fringe Center]. (Abby)

> I heard how [the Coalition] used to hold their meetings at [the Fringe Center] and the police used to come and take down the numbers of all the cars. (Shelly)

The second warning quickly followed. A participant in the Sunday forums heard from his mother, a former police officer, who learned from her former colleague that their family car's license plate number was being investigated. That participant had driven the car to the Fringe Center to attend the Sunday forums. Of all of the stories about surveillance, this "license plate" incident is the most memorable. Interviewees who joined the movement much later most frequently recounted this story as a warning tale passed on by old-timers.

The Coalition's unlicensed newsletter also fueled the panic. The group usually distributed copies of the newsletter only at the Sunday forums to avoid openly violating the laws restricting publications. One day, a forum participant took copies, intending to pass them out to others who were not at the forum, but absentmindedly left the whole stack in the restroom of a bookstore near the Fringe Center.

> And it was just horrifying to us because it was an illegal publication. We didn't have a [government-issued license] number for it, and of course, its content would raise a lot of eyebrows. (Trey)

To make matters worse, a journalist friend tipped them off about a local tabloid's plan to run an exposé of their Sunday gatherings. In those days, the Coalition's members, including some of their leaders, still kept their sexuality a secret from employers or families. As a group, they were unprepared for, even afraid of, media publicity.

From Making Advances to Questioning Survival

The combination of unwanted media exposure and state surveillance contributed to the making of a perfect storm. The fear was palpable. Attendance at the Sunday forums fell. The Coalition had no choice but to adjust their tactics accordingly. From focusing on movement advancement, they turned around to ensure the group's survival, the other tenet of pragmatic resistance. Even though they shunned direct engagement with the state, they had to think about how to respond to authorities, and by thinking through those responses, the question of legal legitimacy arose.

Fending off a nosy tabloid was the easier challenge. The Coalition leaders informed Sunday forum participants that the upcoming gathering was canceled. Without any visual images and details of an actual event taking place, the tabloid had nothing to sensationalize, so the Coalition managed to stymie that imminent threat. This tactical response to local media contrasts sharply with those in later stages of the movement, when fear subsided and confidence grew.

Responding to state surveillance was far more complicated. The Coalition leaders prepared for the worst if the police ever showed up to shut down their Sunday forums. They decided that they should obey police orders and not confront them. Otherwise, they worried that the participants who were not involved in the group's leadership would be implicated in the crackdown.

> I know in my heart of hearts that should the police come, I have to be the one, with a few other friends, who must face them and say, "Okay, we are the ones responsible. The rest aren't." . . . Then everyone can disperse and we will talk to the police. . . . And if the police say, "Disband," we will disband. But if the police . . . say, "You guys have done something illegal. We're going to press charges," then we just have to face those charges. . . . We're not going to deny that we were meeting there to talk about postmodern art. (Oliver)

This position may seem weak, despite the display of courage and responsibility. Alternatively, the tactic aims to contain the damage; rather than put at risk the entire group of people the leaders had tried hard to cultivate, it gives the fruits of their labor a better chance of survival and revival. In this light, the tactic conforms to the core characteristics of pragmatic resistance—refraining from actions that are blatantly confrontational or threatening to the existing political order.

Inherent within these responses to a police crackdown is the realization that the Coalition lacked legal legitimacy, one of the four vital political norms. This was why the members felt disadvantaged in the face of strict law enforcement.

> So the question [was] how do we not run afoul of the law and have the whole bunch of screaming queens hauled into the detention center? It's funny now. But at that time, I think the whole atmosphere was so different. (Quentin)

The lack of legal status for gay activist organizations became a constant feature in the movement. As the movement developed, activists used different tactics to maintain their organizations in unregistered form. At this juncture of the movement, however, its pioneers had no precedent from which to learn or seek inspiration. Instead, they carried vivid memories of past oppression. The crackdowns of previous decades were close to the hearts of some, and the Tanjung Rhu arrests remained fresh. There were only two options that gay activists of the early 1990s could envision for their movement: Either disband and scuttle their efforts or deploy pragmatic resistance, make use of legal restrictions to register the Coalition with the government, and thus gain legitimacy and self-preservation. The movement arrived at a turning point.

Shifting Tactics in Response to Fear

Because of the rising fear, gay activists shifted tactics for the second time in these early years. The first adjustment followed the Rascals letter campaign to escalate consciousness-raising and community building. This one initiated direct engagement with the state for the first time since Rascals and also reshaped the movement. But it arose out of the need to survive, a situation that I contrast with the second registration attempt in 2004.

The Coalition's leaders were split over whether to register the organization. The founding cohort, who met in living rooms and cafés, preferred to stick to community building; officially confessing the group's existence by applying for registration was too bold a tactical shift for them. However, the camp that pushed for registration, led by Oliver and Trey, prevailed in the end. As a gay man, researcher, and former journalist, Oliver joined the Coalition to work on social justice. Trey joked that he was lured to his first Sunday forum under "false pretenses," thinking he could find romantic possibilities to recover from a bad breakup. But he had also grown up in a "relatively political" family and was conscious about the ways in which societies were organized. To Trey, the inward-looking tactics had reached an impasse and a change in direction was needed to keep pushing boundaries. To him, that meant, "We needed to become legit, and that meant we had to form a proper society and get it registered under the law." This motivation differed in the transition years, when the Coalition attempted registration again.

The registration process, long and drawn out, illuminates the nuances of pragmatic resistance and reveals familiar movement characteristics of the time—the timidity and fear among activists, even those who pushed for registration, the state's condemnation of homosexuality and their movement, and the lack of grassroots support and allies. Although registration under the Societies Act was the obvious choice, Quentin first tried to pass the Coalition off as a company seeking registration with the Registrar of Companies. That attempt was quickly aborted. Before applying for approval to register as a company, an entity first needs to seek approval for the company name itself, a process that routinely takes no more than three days. Three months later, the Coalition was still waiting for a reply. The official interim reply was that their application was pending; unofficially, Quentin heard that it had become an issue circulated among various ministries. Another three months later, the group finally received a reply. The government rejected the Coalition's application—which, strictly speaking, was only for a company name at that stage—on the grounds that the group had an "unlawful purpose" and was "prejudicial to public peace, welfare or good order in Singapore" "or contrary to national security, or interest."

The futile attempt sent a clear signal: The state already knew who they were, and pretending they were something else was pointless. So the Coalition's leaders decided that they just had to go for the Societies Act. But they faced the next hurdle. The application required ten signatories, complete with their identity card numbers.

> I don't know whether the rest have told you, but it was damn hard to get ten people out of the whole of Singapore. (Tony)

Few people who attended the Sunday forums were willing to volunteer, for fear that official affiliation with the group could be used against them in the future. Tony was concerned but willing to take the risk for an important cause. Others, even some within the Coalition's leadership, hesitated. After much difficulty, Trey, Quentin, Oliver, and the rest of the core group managed to scrape together nine names.

That left the tenth and final slot. At their wits' end, they circulated an appeal in the Coalition's monthly newsletter. A young lawyer, Brett, had been attending a series of "ex-gay" seminars organized by one of the evangelical churches. The seminars did not quite have the intended effect, and Brett left them behind in the mid-1990s and started cruising. That was when he bumped into friends whom he met at the church's events. They told him about the Coalition's Sunday forums, which he then attended. One Sunday, he picked up the newsletter and read the appeal. Not believing that he could get into trouble for filing a regulatory application and wanting to do something meaningful, he contacted Trey. The Coalition finally found the tenth signatory.

In later phases of the movement, the relative ease in finding signatories for other applications and petitions stands in stark contrast to the Coalition's difficulty with collecting ten signatures for the registration. Future activists who play key leadership roles and shape the movement also cross over from the "reparative therapy" programs run by conservative, anti-gay churches. As the movement escalates, these churches also coalesce into a visible counterforce.

The state's reactions to the Coalition's application and gay activists' subsequent responses contrast with those that come several years down the road. After months of preparation, the Coalition submitted the registration application in November 1996. The application stated that it was a group for promoting "awareness and understanding of the issues and problems concerning gay, lesbian and bisexual persons," and listed the ten Singaporeans as proposed members. This was the boldest tactical move the movement had taken, asserting the freedom to associate and organize for social change on issues that the state deemed to be taboo. Meanwhile, true to the essence of pragmatic resistance, the Coalition deliberately confined membership to citizens to show that theirs were domestic concerns and to avoid accusations of foreign interference.

A few days later, around midnight on a Saturday, three plainclothes officers knocked on Trey's apartment door. Trey answered, and they told him to go down to the police station on Monday morning to give a statement. Although he was nervous, looking back, Trey thought that the interview went through "a routine checklist of questions," such as how the group was formed and what they wanted to do. The police, of course, did not need to knock on Trey's door while he was dressed in pajamas in the dead of night, but neither did they drag him away without a legally substantiated reason. True to their state's rule-bound nature, they were carrying out intimidation within legally prescribed authority. After Trey's interview, the inspector wanted to interrogate a second signatory, and according to Trey, he randomly selected another person off the list.

Then the Coalition waited and waited. The group even sent a reminder letter. Half a year later, the Coalition received a rejection letter that warned the group to "cease all activities in connection with the society." The Coalition wrote to ask the Registrar for the grounds of his decision. The Registrar replied that he was not required to give a reason. The Coalition then appealed to the Ministry of Home Affairs, the Registrar's parent ministry, and finally to the Prime Minister's Office. In the three months that followed, a string of rejections descended on the Coalition, one after another, all saying the same thing: Stop now or face tough legal consequences. More frustrating than the rejection was the categorical stonewalling. Beyond the now-familiar provisions quoted verbatim from the Act on "good order" and "national security," the Coalition could not obtain any clear reason for the rejection. They also asked the minister and prime minister what the government wanted the group to do if registration was unsuccessful. The answer was reticence.

Registration was a tactical move of pragmatic resistance that leveraged legal legitimacy to ensure survival. The Coalition's leaders also obeyed law enforcement and did not openly resist it when interrogated. Following the rejection, they deployed further tactics of pragmatic resistance to object to it. While they questioned the state's authority and challenged its decision, they did not do so publicly, but went through administrative processes provided by law. They focused on the specific issue of registration and did not argue broader principles of rights or civil-political liberties. Their first appeal letter to the minister stated, "We would have thought the spirit of the Societies Act is to provide a framework for responsible free association," instead of pointing out that the Act and the particular rejection fundamentally curtailed their right to association. In their second appeal letter, they played to the political norm of preserving social stability, arguing that approval would enhance it by protecting secularism and promoting diversity:

> To grant our appeal is simply to act within the finest traditions of a dispassionate secular government. . . . Singaporeans are diverse. We are of different races, faiths, cultural orientations (even among the same race). To recognise that there are gay and lesbian Singaporeans too is nothing new. Singapore society strives to accommodate diversity: promoting tolerance and mutual respect. (Appeal Letter to Minister for Home Affairs, Coalition, May 31, 1997)

Finally, to the prime minister, they opined about Singapore's international image as a place of rule of law and lamented how the decision could damage Singapore economically:

> It is a laudable aim to make Singapore attractive to top talent from around the world, but some top talent happen to be gay or lesbian. Increasingly, senior level decision-makers in multinational corporations, in universities and even governments, are open about their sexual orientation and Singapore will not be an attractive environment if it is perceived to be homophobic. Even gay and lesbian Singaporeans now studying abroad consider favourably the idea of never returning. Such loss of indigenous talent, year in, year out,

generation after generation, is something Singapore can ill afford. (Appeal Letter to the Prime Minister, Coalition, July 2, 1997)[14]

As the Coalition's leaders waited for the registration outcome and filed appeals, they shut down the Sunday forums. After all, if they were seeking to organize legally, they felt that they should not be seen as carrying out what they had not yet been approved to do. The organization was not only losing participants because of surveillance scares but also experiencing leadership attrition. Mitchell withdrew after the tabloid scare. His father warned that he would be "screwed" if the police found out. He eventually returned to Australia to pursue his graduate studies and took up Australian citizenship. Others moved on. Keenan focused on his career, whereas Viraj left Singapore to find work. Si-Yuan, Li-Ling, and Cheryl pursued graduate studies overseas. Kang did the same, and so the Harbor faded away. Gillian started growing commercial party spaces for women instead. As its key players dispersed, Argot lingered but was eventually replaced by new lesbian groups. Those who disagreed with the Coalition's new direction of registration also drifted away. Nonetheless, whatever the reason for departure, most of them maintain friendly terms with the remaining leadership.

The rejection of registration brought the movement to a critical juncture. Now that they were officially denied by the state, the Coalition's leaders felt even more strongly that they could not flout the legal warnings and resume physical gatherings. This reaction contrasts with their response the second time around, in 2004. After exhausting all administrative avenues of appeal, the movement felt stuck by 1997. They did not, however, turn toward litigation and seek judicial review of such an administrative decision. The registration process—from making the decision to pursue registration to the actual attempt, outcome, and appeal and the government's stonewalling—brought the first phase of the movement to a close.

Hence, Singapore's gay movement emerged with trepidation in the early 1990s. The surveillance, registration, and warnings of legal sanctions acutely sensitized gay activists to the importance of legal legitimacy and influenced their future tactical choices. Those who pressed forward after the registration attempt remember their experiences with local media bias and state condemnation of activists as threats to state and society. Pioneering activists of the early 1990s in Singapore thus seeded a movement that continues to develop along the three themes of pragmatic resistance as they and newcomers strategically adapt to new signals and carry over lessons from this period.

4

Cyber Organizing

By the late 1990s, Singapore's gay movement shifted to the Internet as a means for organizing and for deploying pragmatic resistance. In this chapter, I examine this shift and show how the three patterns of change noted in the previous chapter evolved along with the strategic adaptation of pragmatic resistance. I also examine how gay activists in Singapore generally organize through the Internet.

Mindful of threatening signals, gay activists tactically adjusted to the newfound medium of the Internet and continued to mobilize away from public view. While the movement still lacked visible grassroots support and allies, it was expanding in outreach and organization numbers through cyber organizing. Political and local media spaces remained largely closed off to the movement, and fear lingered. Gradually, however, as gay activists noticed that the state largely left them alone and "nothing happened," they built up confidence and kept the movement in continuous interaction with state and society (though not in direct challenges), thus preparing it for future tactical escalation.

The Singaporean state made the Internet publicly available in the mid-1990s. It wanted to ensure that Singaporeans kept up with technological developments and maintain Singapore as an international commercial center. But it faced a conundrum: Opening up the island to the Internet meant losing control over information. So it settled on a compromise. As a symbolic stance, government censors blacklisted and blocked out 100 websites, mainly pornographic sites and sites that espoused racial or religious hatred, and proclaimed a "light-touch" regulatory approach (compared with the approach taken with other media). While Internet censorship retains the familiar rules against positive portrayals of homosexuality, regulatory enforcement concentrates on content about racial or religious hatred, local politics, and child pornography.[1]

The Internet opened up access to information about homosexuality, allowing gays and lesbians in Singapore to circumvent state censorship over print and other traditional media and connect with one another.[2] The situation contrasts starkly with the days of pre-Internet Singapore. In those days, my informants and respondents consulted medical encyclopedias to find a definition of *homosexuality*. They explored bookshops and the National Library for books categorized under euphemistic labels, such as *youth studies* or *alternative studies*, tucked away in dark corners of the room. To meet other gays and lesbians, they scoured for cryptically worded personal ads in magazines or on *Teletax,* a television service that provided text-based information such as local weather, traffic updates, and winning lottery numbers.

Furthermore, the Internet provided an efficient means of communication and publicity. During the movement's timorous beginnings, activists relied on word of mouth because they did not dare to and could not advertise in mainstream media. The Coalition maintained a "phone tree." Each person on the "tree" was responsible for calling a designated list of people, each of whom was, in turn, responsible for calling another predetermined list of contacts. Those telephone calls relied on fixed landlines at home or in the office, not cell phones, which were big, heavy, and still too expensive to be widely popular. Other organizers discreetly passed out name card–size invitations on the streets to people who, in Gillian's words, "looked like family."

Tactically Adjusting to the Internet

The Internet's potential, its increasing popularity,[3] and the state's laxer controls signaled an alternative opening for gay organizing in Singapore. With the encouragement of tech-savvy friends, the Coalition's leaders broke up its operations into two parts. They transformed the Sunday forums into a virtual forum. Known as Singapore's longest-surviving gay mailing list, Talklist remains active and retains archives of its message threads dating back to these early days. Trey claimed to be the only Coalition leader who was willing to learn about building websites back then, so he took over the newsletter and turned it into his online commentary.

Other organizations surfaced on the Internet as well. Access to information on the Internet helped gays and lesbians in Singapore to understand and accept their sexuality. Some became politicized after coming to see themselves as entitled to rights on the basis of their sexuality. Those who joined the movement usually first came into contact with an activist or an online group in Singapore. During cyber organizing, the strongest connecting point was Talklist. Several organizations that formed at this time germinated from initial contact on Talklist.

The interactions with gay activism in Singapore encouraged new participants to contribute to the movement, led them to discover mutual interests, or uncovered weaknesses that they wanted to address. They went on to create their own websites or other mailing lists to cater to lesbians, groups with religious concerns, or those with particular interests and hobbies, thus expanding the movement in both the number and diversity of organizations. New participants and groups developed into other connecting points for the movement. When anyone used terms such as *Singapore* together with *gay* or *lesbian* and *group* on Yahoo! or other search engines (Google had not yet appeared), these websites and listings turned up in the search results. People could sign up with a mailing list, exchange messages with other members, or join "live" conversations in "Internet relay chats" or chat rooms (if those features were available). From time to time, group leaders organized small, private get-togethers, such as parties or outings.

Expansion and Diversification through the Internet

> The lesson that I learned from [Talklist] was that it gave people the space to have an open discussion. . . . So eventually we figured out that this whole Internet thing works, because that would be a good start for people to come out to. Maybe improve their self-esteem, by exchanging their opinions and thoughts on the Internet, and then eventually when they have enough confidence, they can come out to meet us. (Stella)

One of the movement's most constant female figures, Stella came out in the mid-1990s. She was looking for support and found Talklist while browsing on the Internet. Although Talklist, dominated by gay men, did not meet her particular needs as a lesbian, it opened her eyes to the possibilities of using the Internet for grassroots outreach. She decided to start Singapore Lesbians Online, one of Singapore's longest-surviving lesbian online groups.[4]

Stella's experience reflects the central theme of pragmatic resistance and the common features of cyber organizing. Like her predecessors from timorous beginnings—Cheryl, Gillian, and Li-Ling—Stella felt that the movement was dominated by men and neglected lesbians. She responded by organizing a new group; similarly, her response did not splinter the movement, but expanded and diversified it. Because she deployed pragmatic resistance, her response also helped to reinforce and perpetuate the strategy.

Through Singapore Lesbians Online, Stella influenced other women to take up gay activism. When Lacey was still studying in Australia, she met Stella and kept in touch with her via its Internet relay chat channel. After Lacey returned to Singapore, the two founded Women's World for lesbians and bisexual women in response to the lack of social spaces outside the limited clubbing and party scenes. To this day, once a month, Women's World organizes an alcohol-free, potluck dinner with a predetermined discussion topic, such as about coming out, sex, or practical relationship issues. Organizers send e-mails to the mailing lists of relevant gay organizations. An interested person sends an RSVP and proposes a potluck item. Then organizers follow up with an e-mail disclosing the location of the event, usually limiting the number of participants per evening to around thirty.

Women's World reached out to young women, some of whom joined the movement too.

> I wasn't out at that time. I was very closeted. So, a few lesbians I knew were basically like my girlfriend, my ex-girlfriend, and people I heard of through the grapevine. . . . [Going to Women's World] was a really huge step for me. But it was really rewarding—I just saw so many very normal-looking lesbians so I came away feeling really empowered, and then after that . . . somebody (in the group) approached me, asking if I wanted to help organize. (Yen Fang)

At first, Yen Fang e-mailed Stella through Singapore Lesbians Online asking for advice on coming out to her mother. Stella sent some information and invited Yen Fang to one of Women's World's monthly gatherings. Over time, as Yen Fang frequented Women's World gatherings and grew familiar with the group, she went from being a mere participant to taking on a leadership role.

The journey of Abby, another lesbian leadership figure, also highlights the common features of cyber organizing. While surfing the Internet, Abby came across Talklist in the late 1990s. The people she met online helped her to accept herself and politicized her views about homosexuality and its relationship to the state.

> I think one thing that hit me when I joined [Talklist] is that these people . . . they decide for themselves who they want to be. And I mean as a Singaporean going through the government school system, I was never taught to think like that. . . . [I]t's just like suddenly waking up. (Abby)

About ten years later, Abby and other women established the Queer Women's Alliance, a key movement organization by and for lesbians and bisexual women.

The people whom Abby met on Talklist founded the Christian Fellowship, the predecessor to the Open Church, Singapore's first and only gay church. It all began with a message posted on Talklist in 1998, calling like-minded people to form a support group on sexuality and Christianity. About six to eight people responded and decided to start the fellowship.[5] These founders turned out to be Protestant Christians who were interested in the intellectual aspects of spirituality and sexuality. Rather than expanding their membership to appeal to gay Christians who were simply coping with personal struggles, their get-togethers concentrated on discussing and intersecting religious texts drawn from Christianity and a variety of other religious traditions, including ancient Egyptian and Islam. Hence, the group in its earliest incarnation resembled the Harbor, and some of these founders also participated in that group. The Harbor, founded in 1994, faded away partly because Kang left Singapore to pursue graduate studies, but also partly because the group lacked mass appeal.

The Christian Fellowship, though, shifted gears with the entrance of Billy, a key movement personality from the late 1990s to the late 2000s. Like Brett, who crossed over to become the Coalition's tenth signatory for its registration application, Billy had spent time with a Christian gay "therapy" program. He was even groomed for the program's leadership. Gradually, however, as Billy expanded his social circles and read more widely, he changed his mind and left the program. He found his way into one of Trey's peer support groups spun off from the Coalition back in the days of the Sunday forums. Then in 1998, about three or four months after the Christian Fellowship had started meeting, he ran into its cofounders at an unrelated event in town.

Billy noticed that gay Christians around him were looking to reconcile their faith and sexuality and saw the potential for the Christian Fellowship to play a stronger role. That meant expanding its numbers, which was not the group's original focus. Soon, the founding members realized that the newcomer had a different vision.

> The big change was when [Billy] came in. . . . I think he understood that most of the members who were coming in were not as reconciled [with their faith and sexuality] as the seven [founding] members and were actually more like him, you know? I think he also had only recently reconciled himself to his sexuality. (Aidan)

> Well, finally [Billy] came in. [The Christian Fellowship] did change radically after that. There was a belief that we needed to expand the numbers. (Frank)

> I said, "Look, this can't go on." Because at the end of the day, all you're going to be is a bit of a holy huddle. . . . One of the results of this happening is that all of the original members left. (Billy)

Billy was driven and determined to get his way. Although this differed from the original group's intentions, he managed to reorganize the Christian Fellowship into cell group–like operations with fixed meeting cycles and clear learning objectives, much like the organizational structure of the gay "therapy" program he left behind. As a result of Billy's intervention, Frank, Aidan, and the rest of the original cohort lost interest in the restructured group, finding it to be intellectually bland, and abandoned it to Billy's management; however, the Christian Fellowship did increase its membership and produce future leaders, such as Xavier.

> This whole process of learning about myself, seeing the importance of addressing issues of self-esteem, accepting myself, having healthy relationships with other gay men—it led me to want to do more, to want to contribute to others. I was telling [Billy] once that if it had not been [for] him, I would not be where I am, so I'm just hoping that I can take the experience and pass [it] on to others who might need it. (Xavier)

Xavier's journey resonates with the experiences of many others who first participated in groups that emerged out of Internet-based discussions and organizing—Yen Fang and Women's World, and Abby and Billy with the Christian Fellowship. Xavier moved on to lead the Beacon's support groups, the secular version of the Christian Fellowship that several of its cofounders initiated in 1999.

Aidan and Frank, along with another friend, Liam, noticed that Trey's informal peer support groups, offshoots from the Coalition's early days, attracted men in their thirties but not younger people. So they started one that catered to gay men in their twenties. The Beacon operated in cycles, each with a fixed number of eight to ten sessions spread over a period of several months. After the first cycle, somebody else who came through the Christian Fellowship's system offered to run the second round, and the group took off as the call for participants for each cycle was met with encouraging responses. Despite its popularity, the Beacon's operations remained rather informal, with undetermined gaps of time between each cycle, because it usually depended on volunteers to lead the next cycle. Again, Billy changed all that.

Similar to the Christian Fellowship's situation, Billy eventually assumed leadership over the Beacon and reorganized it into a cell group–like structure with formalized and consistent operations. The original Beacon cohort stepped aside, giving way to Billy's stronger vision and push. Over the years, the Beacon offered a connecting point where future activists, such as Xavier, first passed through as participants and then volunteered to take on leadership roles within the group as their way of "giving back" to the movement. Participating and leading the group also exposed them to activists from other organizations and built a tight web of interpersonal relationships across the movement.

Meanwhile, the Sports Club, another group that germinated from Talklist conversations around the time of the Christian Fellowship's and the Beacon's formation, connected men and women who were sports and outdoor enthusiasts. Although this group was seemingly less serious than the groups that focused on gender or religion, the Sports Club's casual activities also helped to add new members to the movement through similar patterns of initial contact and politicization. Playing a game of badminton, swimming at the Jalan Besar public pool, and going on a hike served a purpose beyond companionship and fun. The activities and meals that followed at hawker centers[6] were interactions that allowed one generation of activists to pass on narratives about gay oppression and earlier movement trials and tribulations to the next. Over local food and beverages such as *hokkien mee* (a type of fried noodles) and *bandung* (a pink drink made with rose cordial syrup and sweetened condensed milk), these interactions gave newcomers a sense of Singapore's gay history, generated awareness of their political and legal conditions, and offered an entry point into the movement. Tai, for instance, started out organizing social events for the Sporting Club. He then joined the Coalition's younger crop of leaders and led the Open Church.

Other groups that formed around this time included the Sutra Fellowship, an Internet-based group aimed at bringing together gays and lesbians who shared the Buddhist faith. Interviewees also recall more short-lived attempts such as an online group for older women, an alternative to Talklist in reaction to its perceived domination over local gay discourse, and an assortment of groups organized around specific hobbies and interests. In addition, two prominent Singaporean gay commercial websites took shape. The first originated as the "personal homepage" of a teenage boy, Jerome. His personal postings and photos quickly attracted a following, and he presented a younger and more social alternative to Talklist. Jerome took advantage of the popularity of his page and transformed it into a commercial website, the Connection Hub. In 2001, Morris launched the Portal, another commercial website. More than social networks for local gays, the Connection Hub and Portal served as connecting points for the movement and attracted people who went on to lead major campaigns later in its coming-out era.

Deploying Pragmatic Resistance through the Internet

First adopted during cyber organizing, the use of pragmatic resistance through the Internet has become a staple for Singapore's gay movement. The movement has developed and changed over the years, but the Internet remains an important means of everyday organizing and communication, a way to obtain access to information, and a tool for recruitment. Almost every movement organization has some kind of Internet presence in the form of websites, blogs, mailing lists, or social media sites, such as Facebook and Twitter. Most of them also cross-list across these platforms.

The public availability of the Internet starting in the mid-1990s, coupled with looser regulatory controls, led to shifts in the environment to which gay activists responded with tactical adjustment. They made use of the new medium to get around laws that restrict freedom of association and push forward their movement. Strictly speaking, their online groups could be construed as illegal, unregistered societies. Their existence could be seen as mocking the state's image of rule of law and the political norm that upholds legal legitimacy. Simply by *being* a collective—organizing, mobilizing, and recruiting newcomers through the Internet—gay activists challenge formal laws that restrict the formation of "societies." By providing access to information and resources that are otherwise tightly regulated, they bypass legal curtailment of speech, expression, and information in other media.

Together, these tactics contradict the political norms that discourage challenges against the existing political order. Internet organizing brings gays and lesbians together to see themselves as a group of people with shared grievances. In the era of cyber organizing, they did not yet openly challenge the existing political order for equal rights, but more and more of them were beginning to think of themselves as entitled to them. They became politicized: They came to see problems that they encountered because of their sexuality not as personal issues but as something in which state and society played a part. Frequent contact with the movement further compelled some of them to join it and eventually take on organizing roles. Hence, the outreach and human connections made through the Internet and the provision of information and resources helped to cultivate grassroots support and boosted the movement base. As was the case with the Christian Fellowship and the Beacon, newer activists even replaced others to increase membership numbers.

> [We do not] have an office. . . . If I host a website, I call it a name that I want to. . . . [T]here's nothing in the law that says you cannot name a website something. (Shelly)

> [We operate] through Facebook, and . . . legally we are not created as an organization, more of a Facebook group. (Brandon)

Singapore's gay activists who first mobilized on the Internet during cyber organizing, as well as Shelly, Brandon, and others who came to the movement later, perceive cyberspace as a safety zone. They interpret the inherent lack of physical contact associated with the Internet as protection from crossing the boundaries that they concurrently push. The delicate balance also explains more broadly how the majority of movement organizations have managed to survive in unregistered form over two decades.

To offset the potentially dubious legality of Internet organizing (and collective organizing more generally without registration status), gay activists simultaneously toe the line or limits of the political norms that constrain political mobilization. Amid their expansion and diversification, two developments illustrate how gay activists toed the line during the period of cyber organizing of the late 1990s. In the first example, Virtual Sister, gay activists limited collective organizing to the Internet. Now defunct, Virtual Sister was an online counseling service set up to help women who were struggling with their sexuality. In 2001, the local media reported the suicides of two young women who jumped off a high-rise building together. One media outlet gained access to the women's flat and asked questions sensationally about why two women who were living together had one wardrobe of supposedly men's clothing and another of women's clothing. The reports also mentioned that the women were wearing red ribbons around their wrists when they killed themselves. To Rani, the red ribbons symbolized a relationship union. She was deeply saddened by the desperation that those two women must have felt. Meanwhile, around her, she noticed the Beacon's social support for gay men but neglect of lesbians and bisexual women.

Rani and her friend and colleague Harriet contacted Stella from Singapore Lesbians Online. The three decided to set up Virtual Sister. Their biggest question was how they were going to operate the group *legally* and avoid state retaliation.

> I think the political climate at that time was just not as conducive to homosexuals identifying themselves and to people being open about their sexuality. We felt that we had to tread very carefully because the last thing we wanted to do was set up something and have it blow up in our faces . . . with authorities clamping down on us. (Harriet)

They were not ready to risk exposure to the state by registering. They approached registered organizations with professional counseling services to explore partnerships, but these organizations balked at any evident affiliation with a gay group that did not even have any legal status (though individual members of certain organizations provided assistance in their personal capacities). In Rani's words, they "wouldn't touch us with a ten-foot pole."

In the end, after checking with lawyer friends, they decided that the safest way was to position Virtual Sister as an interactive Internet space where women could write in with their problems and receive replies via e-mail. Hence, Virtual Sister's tactics resembled those of other Internet-based groups at the time. Rani, Harriet, and Stella made use of a thriving Internet medium to respond to a neglected problem and circumvent obstacles created by legal restrictions on gay organizing. But their tactics did not develop further beyond the Internet. They did not dare to register and test the legal restrictions for a chance at legal legitimacy. In addition, Rani and Harriet had plans to shift the electronic format to a telephone service and then face-to-face meetings, but those plans did not materialize because Stella was unprepared to take the risk for fear that they could jeopardize the movement as a whole.

So personality differences and one interpretation of their environment prevailed to keep Virtual Sister's tactics from pushing the political boundaries of mobilization further. Eventually dissatisfied with the limitations of Internet-based counseling, Rani left the project. Harriet suspended her involvement to take care of family matters. Other women took charge of Virtual Sister for a few years until they too drifted away due to fatigue or other personal reasons.

In the second example, two closed-door sessions by the Coalition in 1999, gay activists toed the line during cyber organizing by conscientiously maintaining the "private" nature of physical gatherings while publicizing them on the Internet. Quentin came up with the idea of holding the two-day discussions with the hope that they would lead to a publication about the struggles of gays and lesbians in Singapore. On the surface, the events were reminiscent of the Coalition's former Sunday forums and were also held at the Fringe Center. However, they are different. The tactic for the one-off 1999 sessions built on the lessons accumulated from the movement's timorous beginnings, including the experiences with the Sunday forums, and tactically adjusted to the Internet as an organizing means.

Quentin publicized and held the two gatherings as "closed-door" events meaning that they were private as opposed to public. Keeping an event "private" gets around the licensing requirement for public speeches and talks and renders those laws inapplicable. Thus, this action is legally compliant because it does not contravene any relevant laws by circumventing them. To make an event "private," activists restrict attendance to "by invitation only" and require guests to "RSVP." On the day of the event, they maintain a guest registration list.

As a classic tactic of pragmatic resistance that recurs in subsequent phases of the movement, the "privatizing" of events is traceable to the days of cyber organizing, when the growing popularity of the Internet first made it feasible. Besides these two events held by the Coalition, regular gatherings by groups such as Women's World, the Sporting Club, and others in this period adopted the same tactic. In subsequent phases of the movement, a typical announcement looks like this:

[Date]
[Time]
[Venue]

RSVP: This event is by invitation only.
As there are LIMITED seats, prior registration is required.

To get an invitation—please e-mail [———] with your name (in full), contact number, the name/s of your guests. (Event #18, Resource Central)

Such announcements are then sent to a variety of gay mailing lists and posted on movement organizations' websites.

We make sure to be very, very careful about only accepting RSVPs. But then they could be linking a closed-door event to 250 people. And so, we maintain the guest list with quite high regard. Or we would send it to [Talklist] of six hundred members telling them it's a closed-door event. You know what I mean? . . . And we'll say that we'll only let you in if you're reading from [Talklist] and you register and you RSVP again. (Aidan)

Although these events are not publicly open to everyone—since invitations and RSVP are required—their organizers are rather generous about who receives invitations and how they can do so: by asking for an invitation. Hence, the organizers can hold well-attended events in a way that challenges the laws restricting speech and the limits of permissible dissent in Singapore. Without violating the laws, the event organizers maintain a semblance of legal obedience and thus "toe the line" that demarcates politically acceptable conduct.

The Coalition's two closed-door discussions in January 1999 fittingly coincided with Quentin's last project for the group.[7] Shortly afterward, Quentin left Singapore to work for an international non-governmental organization. He participated in the registration attempt in 1997, but he had always preferred community building to the direct state engagement championed by Trey and Oliver, who led the registration efforts. Therefore, Quentin's departure also shed remnants of the Coalition's tactics from the movement's timorous beginnings and prepared the group for the transition to the more open engagement examined in Chapter 5.

During cyber organizing, then, gay activists continued their inward focus on community building. Mobilizing through the Internet and using it as a shield also ameliorated any urgent need to attempt direct state engagement or even to apply for a public speech license. Correspondingly, little political or media space opened up for them. In future phases of the movement, newer and bolder tactics appear. Compared with the two examples discussed earlier, they highlight how activists continuously adjust the tactics of pragmatic resistance to strike a balance between toeing the line and pushing boundaries in response to new interpretations of changing signals.

For organizing through the Internet, however, gay activists over the years generally still try their best to follow the law and sometimes even go out of their way to do so. Although none of the organizations involves any sexual activity, the ones that target gay youths set minimum age requirements for participation because they believe that these rules protect them from unnecessary legal problems.[8] Some of these organizations are discussed in Chapters 5–7. Even though activists widely publicize movement events on the Internet, they largely confine the publicity to organizers' websites, mailing lists, and other outlets targeted at gays and lesbians. Organizers do not send out mass recruitment or publicity e-mails to people who are not yet linked into the movement's communication network. A person starts receiving announcements and publicity information after he or she is connected to a particular movement organization by signing up for the mailing list, or in recent years, after he or she becomes a "friend" of the organization or one its leaders on Facebook (in later stages). Of course, different activists have their own interpretations of risks and boundaries, with some willing to venture further than others, but their tactics attempt to balance the potentially non-legal nature of Internet organizing and the unregistered status of movement organizations.

In addition, the more cynical activists also count on the state and the PAP's desire for legal legitimacy at the international level. They point out that the movement's existence shows Singapore as being diverse and cosmopolitan and thus friendly to foreigners and international investment. A clampdown on gay movement organizations that do not pose any real threat to the PAP's political power, simply because they are not registered, may actually make Singapore appear unreasonable.

> We're no real threat to the government. We're not about to depose the government. We're certainly not going to form a gay and lesbian party and take over the government. And they know that. . . . And they know very well that if they clamp down on us, a cockroach little organization like [the Coalition], it'd make them look really, really, really bad in the eyes of the world. (Trey)

To be clear, this view did not arise immediately out of cyber organizing. It was the consequence of sustained interaction, a process to which this movement period contributed significantly. Cultivating a sense of being "allowed" to exist, no matter the cynicism, requires sustained relations with the state to enable gay activists to better learn its boundaries and possibilities *and* for the state (and the PAP) to understand their motives. Despite the lack of direct engagement in the late 1990s, tactical adjustment to the Internet expanded and diversified the movement. Ongoing interactions then become possible, and the resulting reduction in fear helped to pave the way for tactical escalation in the future.

Fear and Learning Not to Be Afraid

The final point to be made about cyber organizing is that the movement's adoption of the Internet was not simply built on newfound opportunities. It was also a tactical adjustment to threatening signals—surveillance, unwanted media attention, and threats of legal sanctions on gay movement organizations. Fear existed during the period of cyber organizing.

Consequently, some groups took precautions to filter their memberships.

> The only way that you could get into the group was to meet with one of the members of the group, and basically be vetted before you got in. [*Laughs.*] It was kind of a "secret society" in some sense. (Edgar)

To join the Christian Fellowship, one had to undergo an interview process. Edgar was initially suspicious of Billy and worried that Billy's former ties to the conservative churches' gay "therapy" programs would bring a negative influence to the group. But the group's apprehensions went beyond unwanted religious influences. The founders of the Christian Fellowship worried about state surveillance and infiltration, which they encountered.

> There were a couple of scary moments. [A man] in his early thirties who befriended me—he said he was very curious, and he was exploring, he wanted to know more, he wasn't sure, and he wanted to see what was going on. And I think for three months he tried to meet me and started being introduced to the other leaders. . . . But eventually, after three months, we found out, he eventually said that he was sent by his boss [a member of Parliament] to sort of gather information . . . and a member of the Cabinet. And not just to find out more information about who the current generation of leaders are—again you can sort of know from the Internet—but to find out who the next generation might be so that they can contend with the issue for the next ten years. So, we sort of freaked. . . . And then he was not contactable after that. (Aidan)

To this day, old and new activists still experience state surveillance and they do not think it has ever ceased. In fact, they believe it has expanded to cyberspace, where their mailing lists and message boards are being monitored. The Coalition leaders believe, for instance, that somebody from the government watches over the messages exchanged on Talklist. Jerome's

Internet-based group was fined because content on its message boards allegedly violated the Internet content code.

Yet, over time, they realized that no serious consequence ensued. The common pattern in their interview responses to surveillance is that "nothing happened."

> Really, I mean [the Coalition] has been operating for so long, we have been very aware that the government keeps track of all our e-mails and places we've been. . . . You know, stuff like that—a big, big file [*gestures*]—and they haven't made a move. (Vincent)

> Nothing happened. Yeah, and I didn't get any note from any [authority] or whatever to take down the [online outreach program] or anything like that. So yeah, it was . . . a safe environment. (Taariq)

When Stella started Singapore Lesbians Online, she was so paranoid that she printed multiple copies of every e-mail she had sent to the list and stashed them away (thinking it might provide her with some evidentiary protection). But then, as the months and years went by, she realized that she had not attracted any trouble from the authorities. The movement is replete with accounts similar to Vincent's, Taariq's, and Stella's and the observation that "nothing happened."

Despite speculations and reports about surveillance, the lack of state reaction reinforces gay activists' belief in the safety of organizing through the Internet and builds their confidence. It is the case even for someone like Jerome, who was fined for violating Internet regulations. He did not retreat, but adjusted his tactic and went on to develop the group into one of Singapore's first commercial gay websites.

This is an important difference between the movement's timorous beginnings and later periods. Rather than back off, gay activists since the time of cyber organizing persist with the very tactics that are under surveillance. Starting with this period, they respond to the fact that "nothing happened" and learn not to be afraid, a crucial change that sets the stage for future transitions into open and direct engagement with the state and local media.

The gay movement's shift to cyber organizing created an enduring legacy for pragmatic resistance by maintaining an inward focus on community building rather than engaging the state or local media. This helped to expand and diversify the movement as well as cultivate a new crop of activists. Despite their limited visibility or grassroots support, gay activists started to overcome their fears because the state largely ignored their organizing efforts.

Therefore, cyber organizing enabled Singapore's gay movement to sustain itself under what activists perceive to be nonreceptive conditions and maintain continuity for future escalation (see also Rupp and Taylor 1987; Taylor 1989). One might argue that by avoiding direct and public challenges they probably missed opportunities to push boundaries further (see also Sawyers and Meyer 1999). Indeed, memories of hostile signals, coupled with the newfound benefits and perceived safety of Internet organizing, might have discouraged action. But one might also make the counterargument that by continuing to mobilize committed activists kept the movement in interaction with state and society (despite the lack of direct and open challenges) and bolstered their confidence. In this respect, although cyber organizing might not have pushed boundaries more boldly, it prepared the movement to scale up in the next period, when gay activists' perceptions of and responses to ever-shifting signals altered in important ways.

5

Transition

From the late 1990s to the mid-2000s, Singapore's gay movement underwent transition. In the face of signals that were sometimes optimistic and sometimes disconcerting, they attempted to push boundaries further while toeing the line. Their strategic adaptation of pragmatic resistance to these shifting currents reshaped the three patterns of change that I have been tracing.

The movement started to mount challenges openly. It was no longer focused inward on community building; although the time frame of cyber organizing partially overlapped with the period of transition and some activists still mobilized with characteristics of the outgoing era, the new characteristics were blossoming as the former receded. Gradually, tactics escalated and the movement continued to expand and diversify. The few courageous responses from allies and grassroots support also offered encouragement and hope. While local media warmed up and provided more balanced coverage, the state was showing tentative signs of acceptance. Politicians, bureaucrats, and activists were learning how to read one another—where one should draw the lines on mobilization and the extent to which the other could simultaneously push and abide by them. On one hand, top PAP politicians and some elements of the government made gestures toward greater acceptance; on the other, a series of administrative decisions continued to hold back gay organizing.

During the transition period, activists discerned different signals from the larger environment; some suggested greater room for dissent while others warned against it. Still under the leadership of Prime Minister Goh, the government introduced a Speakers' Corner in 2000. The new regulations exempted an area at a public park called Hong Lim Park from its licensing rules for speech. Speakers were not required to apply for licenses to speak at this designated spot. Instead, they were required to register in advance with the police and to abide by preset conditions, especially the ban on speech that could "cause feelings of enmity, hatred, ill-will or hostility between different racial or religious groups in Singapore." Meanwhile, an opposition politician, Chee Soon Juan, grew in notoriety. Known for his confrontational tactics, he often provoked the ruling party and state by staging illegal protests and unlicensed public speaking events. These actions led to multiple arrests, criminal convictions, and defamation lawsuits filed against him by PAP leaders.[1]

More directly relevant to the gay movement, a new sign arrived unexpectedly in December 1998. Then Senior Minister Lee Kuan Yew[2] appeared on a CNN "live" interview show. During the viewers' call-in segment, an anonymous caller, whom some Coalition activists know from their former Sunday forums, asked Lee about the future for gay people in Singapore. Lee replied:

> It's a question of what a society considers acceptable. And as you know, Singaporeans are by and large a very conservative, orthodox society.... But what we are doing as a government is to leave people to live their own lives so long as they don't impinge on other people. I mean, we don't harass anybody. (*CNN Q&A with Riz Khan,* Lee Kuan Yew, December 11, 1998)

For gay activists, even though the answer fell short of groundbreaking, it shifted their terrain. Before Lee's statement, nobody could recall a public position by the state or senior politician that did not condemn homosexuality. The gradual alteration in the state's approach toward homosexuality and gay activism is commonly traced back to "LKY's interview on CNN." It heralded a glimmer of hope that things could change.

Local theater groups also saw signs of easing up in the censorship of gay expression and took advantage of this opportunity.[3] In 1999, a local theater company was allowed to stage *Completely With/Out Character,* a one-person autobiographical play about Paddy Chew, who openly identified himself as bisexual and a person living with AIDS. He was the first person in Singapore to do so. Three months after Chew played himself on stage, his health deteriorated rapidly and he died.

In 2003, the government's censorship guidelines recommended that censors give adults more leeway to access homosexual content, if it was not "exploitative."[4] Singapore's censorship guidelines are reviewed once every ten years and take into consideration survey interviews with the population. The new recommendation was a change from the strict prohibition issued in 1992.

Rather than fronting plays with HIV/AIDS or metaphors, theater became more open about gay representation and themes, encouraged by the censorship changes and taking advantage of the state's treatment of theater as niche and limited in audience impact. Eleanor Wong offered a triple billing of the two lesbian-themed plays that debuted in the 1990s together with a new sequel, *Jointly and Severably*. The same company that staged Chew's autobiographical play presented *Abuse Suxx*, which featured two men kissing on stage and confronted issues of molestation, religion, and electroshock therapy. It also produced *Mardi Gras*, a story about a group of Singaporeans and their quest to hold a local gay pride parade, named after the annual event in Sydney, Australia. Alfian Sa'at debuted the first installment of his *Asian Boys* trilogy.

For Percy, a teenager who was coming out at the time and became a gay activist a few years later, the phenomenon that he described as "every other play was a gay play" signaled a changing landscape for gays and lesbians in Singapore. He associated this experience with a turning tide for the movement. Around him, he saw movement organizations springing up and more people working for a common cause in a variety of ways.

Initiating Direct State and Media Engagement

Events that occurred the year following "LKY's interview on CNN" contrasted the transition period from the partially overlapping period of cyber organizing, highlighting how the new period took advantage of political developments and created opportunities to engage the state and media openly. During cyber organizing, Quentin held two closed-door sessions that circumvented the licensing rules for public speeches and avoided direct state engagement, characteristics that typified that era. Four months later, the Coalition's ascending leadership attempted to organize the group's first public "*open* forum." The tactics they deployed for this forum have become the prototype for a particular version of pragmatic resistance, one that appears frequently in subsequent years.

Trey and other Coalition leaders were responding to a state initiative and creating an opportunity out of it. On April 24, 1999, Prime Minister Goh announced the launch of Singapore 21 Vision, a set of principles that declared that every Singaporean mattered and promised to provide opportunities for all. The Coalition decided to find out how much their leaders meant those words. Trey applied for a license to hold a public speaking event and called it "Gays and Lesbians within Singapore 21." Approval was denied, but denial was part of the Coalition's tactical plan.

> If you don't ban us, we win because we get to have our public space and set a precedent and we get to discuss an issue. . . . But if you ban it, ah! Then you pay a price because we'll whine and complain and we'll make noise. You pretend you can't hear, but it's on the Internet forever and also the foreign media might pick it up. (Arun)

Unlike Quentin, who bypassed licensing authorities by making events "private," Arun, Trey, and the rest of the new Coalition leadership initiated action to provoke a response from the authorities. If they received approval for their license, they would indeed set a precedent for the new boundaries and solidify them by holding the forum. Rejection of the license would also make a point because they would expose the state's repression and self-contradiction.

In the process, they forced homosexuality and gay activism to the forefront of public awareness. Starting in this era, the Coalition stopped shying away from rejection by state authorities. This time, the Coalition leaders documented their correspondence with the police on their website.

> The [police's] letter said, ". . . The Police cannot allow the holding of this forum which will advance and legitimise the cause of homosexuals in Singapore. The mainstream moral values of Singaporeans are conservative, and the Penal Code has provisions against certain homosexual practices. It will therefore be contrary to the public interest to grant a public entertainment licence." Most people thought the reasoning was laughable: Once something was against the law, it was no longer permissible to talk about it. ("History," Coalition website)

During the period of transition, the licensing rules required all public talks to be licensed. Without their license, the Coalition did not go ahead with the open forum illegally, and so they played by the legal rules and political norms in this respect. Their decision to shame the state in a public statement about the license denial, though pushing the edges of political boundaries, also maintained features of adherence. They did not take to the streets. Their public criticism focused on the administrative decision at hand—the license denial—and did not launch a wide-scale attack on civil-political liberties or even an attack on the licensing system itself. They publicly placed the blame on the immediate decision-maker, the police, rather than political leaders for the injustices of their government, hence giving face to the ruling party. Throughout the rest of this era and the next, activists from the Coalition and other movement organizations use tactics similar to those of the open forum.

Pursuing Local Media Attention

The open forum also represents one of the first times that gay activists openly engaged local media, something that became more common from this period onward. In contrast to the period of timorous beginnings, when they fled from journalists, gay activists started pursuing their attention. They realized that they needed to admit openly who they were.

> We started out by hiding from publicity and begging the press not to cover us. At some point in time, we were saying that this won't do. We should be out there. If you're going to be an activist, you must be out there. (Oliver)

Trey and Oliver, in particular, were the first few who initiated lunches and dinners with news editors and reporters and tried to demystify their movement by putting human faces and stories to it. They exchanged business cards with reporters, offered contact information, and made sure that somebody in their group was always available to provide attractive sound bites intended to appear in news reports. These interactions helped to dissuade the state-controlled media from seeing the movement as a threat to state interests, so that in time, they would no longer perceive the movement as inherently crossing boundaries and thus as safe enough for balanced coverage, if not positive portrayals.

Singapore's local media have censorship rules that ban "positive" or "normal" portrayals of homosexuality. In addition, their own political boundaries constrain them to a news "reporting" role, not the role of watchdog. Because of these formal rules and political boundaries, gay activists understand that even friendly members of the press cannot embrace the movement openly, so they aim for coverage that at least includes their side of the story. That alone pushes boundaries because such press coverage gives voice to their dissent, and what they say sometimes exposes state repression and undermines its legitimacy and facade of control. To help the media so that the state does not accuse the media of crossing *their* own political boundaries, gay activists take advantage of the newsworthiness of incidents or create it by framing them as controversies involving state action.

Meanwhile, the changing nature of the local media aided these emergent tactics. As younger generations of reporters took up local journalism, they added diversity of opinions to newsrooms. Some of these reporters were gay or gay-friendly. More important, they were increasingly less inhibited about holding and voicing independent opinions on homosexuality.

In the case of the open forum, after the license application was rejected, Oliver and other Coalition leaders used their newfound connections with the local mainstream newspaper, the *Straits Times,* to get news coverage. By applying for a license and being banned, the Coalition's activists implicated government action and generated a "public event." Consequently, the local press felt safe about reporting the news rather than coming across as "publicizing the gay issue," as Oliver, formerly a local journalist, put it.

Trey was interviewed and quoted in the initial news report, and then the story took on a life of its own. Using the license ban as a starting point, the reporter spun off a feature piece on the place of gays in Singapore. More than eighty readers wrote in with an array of views. At a high school seminar, one student asked the Minister chairing the event if he thought that the government should relax its control and pointed to "the gay forum which was denied a permit." The Minister's response exposed the misconceptions that remained within the broader PAP leadership. After saying that a group of people should not impose their "lifestyle" on others, he offered an analogy, saying, "I am an avid golfer, but I do not hold a forum on golfing to say how much I love golf and convince others it is good." However, the exchange wound up in another newspaper report, which led to more readers' responses, which led to a written retort and reiteration, published in the newspaper, by the same Minister within the following week.

From the reconstituted relationship with local media, gay activists read encouraging signs about the state. Although the local media are not state-run, the editorial leadership stays in constant communication with the government. Their editorial decisions reflect to a modest degree the state's position on a particular issue at a given time. In addition, the various ministries and government agencies have officers who are responsible for reading the newspaper's published letters to the editor every day. Sometimes they write to the newspapers to respond to issues raised by letter writers. The newspapers are obliged to print these letters and so become an indirect way of communicating with the state as well. Overall, the increasing willingness of local media to engage gay activists sent the message that the permissible limits for gay activism could be shifting ever so slightly and gradually.

Engaging Political Leadership through International Connections

The open forum brings out another type of tactical escalation that appeared during transition—applying pressure on the political leadership, or PAP leaders, through international connections. However, unlike the direct challenges analyzed earlier, *indirectness* is key to this particular tactic. It plays to the political norm of legal legitimacy, specifically, the state's and PAP's concern with Singapore's *international* legitimacy.

If the Coalition's leaders had successfully obtained the license for the open forum, they would have shared the results of a survey at the event. Along with plans to organize the forum, they conducted a survey that asked Singaporeans on the Internet and the streets to reflect on how they might relate to family members or coworkers who were gay and about equality for gay people. The survey was not designed with scientific rigor, but was simply meant to "present an interesting opinion that would just introduce some doubt into this whole idea that we're a conservative society" (interview with Arun).

The Coalition's survey results coincided with a local university's survey that was reported in the newspapers. The Coalition had alerted press contacts about their survey, so the news report included a paragraph about the Coalition survey for comparison (with the caveat that it lacked scientific rigor).[5] Then a foreign newspaper journalist asked Lee Hsien Loong, a deputy prime minister at the time, about the Coalition's survey results. Lee, perhaps unprepared for the question, gave a vague answer that alluded to the survey's lack of rigor.

The exchange between Lee and the foreign journalist illustrates how the movement makes incursions into the ruling party's top echelons without being directly implicated. Although gay activists were beginning to challenge the state directly, they remained cautious and indirect in one respect—when applying pressure on the leadership. Notice in the example of the survey that they did not pursue a "boomerang effect" (Keck and Sikkink 1998)— making use of transnational activist networks, whose NGOs or third-party organizations then pressurize the Singaporean state. That can create backlash because the PAP and government do not wish to be seen as bowing to external pressures, domestic or international. It offends the political norm of maintaining control and being *seen* as being in control. Even if the leadership is swayed by criticism, changes that occur are not publicly attributed to such pressures. What is more, such actions too obviously come across as confrontational and shaming on the part of gay activists, especially if these activists are seen as colluding with foreign groups.

Instead, gay activists typically try to shame top political leaders through international connections—thus pushing boundaries—by playing to the normative concern with Singapore's international legitimacy, thus simultaneously toeing the line. It was not until 2011 that one movement organization took the risk and used Singapore's treaty obligations to exert international pressure on the state at the United Nations (see Chapter 7). More commonly, gay activists work through personal connections with foreign journalists, foreign state officials, and diplomats. The hope is that their contacts will ask the political leadership questions about anti-gay laws and policies that over time will cause Singaporean leaders enough concern about international legitimacy that they will decide to make changes.

Setting Up Office Spaces

Percy, who observed the bustling of gay organizing at the beginning of this chapter, was new to the movement and had a shorter memory of it, but he was right in that a more diverse pool of activists was emerging during the movement's transition. The phenomenon was a continuation of cyber organizing, when the type and number of movement organizations expanded and diversified. As the movement moved into the transition period, people who were mere participants in earlier years rose to leadership positions and groups that formed during cyber organizing turned into connecting points for future newcomers.

In addition, three organizations came to occupy permanent spaces, adding a tangible, brick-and-mortar feel to the movement and escalating the tactics from the period of cyber organizing. In a state that suppresses collective mobilization through the control and denial of space to associate and assemble, this development pushes boundaries further than ephemerally occupying physical spaces to hold events and activities. At the offices of Resource Central, the Open Church, and the Beacon, newcomers to the movement met activists and some began to take up gay activism.

Resource Central, the first and only community gay library, opened in December 2003. When the HIV/AIDS group obtained new funds for its gay outreach program in the early 2000s,[6] Sirius, the program coordinator, decided to establish a community library. Not wanting this undertaking to be male-centric, he reached out to Stella, who volunteered for the HIV/AIDS group. Stella saw the proposal as an opportunity to build community spaces away from the social night scenes. She brought along Lacey, her trusted collaborator, and Arun, whom she met through the Coalition.

> I still remember walking through the door and thinking "Okay, I'm stepping through the threshold. Okay, I'm now in gay land. I'm away from the straight world." (Fiona)

Resource Central often turned out to be the first gay space into which younger gays and lesbians, such as Fiona, ventured. During opening hours on Saturdays, Stella and her team displayed rainbow banners and postcards and put out informational leaflets and postcards for distribution. People could walk in and check out books or simply meet up. Resource Central also hosted events such as private movie screenings, book launches, and talks. One Saturday, Fiona decided to seek out Resource Central. She came directly from school activities, so she was wearing her high school uniform, something that both she and Stella remember clearly. Fiona had contacted Stella through Resource Central's website, which used to have an online chat room. Stella, the first lesbian to whom Fiona had ever spoken, gave her information about the center. There, Fiona met other people who were her age. She later teamed up with two of them to found a peer support group for gay teens.

Two years after partnering with the HIV/AIDS group, Resource Central split off from it. The separation was partly due to office politics and partly due to factions within the HIV/AIDS group that shunned association with gay activism. As discussed in Chapter 3, the local HIV/AIDS group worried about losing government funding and jeopardizing its legal status by appearing to be mobilizing rights. By becoming independent, Stella, Lacey, and Arun inadvertently took a bold step. Under the auspices of the registered HIV/AIDS group, the center had legal shelter. On its own, it was unregistered, openly gay, and laden with shelves of books about gay culture and gay rights. It also could not afford its own space. To continue operations, the three worked with a gay-owned business that generously offered them free space at its café. The partnership with a legal entity consequently helped them to survive as well.

The Beacon and the Open Church also established offices in the early 2000s and became places with constant newcomer traffic, serving as first stops where men and women sought out social support and young activists first tried their hands at gay organizing. Xavier, Abby, and Tai, who participated in cyber organizing, benefited from their experiences with these organizations. Xavier stayed on with the Beacon to run several cycles of its support groups and cultivated a new generation of activists; some of them emerge in the movement's coming-out phase. Abby went on to found the Queer Women's Alliance in later years, whereas Tai was so inspired that he abandoned a cushy corporate career to train as a pastor and serve the Open Church.

The Open Church, Singapore's first gay church, has its roots in the Christian Fellowship. By the early 2000s, Billy had taken over the Christian Fellowship and restructured it into a cell group format, ironically reminiscent of the gay "therapy" programs of his past. But it merely provided a second home for members; many of them still returned to their own churches for Sunday services. The Christian Fellowship's initial Sunday service, held at makeshift locations, suffered from poor attendance. Eventually, however, the number of members who were ex-communicated from their home churches for being openly gay reached critical mass. The Sunday service finally gained momentum. In 2004, Billy led the group to register as a company (discussed in the next section). Today the church leases the third floor of an industrial building, with space for a congregation in the low hundreds, musical equipment, a kitchenette, a lounge, and a meeting room.[7] In 2011, its community function expanded when it let Resource Central move onto its premises. The community library had to leave the gay-owned café, which could no longer afford the additional rent for the center's space.

Around the same time, Billy also registered the Beacon as a company and set up an office for it. He transformed it from an informal peer support group for gay men into a counseling service staffed by full-time professionals. He also expanded its services to include counseling for women, HIV/AIDS outreach, and training development for mental health professionals. Located in Chinatown, which doubles as Singapore's gay district and includes bars, saunas, and other businesses, the group achieved what Virtual Sister, the defunct online counseling service for women, did not dare to attempt during the days of cyber organizing.

Registering as Companies

Another escalation in tactic that appeared during transition was the registration of movement organizations as companies instead of societies. In a sea of unregistered movement groups, the Beacon and the Open Church are unusual. They are registered as companies with "charity" status. Although this legal status is common among churches and nonprofit agencies in Singapore, this type of registration moved boundaries for the movement. These two organizations are able to represent themselves as legitimate operations that unmistakably revolve around gay issues. The Connection Hub and the Portal also have company status, but this is less extraordinary because they are intended as commercial entities. Nevertheless, this development stands in contrast to the blunt rejection of the Coalition's registration application in 1997.

> I think it's hard for the government to allow [the Coalition] to register because the messaging is very significant. If the government now allows [the Coalition] to register, then it's saying, "It's okay to have a gay organization." (Billy)

The Coalition's experience with registration prompted Billy to try something different from the Societies Act. His choice contrasts with the Coalition's decision to make a second attempt at registration in 2004. As "companies," the Open Church and the Beacon bypass the Societies Act. Whereas society registration governs political associations, company registration suggests to the government that the organizers have no political intention in the narrow sense of party politics. This approach avoids being seen as challenging the existing power structure. Further, the "companies" do not declare themselves on their registration information as representing gay-related issues or advocating for gay equality. The Beacon names its "principal activities" as "community activities" and describes itself as performing "counseling and community work," while the Open Church serves the functions of "community works" and "churches." The wording is crucial because it allows the state to maintain the appearance of legal legitimacy, while giving a nod to international legitimacy by allowing gay groups to exist and organize. These registration details were sources of tension for the Coalition since bureaucrats liberally interpreted the criminalization of certain sexual conduct to prohibit any society that addresses gay issues in any way, including talking about them. Hence, the "companies" heeded the penal law's broader appeal to legitimacy by officially avoiding any mention of gay-related topics on their registration documents.

The successful registration as companies also indicates a shift in the state's position toward gay activism. Before its attempt to register as a society in 1996, the Coalition tried to camouflage itself as a company and sought registration with the Registrar of Companies. As detailed in Chapter 3, the attempt backfired. Because the Coalition had come under surveillance, state authorities already knew what the organization was. In contrast, other than what appears on their official documents, the "companies" of the Beacon and the Open Church do not hide their gay-oriented activities and objectives on their websites and publicity material. The Open Church, the Beacon, and the Portal report ongoing interactions with politicians and bureaucrats, who are well aware that they are gay groups and are registered as companies.

First Involvement of Non-gays

The Open Church also brought to the movement a new source of activists—non-gays who joined as organizers and leaders.[8] Though insignificant in number, the addition of Loke and his daughter, Nina, marks the beginning of this new development. In 2003, Loke, a retired bishop, wrote a letter to the editor to the *Straits Times* in response to Prime Minister Goh's views on homosexuality in a *Time* magazine article (Elegant 2003) that was reprinted in the local newspaper (more on the interview later). Loke argued for diversity and plainly stated his support for gay Christians. The *Straits Times* published Loke's letter with his name and the title of his religious office. The letter and Loke's title caught the attention of Billy and the rest of the Open Church leadership. They tracked him down and invited him to their church. Loke studied liberal Christian theology in North America during the American civil rights movement. Fighting social injustice was his life's work after he returned to Southeast Asia. This type of work also ran in his family. He brought along his daughter, Nina, a straight, married woman with three children, who used to do community volunteer work and was drawn to the marginalization suffered by those in the Open Church. Both father and daughter have since publicly spoken out in support of gay equality and the repeal of Section 377A of the Penal Code.

Registering as a Society (Again)

In 2002–2003, about five years after Lee Kuan Yew's CNN interview, Prime Minister Goh made statements that sent yet another signal about the state's changing position on homosexuality. At the 2002 National Day rally speech, Goh stressed the importance of "cultural vibrancy" and the need for Singapore to have "a few little 'Bohemias,'" perhaps inspired by Florida's book (2002) on the creative classes and the pink dollar that was featured in local newspapers earlier that year. In 2003, Goh revealed to *Time* magazine that the Singaporean government had quietly changed its policy on hiring gays. Even though the criminal laws against same-sex sexual conduct would remain, he disclosed that the government has been hiring openly gay people, even for "sensitive" positions, and said, "So let it evolve, and in time the population will understand that some people are born that way. . . . We are born this way and they are born that way, but they are like you and me" (Elegant 2003).

Local newspapers reprinted excerpts of the *Time* interview and set off a flurry of letters to the editor. Loke's letter, mentioned earlier, was written in response to this statement. A corporate lawyer and former dean of Singapore's oldest law school, Thio Su-Mien, wrote to a local newspaper to warn against succumbing to "the homosexual agenda" that would threaten "the family unit and racial-religious harmony" and declared that she reserved the right to "disapprove vigorously" of "the homosexual lifestyle" (Thio S. 2003). Thio's objection portended things to come in the subsequent phase of the movement—the awakening of a countermovement.

Goh's statement also affected the Coalition. To this group, it provided an opportunity to test whether the political boundaries had indeed shifted to give legal legitimacy to those who challenge the PAP's ruling order. They also wanted to find out how much the leadership's changing position on homosexuality permeated the ranks of Singapore's administration. So they decided to reapply for the Coalition to register as a society.

> The second attempt at registration was [a] "heads I win, tails you lose" kind of situation, which we absolutely love. I mean, you give us the registration, we win. You don't give us the registration, we go and cry in public, we win some sympathy, and we still win. Yeah, so it was a very different approach the second time around. (Trey)

This tactic, similar to the open forum's, is a more daring variation of pragmatic resistance and yet another example of tactical escalation. Unlike the Coalition's first registration attempt and the registration of the Open Church and the Beacon as companies, the Coalition did *not* intend to seek legal legitimacy this time. Regardless of the outcome, the Coalition wanted to create a public event out of the attempt to raise awareness about gay rights through local and international media either by showing that they had made progress or by exposing state repression. Approval was insignificant; after all, they had been mobilizing collectively without registration for almost a decade.

To discuss their plans, the Coalition convened a community meeting at the Fringe Center. Besides Trey and Oliver, the movement's leadership turned up with new faces not seen in its early years. They included Arun and Billy, who had participated in the peer support sessions that Trey used to organize; Tai, who started out socializing with the Sports Club; and Stella and Lacey, who were responsible for Singapore Lesbians Online, Women's World, and Resource Central.

For its first application, the Coalition had difficulty finding the ten required signatories. Back then, the Coalition's leaders had to beg and cajole people. This time, as many as fifty people stepped forward to volunteer as signatories; however, only ten names were used in the application. Likewise, the turnout for the meeting was much larger than that for the former Sunday forums held at the same place.

> There was a room at the [Fringe Center] for this purpose, but the size of the crowd was staggering. It was spilling out, so obviously we could not meet in that tiny room, so we moved to the courtyard. And then it was huge. It was like filling up the space. And then they moved to a compound wall along the courtyard and there's a door in there, and there's a car park behind it. Somebody stood in the doorway and talked to the group. I remember the group of people spilling out around. It was quite a large group. It was very spontaneous, a bit frightening. . . . Maybe up to one hundred. By the end of the evening, who knows? Some people left and came. They kept moving, so some people got fed up. Eventually we met at [a nearby public park]. (Arun)

Although the movement's grassroots support could not be described as widespread, these moments gave hope to activists that they had indeed made progress.

Once again, the state rejected the registration application. But, the formal outcome aside, communication with the state shifted from stonewalling and offering nonanswers to replies that made some minimal effort at providing an explanation. The police also did not come knocking in the middle of the night to demand an appearance at the police station. The Registrar of Societies' first letter, dated March 31, 2004, cited the now familiar provisions of the Societies Act and warned of heavy penalties against unregistered societies; it was almost identical to the rejection letter of 1997. The Coalition quickly wrote back to inform the Registrar that the group would appeal to the minister and asked for an explanation beyond the cited provisions. The Registrar wrote back, reciting the same provisions, but adding, "As the mainstream moral values of Singaporeans are conservative, it is hence contrary to public interest to grant legitimacy to the promotion of homosexual activities and viewpoints at this point in time." The appeal to the minister was rejected two months later.

Rather than retreat, as it did in 1997, the Coalition went public with the rejection. It issued a press release pointing out that the government's decision contradicted recent statements on opening up and tolerance. The *Straits Times* printed a short, factual report about it the next day, and Trey pulled strings to publish a column in the other mainstream newspaper. These tactics could be construed as boundary breaking because they publicly shamed the state. Yet, they adhered to the same political boundaries. The Coalition aired its grievance publicly through media outlets that the state recognizes and controls and did not stage a protest. The press release and Trey's column focused on the poor judgment of the middle management on this particular administrative decision and did not question the legitimacy of the PAP leadership. In fact, they criticized the bureaucrats for failing to live up to the political leaders' more enlightened vision:

> [The Coalition] believes the present decision by the [Registrar of Societies] (ROS) is completely at variance with . . . the implications arising from the government now accepting openly gay persons in the civil service, even in sensitive positions [and] the admission by the Prime Minister that "some people are born that way" and "they are like you and me," in his interview with *Time* magazine. . . . Furthermore, [the Coalition] believes that such a retrograde decision by the ROS is harmful to Singapore's future. (Press Release, Coalition, April 5, 2004)

By exploiting the contradictions between the administrators and the PAP's leaders, these tactics give face to the leaders, maintaining their place of authority. The shaming makes middle management, faceless bureaucrats, look bad, and not those voted into office. It also presents the issue as an administrative problem rather than a political one.

The Coalition's leaders considered their registration campaign a success because it achieved the objectives of testing boundaries and generating public awareness. But the rejection bore different meanings for other activists beyond its inner circle.

> Trying to test the government by registration—I mean, it's a tried and failed method. (Colin)

> The registration, to us . . . I'm not saying that they are failures because some of the failures—it's more because of the government

and all that. Some of their failures spur us on to greater heights, and we take their failures and their successes as a whole lesson and we run with it. (Percy)

Especially as time passed and a new generation of activists came to learn that the Coalition had tried to register as a society twice and was rejected twice, the 2004 story represented a failure caused by a recalcitrant state. It galvanized younger activists, such as Colin and Percy, to inherit and continue the movement's struggles. In the latter half of the 2000s, these two started an Internet broadcast that featured Singaporean gay issues and personalities and also helped with various movement organizations.

For others among the new generation of activists, the 2004 story reinforced the line that government prevented the movement from crossing: formal status for movement organizations and the legal legitimacy that accompanies it.

> We knew that we couldn't register [the Queer Women's Alliance] so soon after [the Coalition] was rejected a few times. So we had no thoughts of registering at that time. . . . I think we've discussed it, but it's never going to happen, so let's just figure out how to do this legally without registering. (Manisha)

The story of the Coalition's failure to achieve registration discouraged them from even bothering to try and turned them toward alternatives. Groups such as the Queer Women's Alliance, founded in the movement's coming-out phase by Manisha, Abby, and a few other women, simply opted for the proven tactic of mobilizing without registration, thus perpetuating that particular version of pragmatic resistance.

Reading Uncertain Boundaries and Misinterpretations

The contention over the legal status of movement organizations reveals a complicated state, led by an authoritarian party and run by a complex bureaucracy, that was shifting its boundaries with uncertainty. Meanwhile, in this mutually constitutive relationship, gay activists were trying to figure out how and where the boundaries were shifting. Missteps occurred as state actors pulled back boundaries from time to time or activists misinterpreted signals and boundaries.

By the mid-2000s, it seemed to activists that the politicians and bureaucrats were reaffirming more strongly where the boundaries would not shift. At the time of the Coalition's 2004 application, the Societies Act was being revised to create a category of societies that were allowed automatic registration. This meant that the Act had to clarify which types of societies fell *outside* of automatic registration and therefore needed to be approved on a case-by-case basis (essentially the old process). As a result, the term *sexual orientation*, for the first and only time in Singapore's legislative history, was inserted into the statute. Any group advocating on issues concerning "sexual orientation" was lumped with groups that concerned themselves with "political," "religious," and "human rights" issues in the case-by-case category. Despite the verbal assurances of the PAP leaders that they did not condemn homosexuality outright, the Singaporean state was learning to cope with collective organizing around the issue.

Two other examples that have implications for the movement's coming out period further expose the government's hesitance about shifting boundaries for gay activism. Both involve bans—one on circuit parties and the other on a fundraising concert—after initial approval for the required licenses was given. The changes corresponded to newly released information about HIV/AIDS infection in 2004. Singapore's Minister of State for Health at the time, Dr. Balaji Sadasivan,[9] announced that there were seventy-seven cases of HIV infection among gay men in the first ten months of 2004 compared with fifty-four cases in 2003 and attributed the increase to the "promiscuous and unsafe lifestyle practised by some gays." In March 2005, he cited an unnamed medical expert on the link between rising HIV infections and circuit parties. HIV transmission in Singapore is not predominantly homosexual,[10] and gay activists believed that Sadasivan's statements were fear-mongering and damaging.

The Open Church was one group that felt the impact of those statements. Its leaders were planning a musical concert featuring a foreign music duo to raise funds for the local HIV/AIDS group and promote safe sex. After Sadasivan's statements, they thought that the event would be part of the effort to fight HIV/AIDS infection among gay men. They were wrong. The event was scheduled for April 3, 2005, and their requisite license was already in hand when the licensing authorities told them in mid-March 2005 that it was canceled. The authorities claimed that they had been ignorant of the musical couple's romantic relationship and that allowing the concert to go on would amount to "glamorizing" or "normalizing" the "gay lifestyle," words that echo the censorship rules.

The last-minute reversal was strange. When the Open Church first applied for and obtained the license, the authorities easily could have checked the performers' professional website and found out about their publicized relationship.[11] Two years later, the Open Church restrategized and successfully staged the concert, with Sadasivan as their guest of honor (see Chapter 7). But in 2005, the ban indicated that political boundaries remained unclear and were vulnerable to regressive shifts.

Another group that felt the negative reverberations of Sadasivan's statements was the Portal. Since 2001, the organization had been hosting commercial circuit parties in Singapore. These ticketed events were far more visible than the regular gay nightlife in Singapore and attracted gay male patrons in the thousands from around the world. All-women's commercially organized parties, though not expanded to the circuit level of the men's, also started becoming more regular fixtures by the early 2000s. From 2001–2004, commercial circuit parties targeting a gay male clientele grew in size, reaching eight thousand partygoers at one point. A string of news features about these events appeared in international newspapers and Western gay media. Suddenly, Singapore looked like the gay capital of Asia.

But this situation did not last. The first warning sign was the banishing of the HIV/AIDS booth at the Portal's August 2004 party. Sirius arrived at the party to set up a booth for distributing safe sex materials, condoms, and gloves, something that the HIV/AIDS group had been doing at these parties. That night, however, a Portal staff member approached Sirius and passed on a disconcerting message. He told Sirius that "authorities" had ordered them to take down the booth because it was not mentioned in the Portal's license for the party. Sirius and his team complied, and the party would be the last held in Singapore. Two months later came Sadasivan's first media statement about gay men and HIV/AIDS. In early December 2004, the police rejected the Portal's license for its year-end party. It was unexpected for the Portal because license approval had become routine by that point. The police claimed that patrons had complained about same-sex kissing and intimate touching at previous parties (a strange claim since most of the patrons were gay and attended the party to socialize with other gay men) and explained that because Singapore was a "conservative and traditional society" these parties went "against moral values of a large majority of Singaporeans." The police also pointed out that the Portal had assured them that the parties would not be "gay," alluding to its tacit agreement not to market the event officially as *gay*. The following year, after Sadasivan's later statements, the police rejected the Portal's license application for another party.

These incidents form a sequence of events that highlight a movement in transition. The actual reasons behind the reversals may never be clear. Many activists attribute them to the HIV/AIDS statements. Others offer a more mundane explanation—that the police officer who usually handled the Portal's license application was no longer in charge and thus these were simply cases of bureaucratic variations with which activists regularly contend. More important, they show that the state and its leaders were struggling with how to respond to a bolder and more confident movement while activists were trying to interpret accurately, respond, and reshape their interactions. Both were constantly adapting and trying to learn how to deal with each other.

From the late 1990s to the mid-2000s, the movement gradually moved into the open. With new confidence, activists began to engage the state and local media directly, employing escalated and more public tactics. Movement organizations occupied physical spaces by opening up offices and saw hints of grassroots and non-gay support as well as more positive media coverage. Political tolerance increased but also receded from time to time, displaying uncertainty toward gay activism.

Hence, the transition period afforded gay activists the opportunity to devise and hone tactics for deploying pragmatic resistance. Each tactic that they deployed gave them a new opportunity to learn how the boundaries of political norms were shifting and how they can be pushed to advance the movement. They carried these lessons and new knowledge into the next stage of the movement, when they eased it fully into the open with a response to the 2005 bans on circuit parties.

6

Coming Out

In the mid-2000s, Singapore's gay movement entered the contemporary era, one in which the matter of survival has given way to the movement's advancement as the primary focus of activists. Chapters 6 and 7 analyze how strategic adaptation advanced the three themes of change in this period. Imbued with a new sense of agency and confidence, gay activists pushed the movement out into the open and engaged the state and media directly. Hence, their tactics continued to escalate with a series of public, landmark events and growing support from the grassroots and allies. The movement also gained broader media and political recognition. Even though bans and censorship still occurred, gay activists were no longer condemned categorically. In addition, perhaps in reaction to the movement's coming out, a countermovement emerged.

This chapter focuses on the first phase of the contemporary period. It examines the events from the first pride festival in 2005 up to the 2007 parliamentary petition campaign to decriminalize same-sex sexual acts under Section 377A of the Penal Code, highlighting the first peaks of the movement's coming out. The outcome of the petition campaign, its encounters with the state, and a rising countermovement created the conditions for the even greater visibility of the Pink Dot events and judiciary challenges that are discussed in Chapter 7.

As the movement transitioned into the contemporary era of coming out, Singapore's leadership was undergoing changes as well. In 2003, Goh stepped down and Lee Kuan Yew's son, Lee Hsien Loong, became the third prime minister. With the younger Lee at the helm, legal restrictions on civil-political liberties were loosened up.

Among these small shifts, two legislative amendments on speech and assembly passed without fanfare, but soon came to play crucial roles for the movement. When the fate of circuit parties hung in the balance in 2005, Parliament coincidentally amended the Public Entertainment and Meetings Act. The amendment (now replaced by and found in the Public Order [Exempt Assemblies and Processions] Order 2009) exempted indoor public talks from licensing, provided that the speakers were Singaporeans and the talks stayed away from topics that "would cause racial enmity" or religion. In 2008, licensing requirements for public assemblies at Hong Lim Park were lifted (now Public Order [Unrestricted Area] Order 2013). This is the park where public speech was first exempted from licensing in 2000. The 2008 amendment extended the speech exemption to "performances" and "exhibitions," which cover assemblies, and similarly required organizers to register in advance with the police and agree to the same preconditions regarding race and religion.

Starting in the mid-2000s, a crop of newly appointed judges also ascended to the highest Supreme Court bench.[1] Even though their decisions have yet to swing definitively in favor of constitutional liberties over state interests, their judgments were starting to demonstrate greater effort to bring Singaporean constitutional jurisprudence more in line with developments elsewhere. Compared with previous judgments, these decisions appeared to give more thoughtful consideration to the constitutional freedoms at stake (before holding that competing state interests should nevertheless prevail).

These slight shifts are limited and even seem tokenistic to harsher critics in the gay movement. However, they also suggest opportunity. While remaining circumspect, gay activists take the shifts in stride, creating or seizing whatever opportunities they can.

Protesting with an Annual Pride Festival

> We always like to ride on controversy. Okay, so what can we do, if we cannot have a party? . . . [A]nd also of course, we need to test the licensing again. Where are the limits of the licensing? (Vincent)

Although Vincent and the rest of the Coalition did not organize the circuit parties, the ban and the coinciding license exemption for indoor public talks presented a new opportunity to test political boundaries. The activists wanted to find out how far they could push for gay-related speech and assembly, which were denied in the form of large social gatherings (and the new exemption does not include events such as exhibitions). So they decided to organize a gay pride festival. If the event proceeded without state intervention, they would set a precedent for gay speech and expression; if it was prohibited, they would use the proven tactic of exposing state repression and ride on the controversy to bring media and political attention to the movement's grievances.

The pride festival opened on July 29, 2005, and lasted through August. The Coalition deliberately chose this timing to coincide with Singapore's National Day celebrations on August 9. The festival featured art exhibitions, literary talks, poetry readings, theatrical productions, and forums and ended with a barbecue. For the first time in the movement's history, multiple movement organizations collaborated on a month-long activity that received local media publicity. The Coalition issued a press release, and local newspapers reported on the launch. At festival venues, movement organizations—most of them unregistered—displayed their logos on festival banners and flyers. Although the Coalition had not initially intended the festival to be an annual event, they soon received requests to hold it the following year. An annual Singaporean gay pride festival was born.

Not all activists agree with the pride festival. Stella and Lacey worry that it dilutes the movement's impact if gay activists are seen as fighting for huge parties for gay men. The two women joined the Coalition's leadership in the early 2000s to help the group reach out to lesbians, but exited a few years later, unhappy about its domination by opinionated gay men. The disagreement over the pride festival shows how fissures within the movement, between gay men and lesbians or otherwise, usually play out: The process does not interfere with the movement's pragmatic resistance, but maintains it. These disputes are not rooted in deep ideological rifts, such as between radicalism and rights-based activism. Rather, they concern how best to achieve the movement goals of acceptance, equality, and legal reform, which remain constant among the activists, including lesbians and gay men. So even when groups of activists disagree, one group does not splinter off to mount a separate collective struggle. The response is to "agree to disagree" and continue working toward the same goals by deploying their own variation of pragmatic resistance. This was the case with Gillian, Cheryl, and Li-Ling, who started women's-only groups during the movement's timorous beginnings. In Stella and Lacey's case, the organizations led by them do not join in the annual pride festival; occasionally, they provide logistical support to participating youth groups, which they believe should be encouraged, but decline any formal affiliation with the festival as a principle of their long-standing position.

Regardless of the difference in opinion about its genesis, the festival is an early symbol of the movement's coming out. The inaugural event risked crossing the boundaries of political norms. It could have been perceived as a petulant outburst and thus as too confrontational. If the party bans had occurred in an earlier period of the movement, the response might have been to retreat, just as the Coalition itself did when its first registration application was rejected. In fewer than ten years, its leaders pounced on the bans as an opportunity. Seen in this light, answering the bans with an openly gay and proud festival in the midst of National Day celebrations was far more assertive than the movement had ever been.

Yet, its preferred form of protest remains pragmatic resistance and adheres to the limits of political norms. The objections follow the existing tactical mold of focusing on a specific administrative decision—the party bans. The Coalition neither staged a street demonstration nor questioned the legitimacy of the ruling party. In one of its press statements, the Coalition stressed that the festival was nevertheless "not a retaliation" and that "without defying any laws, the community [would] seek to make its point through the avenues available to it." (Press Statement, Coalition, July 29, 2005).

Instead, as publicized in the inaugural press release, the Coalition bolstered the movement's legal legitimacy by using and following the licensing rules. Because the new exemption applied only to indoor public talks featuring Singaporean speakers and not art events, such as poetry reading and photo exhibitions, the Coalition went ahead and applied for those requisite licenses. These actions resonate with the state's immediate responses, which emphasized formal legality and political boundaries. When asked about the festival's launch, one member of Parliament commented, "There is freedom of speech here as long as speakers don't incite violence and are sensitive to the views of others." In one illuminating encounter, the regulatory agency in charge of approving art events contacted the poetry reading's organizer, Winston, and urged him to apply for a license because the event fell outside the scope of the new exemption. Winston was one of the newer activists who had just joined the Coalition. He refused to relent and stood his ground against the regulator's reasoning until more seasoned Coalition activists persuaded him to resolve the dispute in line with the tactics of pragmatic resistance.

> It was either a telephone call or an e-mail saying, "We know that you're organizing this. We need you to apply for a license." It was

very politely worded, and of course, my first reaction was really negative because I thought, "Oh, this is horrible. They'll just ask me to go through this formality and then they'll deny us a license and then all the effort will have been in vain." (Winston)

It's so stupid, isn't it? [*Laughs.*] It's all standing in a room and talking, so why is it in one category there's no need for a permit and in the other category it's just your bureaucratic claim? So for a while, [Winston] refused. So (the e-mails went) ding-dong, ding-dong, ding-dong. And I was in the loop reading all the e-mails and the [civil servant] actually sent an e-mail quite close to the event—four days before—saying that there was still time to apply for them to— to, err, to allow it. I think that was the strongest hint: "Please send in your form!" So I said to Winston, "Listen. Give them what they want. Fill in the forms." [M]y god, they passed that thing in double-quick time. (Oliver)

By insisting on adherence to rules, despite the shift toward relaxation, the state continues to maintain control over the circumstances under which civil-political liberties may be exercised or, conversely, restricted. Not all of the applications for licenses required for festival events since 2005 were approved—the rejected ones include other art events, film screenings, and talks by non-Singaporeans. However, what is important is the crystallized relationship between gay activists' tactical responses and the state's subsequent reactions. These are examined through exemplary incidents that are discussed later in this chapter.

Confronting Surveillance

Despite the greater sense of freedom to speak out, gay activists consistently report state surveillance at the annual festival. After all, preserving the ruling party's power and its appearance of being in control remains an intact political norm. But unlike the old days when surveillance triggered apprehension, activists no longer cower. Instead they confront it with the learned tactics of pragmatic resistance, accumulated from their experiences in the past.

First, this is possible because since the mid-2000s, fear of surveillance has largely subsided among activists, regardless of their age, length of time in the movement, or any other demographic factor. Here, a generational divide highlights the movement's rising confidence in less than two decades: Those who joined the movement during the period of cyber organizing or later were less afraid from the time they first took up gay activism, whereas old-timers who entered the movement in the early 1990s eventually overcame their fear and grew in confidence as the movement survived and endured.

> [Trey] and [Abby] told me that once in a while there will be someone in a car waiting outside. You don't have to worry about them; you can even invite them to come in. They're just there to follow orders to track you down. (Warren)

Warren's experience is typical. Newer activists like him sometimes are oblivious to surveillance, and the more seasoned ones have to tell them how to spot undercover police and how to handle them.

Second, like memories of the license plate story and the Tanjung Rhu arrests, the learned tactics of pragmatic resistance are propagated through intergenerational relationships among activists. Activists such as Warren learn to treat surveillance as a routine occurrence that is not to be feared, viewing the officers as simply doing their jobs.

> I hope they had a good time. They have nothing on us. They can take their notes and that's all. They're just doing their job. (Yen Fang)

> He's a very typical straight guy. He's quite friendly. I talked to him. I was like, "Eh! You got a haircut." [*Laughs.*] . . . We don't try to make enemies or be hostile. There's no point. I mean, he's just doing his job. (Adalyn)

Especially when they make light of the officer's job, gay activists diminish the fear associated with surveillance, its most powerful weapon in paralyzing collective organizing. It is a tactic that emboldens a marginalized group of people to continue to mobilize and not back off from shows of power. This technique does not involve confronting the police or questioning their power to intrude on the movement's activities, but allows the police to act within their authority. Because they play according to the political norms—being nonconfrontational and maintaining the appearance of deference—in return, the state plays by the same rules and refrains from further repression, thus allowing the movement to perpetuate.

Further Expansion and Diversification of Movement Organizations

As the pride festival took off, other organizations achieved further milestones and new activists and organizations appeared between 2005 and 2006. The Beacon released the first collection of real-life coming-out stories in Singapore. Names and photographs accompanied each of the fifteen stories, which included fourteen men and women and one mother with two gay sons—an ironic juxtaposition with the days of the Tanjung Rhu arrests, when local newspapers published the photographs of men arrested in entrapment operations. Percy and Colin, who joined the movement when it was transitioning out of Internet retreat, set up a live Internet radio show, or podcast, on Singaporean gay issues and happenings.

In 2006, the movement's most outspoken women's group to date, the Queer Women's Alliance, emerged. Angered by offensive "trolling" remarks on Talklist, Abby—who joined the movement through the Christian Fellowship—e-mailed a few other women and invited them to meet for dinner. Like the pioneers of earlier groups, they wanted to give lesbians a stronger presence in the movement. They also wanted to go further than their predecessors who focused on social support. Abby and other cofounders joined the Coalition's leadership, marking yet another attempt by the Coalition to reach out to lesbians. This may well be the more successful attempt because the leaders of the Queer Women's Alliance are interested in engaging the state directly, and this brings them more in line with the Coalition's tactical choices.

Since its formation, the Queer Women's Alliance has collaborated with the Coalition on the pride festival. They have published a coming-out book authored in the name of the Queer Women's Alliance (despite being unregistered), conducted nationwide surveys about female homosexuality, and held annual holiday camps for its members.[2] In later years, its leaders play key roles in Section 377A litigation campaigns and for the first time speak out at the United Nations against the Singaporean state's anti-gay discrimination.

Two new types of movement organizations also sprang up in the second half of the 2000s—gay-straight alliances and youth groups. Family and Friends was one of the first gay-straight alliances set up by non-gays. It started with Stella and Ming Choo, who initiated a Mother's Day forum in 2006 for mothers to share stories about their daughters' coming out. At the forum, Ming Choo, a mother whose children are gay, met the Open Church's Nina as well as Ai-Mee and another woman, both of whom have gay brothers. The four of them decided to set up Family and Friends as a resource center for families and friends of gay people. In 2008, Warren and Yvette, with the encouragement of Abby and her peers at the Queer Women's Alliance, set up another gay-straight alliance.

Before the period of coming out, no movement organizations specifically reached out to gay young people in their teens and early twenties. Older activists were either uninterested in this group or reluctant to take it on for fear of being accused of influencing or "recruiting homosexuals." By the mid-2000s, however, they realized that people were coming out at younger and younger ages. Generational gaps occurred as a result of different concerns and interests. The younger generation thus stepped in to fill the void themselves. These groups include Youth Support, which Fiona and two gay men established. Fiona was the high school student who contacted Stella on the Internet and then visited Resource Central, where she first met her cofounders.

New movement organizations such as the Queer Women's Alliance, Family and Friends, and Youth Support are a few examples of how the movement expanded and diversified in the number and type of organizations. Like the earlier groups, they help to cultivate and attract a wider pool of activists. Some of these newcomers later lead two of the most momentous movement events to date—Repeal 377A and Pink Dot.

Speaking Out and Getting Around Bans

The annual gay pride festival in August 2007, leading up to the Repeal 377A campaign and the October 2007 parliamentary debates, exemplifies other ways in which movement tactics escalate in the contemporary era. The government did not clamp down on movement organizing when the Repeal 377A campaign, examined later, challenged openly for legal reform; however, its bans on several festival events demonstrated concern over maintaining its perception of social stability. In turn, activists' responses highlight a classic tactic of pragmatic resistance that has become a standard approach to circumventing legal prohibitions on civil-political liberties. The tactic has several variations, but the main characteristics involve getting around the legal restriction by obeying the law literally and sometimes simultaneously making use of another law, such as an exemption. The effect is that the actions toe the line by following the law and avoiding confrontation while simultaneously pushing boundaries by holding the event in spite of the prohibition.

In one example, the police withdrew the license for a talk scheduled to be given by a foreigner on the legacy of British anti-sodomy laws. According to the police, the talk would amount to letting a foreigner interfere in domestic politics, a major taboo for the Singaporean state because Section 377A was politically contentious in 2007, the year of the Repeal 377A campaign. Several Coalition activists claimed that they had learned from unnamed sources that someone from the right-wing Christian countermovement (discussed later) had used political connections to influence the licensing decision, but these suspicions cannot be confirmed.

More important, however, was the activists' response. Because they were Singaporeans and thus did not need a license to speak, Trey and Oliver paraphrased the foreigner's paper and held the talk in this alternative fashion. In this classic representation of pragmatic resistance, when a public talk license is denied, gay activists convert the event into one featuring a Singaporean speaker. The new speaker first explains to the audience that he or she is standing in for the original speaker because the organizers were denied a license to feature the noncitizen. As a Singaporean, the speaker simultaneously takes advantage of the exemption for citizens *and* obeys the license prohibition. After reading the prepared speech, the Singaporean speaker then opens up the session to questions, signaling the end of the "talk," so that the original, noncitizen speaker, if he or she is sitting in the audience, goes on to interact with other attendees.

Another variation is to convert a prohibited exhibition or artistic event into a talk about the prohibited works, thus taking advantage of the same exemption.[3] One activist turned his photographic exhibition into a talk about the photographs, in the process showing the photographs to explain the subject matter. In 2005, if Winston's poetry reading had been denied its license, he and Oliver would have reframed the event as a talk about poems.

> [If the regulator] says "no," then plan B goes into action. What is plan B? We'll still go ahead and hold this poetry reading, but we won't call it a "poetry reading." We'll call it a "talk about poems." You guys will go on stage and say, "Today I'm going to talk about my poem, but before I talk about it, I've got to recite it." Then you recite! (Oliver)

In 2007, this classic tactic culminated in the Pink Picnic and Pink Run, both of which gay activists remember fondly. The Sporting Club was planning to hold the picnic on August 9, Singapore's National Day, and hold the five-kilometer run on August 11 at the Botanic Gardens. A few days before August 9, a letter from the director of the National Parks Board dated August 3 arrived at Trey's office. Trey was not organizing either event, so he contacted Tai, a Sporting Club organizer and fellow Coalition activist. The letter stated, "We do not want [the Botanic Gardens] to be used as a venue for interest groups to politicise their cause."

Although the laws on illegal assembly could arguably be invoked, no specific license or permit is required to have a picnic at the Botanic Gardens, and the National Parks Board's authority to prohibit a group picnic is perhaps tenuous. Informants suspect that the letter was probably triggered by yet another complaint from someone known to be part of the Christian Right countermovement because this is a typical tactic of theirs. One informant went so far as to claim that a movement participant was an employee at the National Parks Board's office and happened to be standing at the fax machine when the complaint letter came through! In the end, regardless of the board's dubious legal authority, Tai posted a message online to announce that the picnic was *officially* canceled but also said that everyone was nevertheless free to picnic at the park as private individuals. Before the ban, Tai had anticipated thirty to forty picnickers. After news of the ban quickly spread across the Internet, about 150 people showed up. Some wore pink. Others wore different colors of the rainbow. The police were there to film the picnic, but did not stop anyone from participating. Since the popular reception in 2007, the gay pride festival annually features an "unofficial Pink Picnic."

The Pink Run replicated this tactic. Because the National Parks Board also prohibited the run at the Botanic Gardens, Tai and fellow organizers moved the run to Robertson Quay, a popular jogging area by the Singapore River. Around eleven o'clock the night before the event, a police officer called Trey, who was also not in charge of the run. The officer insisted that Trey inform the run's organizers that it was "against the law." Trey simply replied that the police could do so on their own and that he had no legal obligation to help them. He then contacted Tai to warn him.

On the day of the run, Tai and Fabian arrived at Robertson Quay to find ten to fifteen plainclothes officers, some with video equipment, waiting for them. One of the officers approached Fabian and told him that the run was against the law, even though he could only vaguely allude to illegal assembly laws when Fabian asked him to cite a specific provision.

> So I said, "Okay, I can call it off, but they're still free to run as they want, right?" I mean, this is a park by Clarke Quay—Robertson Quay. Anybody can run. There's lots of runners around. If they want to run, I'll just tell them it's not an organized run anymore. They basically have nothing to say to that. . . . I just went there and

said, "Okay, guys, the event is off, but if you want to run, continue running." And then everybody ran. (Fabian)

With both the picnic and the run, gay activists walked a fine line to maintain the norm of nonconfrontation and authorities' sense of rule-boundedness and managed to stage public events in the face of executive bans without disobeying them or violating the law.[4] Although the tactic was no longer novel by 2007, older activists such as Oliver were impressed by the confidence of their younger counterparts. Ten years earlier, Oliver felt that he might have at least paused to contemplate the ban, whereas the younger activists immediately questioned the legitimacy of the decision among themselves before responding tactically with pragmatic resistance. They were pushing boundaries further outward with rising confidence.

Partnering the State and Overcoming Bans

Besides getting around legal prohibitions by literally obeying the law and making use of other legal rules, gay activists developed another tactic in the coming-out years—partner the state. This is different from other forms of engagement such as speaking out in Parliament or challenging government decisions in public. Partnering means that gay activists overcome legal obstacles by cultivating working relationships with government agencies; they frame a particular issue that an agency can find mutual interest in addressing and position their groups as having the capability to help the government achieve that goal.

So far, the tactic has most commonly involved HIV/AIDS.[5] Gay activists see the government as caught between pragmatically trying to prevent the disease and wanting to avoid seen as endorsing illegal activities, which still include same-sex sexual conduct between men. The PAP relies on being legally reelected to power and perceives the general public to hold conservative views that include disapproval of sexual activities involving marginalized groups. The dilemma for the government is to address HIV/AIDS without being seen publicly as reaching out to—and thus apparently condoning—risk groups that it has identified, including gay men, sex workers, and intravenous drug users. With this understanding, gay activists convince public health agencies that they are in the best position to reach out to the gay community and that the government can provide them with financial resources and cooperation without having to get their hands dirty, so to speak. This tactic toes the line by avoiding confrontation and reaffirming existing power structures—activists do not challenge the initial restrictions or bans, but work *with* authorities instead. However, this approach also pushes boundaries because it subtly makes the state cede ground to collective mobilization in areas that the PAP finds worrisome for its political hegemony.

One early example of partnering goes back to the Open Church's HIV/AIDS fundraising concert that was banned. In 2005, after the group obtained the requisite license, the police withdrew the license at the last minute, claiming that they had not known of the musical performers' openly gay relationship (see Chapter 5). The ban also coincided with the minister of state for health's statements on rising infection rates among gay men. Two years later, during the Repeal 377A campaign and the excitement around the pride festival of 2007, the Open Church was working behind the scenes with the Ministry of Health to restage the concert.

After the 2005 ban, the Open Church's leaders refined their tactic by cultivating a friendly relationship with the Ministry of Health. They contacted Sadasivan and initiated conversations behind closed doors. They persuaded Sadasivan and public health officials that gay movement organizations could work together on HIV/AIDs. Then several activists, Sadasivan, and his officials went on an overseas trip together to learn how other governments worked with gay groups to address HIV/AIDS. Since then, movement organizations that work in part on HIV/AIDS issues have partnered with public health agencies to implement HIV/AIDS outreach programs for the gay community. The license for the Open Church's concert also came through without a hiccup when the group reapplied. Finally, the Open Church was able to restage the banned concert, featuring the same performers, on December 13, 2007, seven weeks after the Repeal 377A campaign ended with heated parliamentary debates.

Repeal 377A: Petitioning for Legal Reform in Parliament

The Repeal 377A campaign of 2007 was the first time that gay activists openly challenged for legal reform in Parliament. It was also the first time that the movement amassed vocal and public support from its grassroots base of gays and lesbians as well as non-gay allies. Further, it remains the movement event with the most extensive local media coverage, giving voice to campaign leaders and their supporters.

The campaign started when the Ministry of Home Affairs announced a comprehensive review and amendment exercise for the Penal Code in November 2006. At the time, two criminal provisions against same-sex sexual conduct remained in the Penal Code. The first provision, Section 377 on "carnal intercourse against the order of nature," covered both consensual and nonconsensual sexual conduct such as oral sex and anal sex between partners of different sexes or between men. The second provision, Section 377A, outlaws "gross indecency" between men—regardless of whether the act is private or public or consensual—and can extend to non-intercourse scenarios such as kissing and other displays of physical intimacy. The punishment under Section 377A is imprisonment for up to two years. Under Section 377, punishment encompassed a broad range that included life imprisonment, imprisonment for up to ten years, and a fine.[6]

The Ministry of Home Affairs proposed to remove Section 377 from the Penal Code, deeming it out of date for *heterosexual* sexual relations. However, Section 377A was to be retained, effectively singling out men who have physical intimacy with men. Along with the announcement, the ministry launched a public consultation exercise to solicit feedback on the proposed revisions, a common practice since the Goh administration to allow the PAP government to appear more attentive to citizens' wishes. The discrepancy associated with repealing Section 377 but retaining Section 377A was deliberate and glaring, and gay activists took notice.

Morris, who was in charge of the Portal, called a meeting of movement leaders. Parker, a lawyer, was already drafting a response for the Open Church, so the group that met at the Portal decided to adopt it for the public consultation exercise.

> We didn't ask for a Penal Code review. But they reviewed it, and there was this big, glaring omission. We felt that if nothing was said, it would just be like every other review, which means it would just get rubber-stamped and it would pass. And that would indicate to everyone that we're just going to take it lying down. If anything, we needed to be on record saying that a number of Singaporeans felt that it was not right. (Morris)

Half a year went by before the ministry announced the results of the consultation: It will retain Section 377A. It noted that opinions were divided, but because the majority supported retention, the government had best "let the situation evolve." The ministry moved ahead to submit the Penal Code amendment bill, leaving out the removal of Section 377A, to Parliament for a second reading. Of the three parliamentary readings of a bill, the second is usually the most substantive because that is when its contents are scrutinized and debated.

Parker and Morris sensed that time was running out to make their voices heard. Submitting public consultation papers was a muted gesture. Their paper was posted on the ministry's website, but they did not occupy government or public attention. What they wanted was to demonstrate their objections and have them heeded.

The two looked around for options and noticed a little-used legislative procedure, the parliamentary petition. It had only been put into action in independent Singapore once, for a private bill. According to Singapore's Constitution and Standing Orders of Parliament, a member of Parliament (MP) may present a signed parliamentary petition. The Public Petitions Committee is required to consider the petition and submit a report, and then the sponsoring MP may table a motion for debate. This is what they were seeking—a visible political platform and a captive audience. All parliamentary debates are entered in *Hansard,* the legislative body's official records, so a petition offers an opportunity to document the issue and its arguments as they stood in 2007 for future reference.

They set out to find sponsor in Parliament, someone to present the petition, as required by the rules. After profiling a few candidates, they decided on Siew Kum Hong, a nominated member of Parliament (see Chapter 3). As early as 2003, Siew had written publicly in response to the Christian Right's objection to Goh's statement on gays in civil service. As a straight man, he believed that the issue of discrimination against gays concerned all Singaporeans. He was also spotted speaking at a gay literary book launch and a public forum about the Penal Code amendments. Although nominated members of Parliament have no power to vote on Constitutional amendments, supply or money bills, or votes of no confidence on government, they have the same power as elected MPs to introduce bills, present petitions, and table motions for debates. Invented as a tool of containment and co-optation, the nominated member of Parliament scheme ironically played a central role in the gay movement's biggest parliamentary campaign.

The next issue was numbers. A parliamentary petition does not require multiple signatures. But Parker and his team felt compelled to send Siew into Parliament with at least some degree of popular support, so the campaign team launched a signature drive. One of the team members, Zac, set up Repeal377A.com to collate and disseminate information, issue press releases, and post an open letter to the prime minister.[7] He also called on his contacts in the local entertainment industry to produce a rap music video featuring local celebrities and performers and distributed it on YouTube. Local playwright Alfian Sa'at staged a new installment to his *Asian Boys* trilogy that raised direct questions about Section 377A, and the production company held a forum to call further attention to the discriminatory law.

For a petition signature to be officially accepted, it must be handwritten and submitted on an original hard copy of the petition. By the time the campaign team launched the signature drive, it was already early October 2007 and the second parliamentary reading of the Penal Code amendment bill was scheduled for October 22–23. Pressed for time, activists, grassroots supporters, and non-gay allies spent the next fourteen days canvassing their workplaces, schools, and popular bars. The response they received stood in stark contrast to the Coalition's desperate quest for ten signatories for its registration application in 1996–1997. The simple act of penning one's signature allowed gays and lesbians in Singapore as well as a broader straight alliance to demonstrate and foster a sense of community.

> People who went around on their own accord didn't know anybody, were not connected to anybody, because they felt it was so right. They went around collecting fifty signatures, one hundred signatures, and all these little stories of the mother, the aunt, the old lady . . . they signed the petition. (Ai-Mee)

Gay men and lesbians, their families, and straight friends and strangers came forward. Gay-friendly businesses volunteered to be designated collection centers. Overseas Singaporeans hired courier services to deliver their signatures to the collection centers. Singaporeans living in nearby countries traveled home to turn in theirs. Touching stories abound about how family members signed right next to the name of their gay son, daughter, or sibling. One activist kept a petition sheet for his and his mother's signatures only, and he did not allow anyone else to sign it.[8]

Within two weeks, the campaign collected 2,519 signatures. On October 16, 2007, a week before the bill's second hearing, Siew walked into Parliament to submit the petition.[9] It was a historic moment. For the first time in Singapore, a parliamentary petition was submitted with popular support. It was also the second time in history that a petition was submitted through this procedure.

By making use of parliamentary proceedings rules, Repeal 377A activists pushed political boundaries to reshape how they publicly air their grievances.[10] They forced the entire legislative body and the administration, which refused to propose repeal, to pay attention to decriminalization. For the first time, before a right-adverse state, the gay movement made a public claim clearly articulated in the language of rights.

The petition's text reads, in part:

> The continued existence of Section 377A will prejudice the rights and interests of homosexual and bisexual men, in an unconstitutional manner. . . . Such discrimination infringes the right of homosexual and bisexual men to equal treatment by and protection before the law, as set out in Article 12(1) of the Constitution of the Republic of Singapore. (Repeal 377A Parliamentary Petition 2007)

When the campaign leaders' understanding of Singapore's political realities is considered, the astute use of legal procedures becomes even clearer. From the beginning, Parker, Morris, Siew, and Ai-Mee, who joined them as a lead petitioner, were clear about their objective. It was to make the government pay attention to their objection. It was never to win the law's repeal. In fact, they had no expectation that the law could be repealed in this manner. The four of them knew that the PAP government would not change its position, especially after a challenge as public as a petition to call for the reversal of a decision that it had already announced. That would make the government and party appear weak and vulnerable to pressure by interest groups. In addition, similar to the convention of English political parties, if a party's whip is not lifted, MPs of that party are expected to vote according to party line. This means that PAP MPs will follow their party's discipline and vote uniformly. In Singapore, this usually reflects the executive's position. Siew, in particular, knew that the PAP party whip would not be lifted on the Penal Code amendment bill; in Singapore, it is rarely lifted on any issue. Besides, a parliamentary petition simply means setting out one's grievances and requests for relief. It does not mean that the bill, going onto its second reading, would be altered to accommodate the petition. A petition also does not require Parliament to vote for or against its proposition. It only enables a motion to be tabled to debate the issues raised.

Furthermore, because the parliamentary petition *was* news—in fact, it was part of parliamentary proceedings that local media usually are obliged to report—Repeal 377A pushed boundaries with the amount of dissent that it induced state-controlled media to publish. Since the period of transition, gay activists have started to engage local media, which they believed were slowly shifting in their favor. During Repeal 377A, they solidified the movement's media tactics to spurn public discourse on gay issues. The petition first led to a legitimate news event. After local media reported on news about the campaign, readers with viewpoints all across the spectrum, including Christian conservatives, wrote letters to the editor to have their say. Thus began the pattern that Stella and others who were not involved in the campaign astutely observed and followed.

> Usually the pattern that [the media] would go through is that they will publish some really, really offensive gay letter, an offensive homophobic letter. That would be a prompt for us to write in, and then they would feature really, really positive and well-reasoned strong letters. (Stella)

Activists wrote letters extrapolated from news reports or responded to someone else's published letters, triggering subsequent events and responses. Compared with previous years, media coverage on local gay issues multiplied by nearly three times in 2007. Of all of the newspaper articles about gays or local gay rights in 2007, two-thirds of them concerned Section 377A or the repeal petition.

For two consecutive days, October 22–23, 2007, Section 377A dominated parliamentary debates during the second reading of the Penal Code amendment bill, even though it was not officially part of the bill.[11] Seventeen of the twenty-one MPs who stood up to debate on the bill considered Section 377A. As a contrasting example, unfortunately, the debate over whether to have stricter penal laws against martial rape did not receive as much attention. Women's rights groups had voiced their criticisms during the public consultation phase; however, unlike Repeal 377A advocates, they did not take advantage of the parliamentary petition process.

Only three of these MPs, discounting Siew and the prime minister, openly supported repeal of Section 377A, but the campaign walked away with an unexpected gain. It reached its high-water mark when Prime Minister Lee Hsien Loong finally stood up to give a speech that clarified the state's position on homosexuality: Gays have a place in Singaporean society, and Section 377A is not to be enforced against gays in consensual, private situations; nevertheless, their interests still may not trump the majority of citizens who have yet to accept homosexuality. Looking back at "LKY's interview on CNN" in 1998, this position is nothing new. Before the campaign, the prosecution had also been applying Section 377A mainly to cases involving nonconsent or minors (L. Chua 2003; but see Amirthalingam 2008; Hor 2012). With Lee Hsien Loong's statement, however, this known practice crystallized into what became known as the *policy of nonenforcement,* one that returns to the public spotlight in 2010.[12]

Given the public nature of its petition, the demand for political attention, and the call for recognition of rights—but at the same time recognizing that success was unlikely—the campaign may seem confrontational on the surface. However, it was tempered by a combination of tactical moves. Repeal 377A activists used legal procedures to file the petition[13] and did not demonstrate on the streets. Even though the campaign attempted to justify repealing Section 377A on the basis of rights, its public statements moderated the arguments by linking repeal to the acceptance of diversity as the cornerstone of social stability and portrayed the issue as having a broad effect on Singaporean society.

> Singapore society has matured very quickly over the years, to be more inclusive and accepting of people from all walks of life. We are seeing parents of gay children publicly voicing their support by signing on the petition, and we have been receiving heartfelt comments by family and friends of gay persons on the Repeal377a.com site pleading for the section to be repealed. This is a call by Singaporeans to embrace the diversity within our society. (Press Statement, Repeal 377A Petition, October 18, 2007)

Further, to send the signal that Section 377A did not polarize society, Parker and Morris intentionally recruited their third leading petitioner from Family and Friends and settled on Ai-Mee, one of the founders of the gay-straight alliance. A married, straight woman with a gay brother, and pregnant at the time, Ai-Mee fronted the campaign to stand for the message that it was more than a "gay thing" to appeal to non-gay allies.

Countermovement

The movement's coming out, especially Repeal 377A, corresponded to an upsurge in a Christian Right countermovement that included a segment of Christians who are minority members of a minority religion in Singapore.[14] Before Repeal 377A, these opponents confined their views to sermons, churches, and "reparative therapy" programs, with only occasional glimpses in letters to newspapers editors. Repeal 377A drew them out and became the first public and protracted conflict between movement and countermovement.

A tactic of this countermovement is to portray their objections as representative of those of Singaporean society and cultivate fear among parents about the danger of gays to their children and harm to "family values." During Repeal 377A, Keep377A.com and Support377A.com appeared on the web, resembling Zac's Repeal377A.com in design and look. Supporters of Section 377A launched an online signature drive for an open letter to the prime minister. Then the conflict made its way to the Parliament floor, where Nominated Member of Parliament Thio Li-Ann, a human rights and constitutional law professor and the daughter of Thio Su-Mien, spoke out against repeal and equal rights for gays. She referred to the Bible to support her opposition, and warned against succumbing to "a radical, political agenda which will subvert social morality, the common good and undermine our liberties"[15]—arguments that resonate with how American conservatives recast equal rights for gays or other minority groups as "special rights" (Dudas 2008) and their claimants as people with illicit or immoral purposes (Goldberg-Hiller and Milner 2003).

Tackling such a countermovement can be difficult. Attacking a minority of right-wing Christian opponents too aggressively risks appearing to be sowing social discord among religious faiths. Therefore, gay activists deploy a delicate version of pragmatic resistance captured in the statement issued after the Repeal 377A parliamentary debates.

> The intolerance and ill-will demonstrated by a few of our opponents clearly attest to the fact that we cannot be silent. Such fundamentally extreme views against homosexuality splits [sic] families apart and causes [sic] much harm to us as individuals, professionals and as a community. In fact, these are the very actions that cause divisiveness and polarise our society. (Press Statement, Repeal 377A Petition, October 24, 2007)

The statement portrays to the government and the public that the Christian Right countermovement threatens social harmony, whereas the gay movement embraces and promotes it. The tactic borrows the state's hand to tackle the opposition by triggering the political norm of preserving social stability.

Coming out in the contemporary era with bolder tactics, such as the annual pride festival and Repeal 377A, Singapore's gay movement inadvertently spurred a countermovement. The petition campaign became the first public conflict between the two sides, perhaps because the prospect of repeal heightened the opponents' perception of threat to their interests (see Meyer and Staggenborg 1996). The conflict and the petition's outcome helped gay activists to reach a more sophisticated collective understanding of the complicated politics surrounding the repeal and the Singaporean state's position on homosexuality. They learned that repeal would be controversial and cost the PAP political capital. They also experienced the ability of the countermovement to rouse panic and fear among parents, a formidable constituency among PAP electorates. While activists believe that Singapore's influential former prime minister, Lee Kuan Yew, his son and current prime minister, Lee Hsien Loong, and others within the PAP's top ranks are not religiously motivated, they recognize that conservative Christian elites who oppose repeal represent a faction of the party. Rather than risk political capital within the ranks and with the populace, the PAP leadership negotiated the political compromise of a nonenforcement policy, despite the potential cost in international legitimacy. Gay activists applied this political lesson to tactical readjustments as they carried on with the movement's coming-out journey and developed two new pathways of tactical escalation, to which I next turn.

7

Mobilizing in the Open

This chapter continues to show the ways in which the contemporary period develops along the three themes of change summarized at the opening of Chapter 6—coming out into the open, holding public events and enjoying growing support, and receiving broader recognition from the state, the media, and even a countermovement. But the developments examined in this chapter also highlight differences in tactical direction that occur as activists make adjustments based on lessons learned from earlier tactics. After analyzing these changes, I step back at the end of the chapter to examine the implications of pragmatic resistance.

Repeal 377A and interactions with the countermovement refined the movement's understanding of the state's position on Section 377A and homosexuality and influenced gay activists to develop two new and distinct paths of tactical escalation. First, the legislative and executive reactions signaled that the law would not be repealed unless mainstream values seemed to shift in favor of doing so. Since then, one part of the movement has channeled efforts toward amassing a visible support base of non-gay allies and demonstrating that their cause promotes social harmony. Among them, the most representative is Pink Dot.

Second, the political climate during and after Repeal 377A led a minority of gay activists to find courage and hope in the possibility of repealing Section 377A through the courts. These activists interpreted a preference among a faction of PAP's leadership for the judiciary to determine a politically inconvenient matter, believing that these politicians favored repeal but did not wish to expend political capital on its behalf—a view in line with studies about the delegation of controversies to the judiciary to avoid political fallouts in both democratic (Tate 1995) and authoritarian regimes (Moustafa 2007; Ginsburg and Moustafa 2008). Such optimism began to be tested in 2010, when a gay man was charged under Section 377A, offering an opportunity for litigating the law's constitutionality.

The year following Repeal 377A was a relatively uneventful one for the movement, but it was also the year when the government once again tweaked the licensing rules for speech and assembly under Prime Minister Lee Hsien Loong's administration. With the extension of the 2000 Hong Lim Park licensing exemption on public speaking to "exhibitions" and "performances," the practical effect was that organizers did not need to apply for licenses to hold assemblies at the park as long as they registered in advance with the police and agreed to the same preconditions regarding race and religion. The impetus for Singapore's first public gay rally, Pink Dot, can be traced back to these changes that took place quietly in November 2008.

Innovating a Public Gay Rally

News of the new Hong Lim Park exemptions caught Nelson's attention: Why not hold a gay pride parade at Hong Lim Park? Nelson's idea did not come to fruition, but it provided the catalyst for Pink Dot, the first public gay rally in Singapore. From the initial inspiration to the first formation of Pink Dot in 2009, gay activists faced and tackled differences among themselves, led one version of pragmatic resistance to prevail over others, and even inspired similar events around the world.[1]

A gay man in his fifties, Nelson considered himself an archivist of the movement, filming every event he attended, posting the videos on YouTube, and creating Internet entries to document local gay culture and history. Up until that point, he had not taken on any leadership or organizational roles. Yet, his motivations for wanting to hold a pride parade reflected the creative spirit of pragmatic resistance: He wanted to make use of the new exemption rule—ultimately a form of legal control—and expand collective mobilization's acceptable political limits, which have conventionally repressed large-scale public gatherings. At the same time, he internalized the survival instinct of the movement's overarching strategy.

> If the government hadn't liberalized Hong Lim Park . . . then I would think that it would be confrontational, and it would be illegal, and I wouldn't have done it. But because it was legal, that's why I decided to do it. I thought it was a great opportunity to do it in a legal way. (Nelson)

As much as Nelson wanted to hold a pride parade, he was not going to break the law to do so. He had no intention whatsoever of holding the proposed parade outside of the designated park because that would be "illegal" (and he wrote off the possibility that a permit would be approved for any street demonstration) and would cross the boundaries too blatantly.

Nelson first broached the idea of a pride parade on Talklist and registered with the relevant authorities to hold the event on November 15, 2008. Local journalists found out and reported Nelson as saying that he would hold speeches on gay rights and march around Hong Lim Park to protest Section 377A. Nelson also admitted to the press that he had limited support—only one written and fifty verbal confirmations. Support for Nelson's idea was weak. More seasoned activists questioned the viability of having a pride parade. First, a "parade" connotes moving linearly toward a destination. But Hong Lim Park is a contained area of approximately 2.3 acres, only a little larger than two American football fields. Obeying the rules would mean parading around the park, literally walking in circles. The idea did not seem to make sense to them. Second, those who later transformed Nelson's idea into Pink Dot did not believe that Singaporeans, gay or straight, would turn out to march in a parade. They felt that Singaporeans would shun the political stigma attached to demonstrations and protests after seeing how opposition politicians who staged streets protests without permits have been prosecuted, convicted, and consequently delegitimized.

When Nelson did not seem to mind the lack of cultural resonance, Winston and Morris decided to step in.

> I was horrified by the silence, the dead silence that seemed to surround what he was trying to do. . . . So my thought was I don't want [Nelson] to fall flat on his face. Even though he is perfectly fine with falling flat on his face, I don't want him to. . . . I don't know whether you could say it was for a selfish reason, but I felt it was important that [Nelson's] event not fail because it would be taken as representative of the [gay] community as a whole. And I didn't want to give the Christian Right any more ammunition than it already had, in that sense, or any chance to gloat and say, "Oh, see how little

support gay people have" or "See how divided they are," and so on. So, I felt that if we had an event and something as public as at Hong Lim Park, it had to be a success, and it had to be a show of strength. (Winston)

Winston and Morris met with Nelson and convinced him that numbers were important because they needed the media to cover the movement positively. The two called a town hall meeting of activists to brainstorm ideas. For a while, people at the meeting were stuck as they searched for an alternative to a parade, something that could still show strength in numbers but would not be associated with a demonstration. Then Eu-Jin, who started getting involved with the movement after joining the Portal, came up with Pink Dot.

I said, just have something that is so simple that anybody, all ages, can come, without any preparation. They just need to come knowing why they're there. And why they're there should be so simple that they can say it in one sentence: that it's to support the LGBT community in Singapore. (Eu-Jin)

According to Eu-Jin's idea, all participants needed to do was show up at a designated time at the park to form a human pink dot that would be filmed and photographed aerially from a hotel building overlooking the park.

If they knew about it an hour before because someone just told them about it, they could still come and do it because there is no need for any prior rehearsal or preparation. It's as simple as that. And then at the same time, it has to be something that will register visually to everyone the next morning and maybe for many years to come. (Eu-Jin)

Thus Pink Dot was born and Nelson's pride parade was "hijacked," as both he and the Pink Dot organizers admitted independently of one another. Compared with Winston, Morris, Eu-Jin, and other activists linked to movement organizations such as the Coalition and the Portal, Nelson at the time lacked the necessary social connections and clout within the movement. His communication with local media also indicated that he had less regard for the political norms on nonconfrontation, signals pointing to the rise of the Christian Right countermovement, and the movement's overall strategic position. Consequently, he did not persuade other activists to support his idea. Other activists before Nelson, such as Trey and Billy, also introduced unpopular ideas but ultimately mustered support to implement them—Trey insisted that the Coalition apply for society registration, and Billy restructured the Christian Fellowship and the Beacon. Besides the ability to sway others to accept their tactics as most conducive to the movement's survival, advancement, or both, they also did not back down. This was not the case with Nelson.

> I had to bow down to the wishes of the majority. Yeah, I had to toe the "party" line because most of them didn't want the thing, the protest message at all. . . . [Pink Dot was] a dilution of my original intention. But that's what the majority wanted, so I was willing to go along with it. (Nelson)

Nelson's pride parade could have gained ground in the end or he could have broken off from the group to organize a pride parade, but he did not. He was willing to assimilate and go along with the majority's preference. He worked with the rest of the Pink Dot organizers, who honored him as the progenitor at the historic event.

At the juncture immediately following the town hall meeting, however, the event was still in its infancy. With Nelson's concession, Pink Dot organizers moved the proposed date from November 15, 2008, to Valentine's Day on February 14, 2009. However, more took place in 2009 before Pink Dot returned to the spotlight.

The AWARE Saga: Fending Off the Countermovement

A lot of what happened in the interim had to do with the AWARE saga. Involving Singapore's largest and mainstream women's organization, this incident started with no apparent connection to the gay movement. As it unfolded, it became clear that the rise of the movement served as the impetus; the way in which the events developed and concluded also implicated the movement as gay activists, especially lesbians, took on the fight as one against the countermovement. Just two years after Repeal 377A, it was the biggest public contention between movement and countermovement that did not directly involve the state. The outcome warned gay activists of the countermovement's strength but also further clarified the state's complicated position on homosexuality.

The saga is complex, involving issues wider than the scope of this book.[2] In sum, a batch of new members who joined the organization just in time for elections took over AWARE's leadership, the executive committee ("Exco"), by voting in their own people in March 2009. Eventually, these usurpers introduced their "feminist mentor," Thio Su-Mien, who had written to the press to warn of "the homosexual agenda" and whose daughter, Thio Li-Ann, spoke up against repealing Section 377A in Parliament. The new Exco revealed their intentions: AWARE, they alleged, had lost direction and succumbed to the single purpose of promoting homosexuality. They pointed to several factors: the involvement of former AWARE president, Ai-Mee, in the gay movement; AWARE's affiliation with the Mother's Day forum initiated by Stella and Ming Choo; and the neutral treatment of homosexuality in the optional sex education program that AWARE offered to public schools.

The relevance of the AWARE takeover to the gay movement became clear. Gay activists and curious reporters investigated the backgrounds of the new Exco members and made the following connections: Several of them had written letters to the press during Repeal 377A to espouse anti-gay views; the new Exco president is married to the nephew of Thio Su-Mien; and most of the nine newly elected Exco members attend the same church reputed to run the ex-gay "therapy" programs in which gay activists such as Brett, Billy, and Xavier used to participate. Stella and activists from Women's World as well as Abby and her team from the Queer Women's Alliance rallied around AWARE's old-timers to organize We Are AWARE to fight the new Exco. They recruited women to boost AWARE membership in their favor and invoked the organization's constitution to call for an extraordinary general meeting. On May 2, 2009, AWARE members cast votes of no confidence at the extraordinary general meeting and expelled the new Exco with voting results of 2:1 against them,[3] ending a two-month-long power struggle.

The AWARE saga illustrates the uneasy relationship between the women's organization and the gay movement. From time to time, the organization has pro-gay leaders and members who participate in the gay movement. Ai-Mee and Stella are such examples. However, the organization does not have a pro-gay reputation (hence gay activists found the new Exco's motivation for taking over AWARE somewhat ironic). After putting in long hours for We Are AWARE, lesbian leaders such as Stella and Abby realized that AWARE went back to business as usual, relegating lesbians to the sidelines. One explanation for the relationship may be ideological differences—that is, AWARE's influential old-timers do not embrace sexuality-based politics. When the Queer Women's Alliance reached out to AWARE, one of them tried to clarify that AWARE's agenda is driven by "issues" and therefore cannot champion any particular group, such as one organized around sexuality.

Another explanation may be that AWARE does not want to be seen as a lesbian group. Its leaders worry that this association can compound AWARE's challenges in a deeply patriarchal and heteronormative society (Lyons 2004). After all, AWARE's leaders are also mobilizing under the same authoritarian rule and formal legal conditions (though their interpretations of norms and signals may vary from those of gay activists).[4] In fact, their manner of fighting the new Exco resonates with the gay movement's pragmatic resistance—We Are AWARE abided by formal rules and regulations and followed their organization's procedures to vote out the usurpers.[5]

In addition, the motivation for the new Exco's takeover and its aftermath may have given AWARE even more reason to hold gay activism at arm's length. Although its old-timers and supporters expelled the new Exco, they lost one important battle to the countermovement: The negative publicity about AWARE's voluntary sex education program and parents' complaints pressured the Ministry of Education to suspend it (another ironic twist since the PAP government prides itself on not yielding to pressure from interest groups). A year later, the ministry announced new rules allowing only ministry-approved vendors to provide sex education programs and requiring the providers to inform students that homosexual acts are illegal. Of the six qualified programs announced in 2010, four are known to have conservative Christian affiliations.

At this point, to address the book's central theme of pragmatic resistance, I want to highlight how gay activists interpret signals from the AWARE saga and how those readings shape future movement tactics. Regardless of the reasons behind the complex relationship between AWARE and the gay movement, the saga sent several signals to gay activists. For one, the aftermath confirmed what they knew all along: They cannot count on AWARE as a consistent ally. This harsh reality affects the tactics of the Queer Women's Alliance in 2011. For another, the AWARE saga solidified for gay activists their understanding of the state's overall stance on homosexuality. Despite losing the battle on sex education, one crucial aspect remains constant. The state maintained the position that while heterosexuality remains the norm, gay people are to be left alone to live in peace. A closer look at the revised sex education policy actually does not suggest otherwise. No matter how inadequate this stance may seem to critics, the fact that it weathered a public controversy in which one side aggressively mounted a majoritarian argument is significant in an authoritarian state where the dominant party ironically relies on winning elections for legitimacy. In fact, during the two-month-long struggle, activists took comfort in PAP politicians' warnings to religious leaders not to create social unrest by mixing religion with politics. Twenty years earlier, when the gay movement first started, such a debate would not even have been possible, nor would activists have fathomed challenging their rivals so openly without fear of attracting negative state reaction (of course, the countermovement might have had no reason to take action, given the movement's timidity back then).

Furthermore, the setback on sex education reaffirmed activists' assessment after Repeal 377A—they must demonstrate stronger non-gay, ally support to rebuke the countermovement. Considering the PAP's adamant stance that it will not pander to interest groups, the Ministry of Education's acquiescence to the countermovement's agenda demonstrated its ability once again to influence a larger population of Singaporeans and a wider electorate of the PAP. Hence, the AWARE saga indicated to gay activists that the movement's challenge is no longer simply about engaging the state directly. It has also become a contest between movement and countermovement to forge alliances with Singaporean society at large, and that entails coming out even more boldly.

Pink Dot: Organizing Singapore's First Public Gay Rally

> Pink Dot had nothing to do with AWARE. The whole event . . . the campaign was conceptualized way before any of that happened. So I think that maybe it was a stroke of luck that it happened, and it got so many people so angry, angry enough that they were willing to step forward and give that little bit of extra volunteer help. . . . And I would say that while AWARE spurred other people to join Pink Dot, it also spurred existing members of Pink Dot to work even harder because, as we discussed, we got angrier, and as we got angrier, we became more and more motivated. (Kurt)

Before the AWARE saga, enthusiasm was flagging for Pink Dot. By then, the event had been pushed back to May 16, 2009, because the first postponement to Valentine's Day coincided too closely with the Chinese lunar new year celebrations that year, a busy time for most Singaporeans. The initial publicity on Facebook showed a roundish cartoon character that looked like a pink cousin of the purple "Ribena berry" (Ribena is a popular black currant–flavored drink), but gay activists outside the Pink Dot team knew little about what was going on. Some still referred to it dismissively as "[Nelson's] thing" and joked about whether anyone would want to show up at Hong Lim Park to take a group photograph. Even the organizing team seemed lackluster. Tasks were not accomplished as scheduled, and people did not show up for meetings.

The AWARE saga, which took place from March through early May 2009, renewed energy for Pink Dot. Coincidentally, the new date of May 16 marked exactly two months after news broke on the new Exco's takeover of AWARE and was two weeks after the extraordinary general meeting that expelled them.[6] Memories of the conflict with the countermovement and excitement from the successful extraordinary general meeting remained fresh (the Ministry of Education did not announce the changes to its sex education policy until a year later). New activists joined the movement because they were aggrieved by the countermovement's role in the AWARE saga. Original Pink Dot team members started returning to the planning meetings, and new ones came calling. In the few weeks leading up to the event, the organizing team hurried to put everything in place.

May 16, 2009: Hong Lim Park, Singapore

About 2,500 people, gay and non-gay allies, flocked to Singapore's first public gay rally. Volunteers wearing cowboy hats covered in neon pink disco dust distributed free pink cardboard fans, balloons, umbrellas, and flyers. Local theater and television celebrities turned up as Pink Dot ambassadors and spokespersons. Families came with their babies, toddlers, and dogs, dressed in shades of pink, to have an afternoon picnic on the grassy grounds. Some brought along rainbow flags.

At 4:45 P.M., the volunteers organized the crowd to make the first of three consecutive formations: "LOVE," "4ALL," and a pink dot. The aerial photography and videography team shot from a hotel room overlooking the park. They used walkie-talkies to communicate with fellow organizers on the park grounds to tweak the formations. People were assigned to stand at designated points on the grounds to make sure that the crowd huddled into the desired shapes. When cued, the crowd held up whatever pink items they had, such as the pink cardboard fans, balloons, and umbrellas, and waved them in the direction of the hotel. In between formations, a traditional Malay music ensemble, an Indian music band, a contemporary dance group, and a Chinese lion dance troupe took turns performing.

Then came the finale, the pink dot formation. Twenty-odd years earlier, Nelson visited Hong Lim Park after reading newspaper reports about police investigations of same-sex activity there and found a cruising ground for years to come. At the same park, on May 16, 2009, wearing a matching pink shirt and pants, Nelson carried the official Pink Dot flag on a staff, climbed onto a wobbly makeshift platform in the center of the pink dot formation, and waved the flag high above his head as the crowd sang "All You Need Is Love." Despite the "hijack" of his pride parade idea, he was beaming and smiling that afternoon. Pink Dot had become one of the "highlights" of his life.

Since 2009, Pink Dot has become an annual event and the number of participants has increased each year. In 2010, about four thousand people showed up to form a pink heart. In 2011, the number swelled to ten thousand. Representatives from various movement organizations, including Resource Central, the Beacon, Youth Support, and the Friendship League, distributed information about their groups and activities. There was no longer any point in trying to shape the crowd into a round dot. From the vantage point of the hotel room where the annual photographs and video are taken, Hong Lim Park looked like a sea of moving pink.

In 2012, Pink Dot organizers decided to move the event to nighttime to avoid the 90-degree-Fahrenheit afternoon heat. This time, movement organizations set up booths in a designated community tent area located right next to the police station on the edge of the park. Volunteers distributed free pink flashlights and cellophane strips (to modify the color of light emitted from mobile phones). Nelson managed the official Pink Dot booth. A concert featuring local performers began at 6:30 P.M. Around 7:30 P.M., fifteen thousand people got ready to form the first-ever nighttime pink dot. The organizers lit a heart-shaped fixture at the hotel window overlooking the park (so that people on the ground would know where the cameras were). On a countdown from ten, the participants raised their pink light devices, pointed them at the heart in the hotel window, and turned on their lights together. Then they broke into the theme song for Pink Dot 2012, "True Colors."[7]

Pink Dot 2009 was a historic moment for Singapore's gay movement. Before that, a public gay rally was perceived as transgressive. Even Pink Dot organizers worried that they were not going to persuade enough people, gay or non-gay, to show up. Just because the law—the 2008 exemptions—suddenly made it a little easier did not necessarily mean that Singaporeans were going to participate in or support public assemblies. Formal restrictions are only one type of barrier. Gay activists also believed that many Singaporeans associated protests with troublemaking, and because protesting without a permit is illegal, this type of assembly could also be seen as delegitimizing the government. By holding increasingly larger Pink Dot rallies each year since

2009, these activists managed to overcome a negative cultural perception against public assemblies.

Indeed, the rallies remain contained by the restrictions on civil-political liberties. One activist not directly involved with Pink Dot described it wistfully as a "party in a prison yard." Pink Dot organizers recognize the tokenistic nature of the Hong Lim Park exemption. Unlike critics who dismiss the new rule, however, they choose to make use of it.

> [Hong Lim Park is] about restricting the space available for free speech to this tiny corner. So in conceptualizing Pink Dot, we wanted to reverse all that. We wanted to do something that was visually stunning so that it would break out of the confines of that space, something memorable, something iconic. (Winston)

By capturing the Pink Dot formations on photos and videos and using the Internet to distribute the images, activists creatively push through the physical constraints of the park and legal rules and nudge the political boundaries outward. Further, *because* they make use of those restrictions, they earn the event cultural legitimacy. In fact, Pink Dot organizers are meticulous about obeying the law.

> Q: Is this event legit or legal?
> A: Yes, of course! We have registered for the event and we shall strive to conduct ourselves appropriately, as set out in National Parks' terms and conditions. Who says we can't behave and have fun at the same time! (FAQ, Pink Dot 2009)

The activists not only register Pink Dot with the police as a public assembly event, as required by the license exemption rule, but also register every person who might be speaking on that day—for example, to make an announcement or give instructions to the participants when making the formations.[8] They also emphasize and abide by one other important rule: Only Singaporean citizens and permanent residents may participate in the assemblies. Interpreting *participation* as joining in the organized formations, every year Pink Dot organizers announce this rule in their publicity materials and "live" announcements.

> Q: Are foreigners allowed to attend?
> A: According to the park's terms and conditions, only Singaporeans and Permanent Residents may participate at the events held

at Hong Lim Park. However, foreigners are most welcome to watch and observe. It is, after all, a public park.
Q: What does "participate" really mean?
A: Well, our interpretation of the term is that foreigners should not join in during the human Pink Dot formation segment of [the] event. (FAQ, Pink Dot 2010)

In 2012, organizers put up signs near the concert stage saying that it would be converted into an observation deck for the use of those who were not citizens or permanent residents during the Pink Dot formation. They made announcements to the same effect before it began.[9] Pink Dot flyers on the day of the event also added a Singaporean touch, noting, "Please remember to keep Hong Lim Park litter-free." Afterward, organizers and volunteers picked up litter and deflated and disposed of stray balloons.

Besides adhering to formal restrictions, the organizers of Pink Dot emphasize its nonconfrontational nature and promotion of social stability while simultaneously expanding the opportunity for political mobilization that such norms constrain. The participants stay within the park and do not march down public streets. The Pink Dot publicity materials repeatedly emphasize that the event is not political and is "not a protest." Event flyers remind participants not to confront or engage opponents if they show up. These precautionary measures against legal violations and transgressive conduct do not merely appease paranoia; the police *do* conduct surveillance on the Pink Dot gatherings. Some police in uniform are stationed in and around the park area and plainclothes officers are present as well (though they are not too difficult to differentiate from the actual participants).

Using the slogan "the freedom to love," Pink Dot organizers further promote the message that acceptance of diverse types of sexuality[10] strengthens rather than polarizes society and that Singaporeans from different backgrounds already accept homosexuality, contrary to the countermovement's argument and the state's worry that Singaporeans remain largely "conservative." For instance, Pink Dot highlights racial and religious diversity. The online publicity videos and on-location activities showcase the participation and support of people identified visually with the major racial and religious groups in Singapore. In the traditional cultural performances, the performers wear their normal clothing, but incorporate generous quantities of pink. Even the eighty-two-foot Chinese "dragon" at Pink Dot 2010 arrived in fuchsia.

Bearing in mind the AWARE saga and the countermovement's claim that homosexuality threatens the basic values of the family unit and thus social stability, Pink Dot links the implications of having "the freedom to love" to relationships with parents, siblings, and friends.

> When we talk about freedom to love, we're not talking about the freedom to love between two men, just between two men, but the freedom to love between parents and their child, a child for his parents, between siblings, and that, if you live a life that is dishonest and if you constantly live in fear that it will be found out that you're gay—it impacts this freedom to love. Can you truly have an honest relationship with your family or siblings or friends if you are hiding one important part of yourself? (Kurt)

Just as Repeal 377A had help from professionals who made a rap music video for the campaign, Pink Dot has help from activists and allies in the arts and entertainment industry to produce promotional videos. Circulated on Pink Dot's websites and YouTube, these videos feature straight allies—parents of gays and lesbians, local artists, entertainers, and celebrities—who speak on behalf of Pink Dot.

Finally, to avoid potential accusations by opponents that Pink Dot imposes Western values—and again allegations of harming the social fabric of Singapore—the organizers reinterpret the meaning of the color pink.

> Pink because it's a blend of red and white and the colour[s] of Singapore's national flag. Also, it is the colour of our national identification cards. More importantly, Pink Dot Sg stands for a Singapore in which all Singaporeans, regardless of their sexual orientation, are free to love and be loved. (Pink Dot Blog, Pink Dot 2009)

Instead of making the color's symbolic connection to discrimination or gay pride, the activists link it to a localized notion of diversity: Pink is the product of mixing Singapore's national flag colors of red and white. They then point out that the color—the result of accepting diversity—is already part of what it means to be Singaporean because it is the color of the identity cards issued only to citizens.

Expanding Use of International Connections

The translation (Merry 2006) by Pink Dot activists of symbols originating outside of Singapore is the most common way in which the Singaporean movement taps into transnational activism and human rights discourse. Singapore's gay activists are influenced by and deploy the ideals of rights and images of the urbanized, Western gay identity, such as the rainbow and the color pink (Altman 2001).[11] Their organizations refer to these terms and use such references as *LGBT* and *coming out* in their communication and organizational materials. However, while they draw from these sources to fuel their movement, they do not adopt the same tactics but readapt them into versions of pragmatic resistance that they believe will both advance and preserve the movement in Singapore.

Furthermore, to avoid allegations that their movement has foreign influence, their organizations are homegrown and for the most part they do not portray themselves as claimants on the international stage (Bob 2009). As considered in Chapter 5, gay activists are aware of how the Singaporean government accused dissident groups of having foreign connections or receiving foreign funds and thus suppressed them for being national security threats. Some of the activists also perceive stereotypical transnational activists as lacking appreciation for the local context and being dismissive of their agency. Often viewed as telling ignorant and oppressed locals what to do, transnational activists are seen as potentially creating problems by not operating according to pragmatic resistance.

For these interwoven reasons, it is a deliberate tactic of the movement to avoid open affiliations with transnational movements or human rights organizations. I explained in Chapter 5 that Singaporean gay activists' international connections are informal and based on personal communication and friendships with foreign media and international activists and organizations. In recent years, these personal connections have extended to multinational corporations that have offices in Singapore and are known to have nondiscrimination policies. For instance, Pink Dot 2011 and 2012 obtained sponsorship from multinational corporations where fellow activists or allies work. I also examined in Chapter 5 how gay activists usually leverage international pressure in subtle and indirect ways to avoid outright confrontation. They build relationships with foreign journalists, diplomats, and state officials; keep them apprised of their movement and concerns; and then wait for them to ask Singaporean politicians and officials inconvenient questions about Section 377A or other unjust conditions.

In 2011, however, the tactics used for international connections became more direct when the Queer Women's Alliance went straight to the United Nations to exert international pressure. Knowing that Singapore, as a party to the Convention for the Elimination of All Forms of Discrimination against

Women (CEDAW), was due to provide its periodic country report, the Queer Women's Alliance filed its own shadow report and its representatives traveled to the United Nations headquarters to give oral statements at the forty-ninth CEDAW session. NGOs of each party state may submit shadow reports that will be considered by the United Nations CEDAW committee alongside the state's official report. The committee may question the state about discrepancies between the official and shadow reports, and the country must respond. The committee then identifies areas of concern and makes recommendations to the state for progress. For the first time in any international legal process, lesbians in Singapore had representation and the Singaporean state delegation had to address their grievances officially and publicly.

The leaders of the Queer Women's Alliance were actually talking to AWARE's representatives about including the group's research in AWARE's more general shadow report. During the AWARE saga, the Queer Women's Alliance gave resources and time to help We Are AWARE expel the new Exco. At the time, Abby was already conscious of the difficult relationship that AWARE has with gay activism—for the various reasons discussed earlier—and was prepared for the organization to distance itself once it was restored. Her worries were confirmed when her group later learned that the mainstream organization was planning to exclude it from the CEDAW shadow report after all. At most, it was going to consign the research to a short mention in an appendix. Frustrated, the Queer Women's Alliance decided to submit its own shadow report and send its own delegation to the United Nations.

The Queer Women's Alliance's sixteen-page document detailed the social, cultural, political, economic, and legal conditions affecting lesbians in Singapore, describing them as "prevalent and systematic discrimination against women based on sexual orientation and gender identity." During one of the sessions, the committee asked the Singaporean state delegation how the government was going to address these problems to reduce stigmatization and promote tolerance. CEDAW is one of only three international human rights treaties that Singapore has ever ratified,[12] and the state is known for claiming that it would ratify only conventions that it was prepared to implement. In 2007, when the same committee asked about the existence of measures to prevent discrimination against lesbians at work, in access to health services, and in society, the state delegation merely responded that "homosexuals were not discriminated against" and insisted that "they had the same right to employment, education, and housing as everyone else." In contrast, in 2011, the state delegation replied:

The principle of equality of all persons before the law is enshrined in the Constitution of the Republic of Singapore, regardless of gender, sexual orientation and gender identity. All persons in Singapore are entitled to the equal protection of the law, and have equal access to basic resources such as education, housing and health care. (Responses to the list of issues and questions with regard to the consideration of the fourth periodic report, Singapore, 2011)

The actions of the Queer Women's Alliance at the United Nations provide yet another example of how gay activists constantly interpret and reinterpret signals and sometimes scale up tactics while maintaining pragmatic resistance. To a certain extent, the Queer Women's Alliance's activists did behave according to the political norms. They made use of official channels provided by the legal procedures of an international treaty ratified by Singapore. While the questions and exposure might have created an awkward situation for the state delegation, these actions were still not tantamount to staging a street protest when Singapore hosts top political leaders from other countries. At the same time, they challenged boundaries. Here was an unregistered organization that directly exposed legalized and state-sanctioned discrimination against lesbians and forced the state to answer the allegations under international scrutiny. A decade earlier, their predecessors were agonizing over whether they could offer telephone counseling services safely without state sanctions. In ten years, gay activists' interpretations of risk and transgression have shifted, as have the political boundaries and the state's position on homosexuality and the gay movement. As both contributors to and beneficiaries of these changes, the Queer Women's Alliance's leaders felt emboldened to make use of international connections directly and speak out at the United Nations.

The rewards of taking this risk may not yet be completely known. Contrary to the state's response, Article 12 of Singapore's constitution on equal protection makes no explicit mention of gender, much less any reference to sexuality or sexual orientation. Hence, the answer can be construed as misrepresentative. Or, it can be seen as a concession, albeit a weak one. Ultimately, the answer may have little effect on domestic legal developments because international treaty obligations must be implemented via amendments or enactment of Constitutional provisions and other domestic laws and policies. Thus far, the Singaporean administration and legislature have shown no sign of taking action. From the 2007 Repeal 377A campaign to the Queer Women's Alliance's adventure at the United Nations, the movement's contention over the meaning of Article 12 has only just begun.

Going to Court

The courts present an alternative to Parliament for activists to seek redress under Article 12. But litigation is not a common tactic for Singapore's gay movement. One verdict had been clear about rights litigation in Singapore. By and large, as discussed in Chapter 2, judicial precedents on constitutional rights have suggested to gay activists that seeking rights vindication through the courts is a difficult tactic.

This outlook, however, started to change in the years following Repeal 377A as gay activists started encountering and reading newer signals. Some of them began to see hope. The political statements emerging from the petition campaign hinted that repeal through the legislative route is foreclosed until and unless a PAP-dominated Parliament perceives sufficient majority support for it. Then, in 2009, the Indian New Delhi High Court struck down the criminalization of private and consensual same-sex sexual conduct as unconstitutional (*Naz Foundation v. Govt. of NCT of Delhi* 2009).[13] In conjunction with the development in India, Singapore's law minister at the time was asked about the future of Section 377A. He reiterated the nonenforcement policy, but went on to say that courts have the power to decide how the provision should be interpreted and applied (Hor 2012). Taken together, these developments led a minority of gay activists to interpret the government as having signaled a preference for courts to determine the fate of Section 377A.

> [That] is the only issue that is ready to be heard in courts. . . . I think the government would like it to be settled in court, not in Parliament. For some reason, I feel that they do think there's some sort of political liability. To take it to court, there would be no political liability. (Parker)

> [Litigation on Section 377A's constitutionality] will excuse the government. . . . They don't have to come out and say, "Okay, we accept it." (Devi)

In other words, although gay activists still generally doubt the efficacy of rights litigation, their readings of newer signals suggest optimism confined to one particular issue—the constitutionality of Section 377A. If the courts were to decide the matter and invalidate the law, the legislature would avoid being held responsible for what they consider a controversial decision that may cost the party electorate votes and expend political capital within party ranks. Regardless of the ruling, the PAP would be able to point to the decision as the consequence of having an independent judiciary, which it fiercely defends as a symbol of Singapore's rule of law.

As this book goes to press, such nascent hope and interpretations of political signals are being tested. On September 2, 2010, a man named Tan Eng Hong was charged under Section 377A for having oral sex with another man in the restroom of a shopping mall on March 9, 2010. Activists criticized the charge, pointing to the prime minister's statement on nonenforcement. After investigating Tan on the basis of Section 377A for almost seven months, the attorney general substituted the charge with a lesser penal provision, public obscenity under Section 294(a) of the Penal Code,[14] though he did not explain his motivations (the prosecution enjoys constitutionally protected discretion, so holding it accountable to the policy may be an uphill legal battle). By then, Tan's attorney had initiated a constitutional challenge on Section 377A, arguing that it violated, among others, Article 12 of the Constitution on the right to equality. So the attorney general moved to strike out the Section 377A constitutional challenge on procedural grounds that Tan lacked legal standing since he was no longer charged or prosecuted under the provision. Soon after, Tan pleaded guilty to the lesser charge. The lower court agreed with the attorney general and granted the strike-out motion pertaining to Section 377A (*Tan Eng Hong v. Attorney-General* 2011). Tan appealed this decision all the way to the Court of Appeal, Singapore's final court of resort.

On August 21, 2012, the Court of Appeal delivered a historic judgment, ruling that a gay citizen has legal standing to challenge the provision for being in violation of the equal protection clause in Singapore's Constitution without having to be prosecuted under the law. It went so far as to acknowledge that Section 377A's extension to private and consensual conduct "affects the lives of a not insignificant portion of our community in a very real and intimate way" (para 99). Even though the decision concerns only the preliminary issue of *locus standi,* or legal standing, it marks an important milestone for Singapore's gay movement. It opens up the opportunity for other gay men to step forward and challenge Section 377A's constitutionality. In November 2012, gay couple Lim Meng Suang and Kenneth Chee Mun-Leon, backed by a group of activists, filed a new case alongside Tan's.[15] On February 14 and March 6, 2013, *Lim Meng Suang* and *Tan Eng Hong* 2013 were respectively heard by Justice Quentin Loh. He dismissed both cases, holding that Section 377A did not violate the constitutional right to equality. Both the couple and

Tan have appealed to the Court of Appeal, which, at press time, is scheduled to hear them jointly in April 2014.[16]

Implications of Pragmatic Resistance

From timorous beginnings to the contemporary era, the three patterns of change—the movement's coming out, tactical escalation and movement expansion and diversification, and opening up of political and media spaces—become increasingly apparent as gay activists strategically adapt pragmatic resistance to their interpretations of shifting signals, including legal restrictions and political norms that constrain collective action and civil-political liberties. Twenty years since Rascals, Singapore's gay activists have developed into a group of people who speak out and organize openly as a collective, standing in stark contrast to their timid beginnings in the early 1990s. They directly challenge the state, publicly engage state actors and politicians, and seek media attention. They have taken the issue of homosexuality from the dimly lit spaces of nightlife and cruising to Singapore's highest lawmaking body and courtrooms, state-controlled media, and public places. Grassroots support from gays and lesbians and non-gay ally support are gaining visibility and strength. From worrying about state retaliation and their movement's survival, activists increasingly channel creativity and resources into advancing it. As Table 7.1 shows, the movement has expanded and diversified in its tactics and the type and number of organizations.

The persistent tactics sustained interactions with the state, gradually enabling the movement to enjoy greater political space. Over time, state officials and PAP rulers learn about the movement's leaders and their motivations, change their perceptions of them as threats to existing political hegemony, and open up communication with activists. Even though Section 377A lingers, the police no longer routinely raid gay businesses or entrap gay men at cruising grounds. Along with the expansion of political space, activists find improvement in local media coverage of gay issues and the movement. While media reporting trends are inconclusive, in a place like Singapore, where the media remain controlled and influenced by the state's position on sociopolitical issues, these trends offer a crude barometer for the opening up of political space.

Therefore, media space itself opened up, moving from derogatory coverage to the inclusion of activist voices. In the early 1990s, local media did not feature coverage of the movement but focused on censorship and issues of morality and sexual deviance. The mid- to late 1990s were quiet years, coinciding with the movement period of cyber organizing. From

TABLE 7.1. TACTICAL ESCALATION, EXPANSION, AND DIVERSIFICATION OF SINGAPORE'S GAY MOVEMENT

	Phase 1 Pre-1997 Timorous beginnings	*Phase 2* 1997–2000 Cyber organizing	*Phase 3* 2000–2005 Transition	*Phase 4* 2005 – Coming out and Mobilizing in the open
Social and/or support services	The Coalition			
	Argot			
	The Harbor			
		Beacon		
		Connection Hub		
		Singapore Lesbians Online		
		Sports Club		
		Sutra Fellowship		
		Christian Fellowship		
		Umbrella		
			Muslim Fellowship	
			Open Church	
			The Portal	
			Resource Central	
			Women's World	
			Virtual Sister	
				Annual Pride Festival
				Biz Tribe
				Brotherhood
				Chalkboard Caucus
				Queer Women's Alliance
				Voicestream
				Youth Planet
				Youth Society
				Youth Support
Efforts to raise social awareness			The Portal	
				Family and Friends
				Friendship League
				Pink Dot
				Repeal 377A
Media advocacy			The Coalition	
State advocacy			The Coalition	
			Queer Women's Alliance	
				Repeal 377A
Courtroom advocacy				*Lim Meng Suang*
				Tan Eng Hong

2003 onward, the spikes in coverage corresponded to significant state pronouncements that indicated shifts in political space and movement milestones, such as the circuit party bans, the inaugural pride festival, Repeal 377A, the AWARE saga, and Pink Dot 2009. Since 2003, gay activists have been identified as such and quoted in news stories. Ironically, perhaps in reaction to the movement's gains in political and media space, an organized Christian Right opposition emerged (see Meyer and Staggenborg 1996), with both sides continuously trying to neutralize each other's claims (Hewitt and McCammon 2004)

> [That line] can't be defined. But if you ask me, I think that line shifts a little further, a little bit, as time goes by. (Rahim)

But how effective are these changes? Rahim, who struggled with his sexuality as a teenager and later started Youth Planet, wistfully captures how gay activists appreciate these three patterns of change. Little by little, the movement achieves progress, but exactly how far those changes go is unclear. The main reason is that the progress primarily consists of informal gains that lie outside of formal law. While the sense of freedom expands as boundaries shift outward, the boundaries themselves are fuzzy and comprise political norms that are socially constructed (and interact with formal laws). Efforts toward toeing the line and pushing boundaries often rely on nothing more than intuition informed by readings of signals and past lessons. Hence, the extent of freedom won is unstable and fluctuates, depending on the interpretations of various social actors, especially activists and state authorities.

If one scrutinizes changes in formal law or other formal institutions, one may conclude that the movement has not achieved much. This concern speaks to skeptics who worry about celebrating covert and subversive tactics—which are plentiful in the tactical repertoire of pragmatic resistance—because they usually do not lead to formal institutional changes (see, e.g., Handler 1992). Although Rascals is credited with stemming the widespread police practice of raiding gay bars, the letter campaign did not alter any law or regulation nor did authorities acknowledge any violation of rights. The result was a letter of apology and verbal assurances—"informal protocol," in Keenan's words. Local media content is still hindered from depicting homosexuality positively or as a normal way of life. The 2003 pronouncement about nondiscrimination against gays in civil service remains just that. No anti-discrimination law was ever passed. Neither was there any instruction—publicly known, anyway—for government agencies to revise their employment policies accordingly. As detailed in Chapter 2, activists report discrimination—either against them or against people they know—by the Ministry of Defence and the Ministry of Education.[17] Gay and lesbian government employees remain at the mercy of politicians and administrators, no matter how open-minded they are or how much they have verbally supported change. At press time, Section 377A of the Penal Code lives on stubbornly as a symbol and a lingering threat. In fact, the attorney general acknowledged in open court that the police still issue "stern warnings" under Section 377A (*Tan Eng Hong* 2012).[18] So long as this criminal provision exists, gays and lesbians remain vulnerable to all forms of discrimination on the basis of their sexuality.

Furthermore, none of the movement's efforts have led to greater recognition of basic civil-political rights that facilitate collective mobilization. Adherence to the licensing rules leaves restrictions on free speech unchallenged. One activist felt proud about Pink Dot, but pointed out its tokenistic nature and confinement to the exempted park. Outside the park, activists still cannot legally march down streets in protest.[19] Most of their organizations remain outside the law, barred from registering under the Societies Act. Public speech remains subject to licensing conditions that control its political content; although the movement transcends the PAP's essentialized notions of racial and religious differences, gay activists remain bound by the rules that prohibit openly critical, intellectually provoking speech about this type of state-imposed ideology on race and religion.

> At any point in time, if someone changes their mind, someone in the government changes their mind, you can be—you're at risk. You can be arrested or whatever. . . . Depending on . . . who is making these decisions or what you happen to say or what you're doing, you may never know. (Adalyn)

As for the informal changes demonstrated by the three patterns, they lack legally binding effect and thus predictability, a problem that gay activists recognize and repeatedly experience. The rules that activists have exploited can easily be removed by the administration, and the legislation be repealed by a PAP-dominated Parliament. The gains that have been made, including administrative policies and bureaucratic practices here and there, do not come with recourse to accountability or formal protection from arbitrariness. This situation is ironic, considering the state's efforts to promote Singapore as a place of "rule of law."[20] Previous chapters recounted several incidents in which licenses—for parties, talks, concerts, and other events—were withdrawn at the last minute or denied after an ongoing series of approvals. Sometimes this occurred because a member of the public (often suspected to be associated with the countermovement) complained to the administration and the person in charge took the complaint to heart or a different officer was put in charge. The licensing exemptions for public speech by citizens and assemblies at Hong Lim Park are executive orders issued by the Ministry of Home Affairs pursuant to the Public Order Act. In the weeks leading up to general elections, the ministry has typically revoked the order exempting Hong Lim Park—to prevent political campaigning in the park—and then reissued it after the elections were held. The tolerated existence of unregistered, non-legal movement organizations faces the possibility, however slight, of the state's invocation of formal legal sanctions. A similar possibility hovers over Section 377A's nonenforcement policy. Ultimately, the situation remains a political compromise. The prosecution has no legal obligation to uphold it; on the contrary, it enjoys constitutional power to exercise discretion in choosing whether to enforce the law strictly.

Hence, one may argue that pragmatic resistance challenges power only in particular and restricted ways and consequently risks losing creativity to routinization. The boundaries of political norms are pushed only to an extent without risking confrontation or jeopardizing the ruling party's perception of control. The incentive for gay activists may be to continue with the strategy that has served them well and safely. For example, the annual pride festival started out in 2005 as a political statement against banning the circuit parties. For the first three years, the festival seemed more cutting-edge as it pushed the state to engage homosexuality and gay activism on broader boundary terms. Since then, it has taken on the feel of a community event, albeit one that has grown in scale, and there is a sense that the state has become used to it. In recent years, officials from the National Arts Council have even been spotted attending the literary events to scout for young talent. The internal conflicts, such as the occasional tensions between gay men and lesbians, also illustrate the tenacity of pragmatic resistance. The conflicts did not splinter the movement into different ideological factions. Whether one side ends up assimilating into the other or both sides continue to implement their own tactics, they conform to the principles of pragmatic resistance. At most, the variations are in tactics, not in strategic overhaul. As time passes, the stakes continue to mount for breaking the tactical routines of pragmatic resistance because the state correspondingly expects this routinized form of resistance. Acting out of character and disrupting the routine and state expectations may attract extraordinary repression. The routinization of strategy and repression, therefore, results in regulating the movement's actions according to the accepted and expected norms (Habermas 1984). It does not mean that the state is no longer controlling—police surveillance persists at the festival and other movement events. The control only *appears* less so because the repression is routinized (Scott 1985). Therefore, it is even less questioned because its violent nature becomes concealed (B. Moore 1966).

Nonetheless, evaluation of the progress of Singapore's gay movement should take into account activists' *interactions with* Singapore's sociopolitical conditions—the curtailment of civil-political liberties using legal restrictions and political norms on nonconfrontation, protection of social harmony, preservation of legal legitimacy, and most of all, continuation of the existing political order. Granted, outcomes and their causalities are notoriously difficult to measure, and outcomes beyond formal institutional changes are even more so (Earl 2000). But using qualitative analysis of original data, I pieced together a trajectory of progress that intersects with activists' diverse experiences and evolving interpretations of their reality. Instead of focusing on changes to formal institutions, as many social movement studies do (Earl 2000, 2004; but see Kriesi et al. 1995; Cress and Snow 2000), or preconceptualizing the meanings of *social change,* I considered social change in terms of activists' subjective meaning making—what they thought was possible, how they thought they could achieve it, and how they evaluated their own efforts.

From the perspectives of activists' contestations on the ground, social change for Singapore's gay movement means more than formal legal changes. With pragmatic resistance, Singapore's gay activists emerge from hard-fought battles, sometimes with inspirational victories and always with lessons to fuel the next encounter and new generation of activists. They continuously reshape the dynamics of pragmatic resistance. Each individual tactic may lead to imperceptible progress; over time, however, they create powerful social change. Looking back on the gay movement's history in the United States, John D'Emilio found awe in its "long stretches of just creeping along. They display less drama and excitement; the kind of change that occurs often escapes notice at the time. But the work . . . is critically important nonetheless" (1998, 262). In Singapore, the gay movement's three patterns of change show that small struggles along the borders have a profound effect over time: They cultivate efficacy, build free spaces to create collective identities, strengthen grassroots and amass ally support, and improve skills in deploying and sustaining tactics that help to open up political and media space under authoritarian conditions.

First, the growing sense of efficacy and confidence behind the movement's coming out represents a type of social change under authoritarian conditions. Sentiments of efficacy echo the idea in social movement scholarship of "cognitive liberation" (Piven and Cloward 1977; McAdam 1999), which is an important element of movement emergence because it inspires people to take up activism. In the Singaporean story, however, cognitive liberation does more than contribute to movement emergence. Repressive laws and political norms in Singapore send signals to discourage collective action. State surveillance heightens the imbalance of power between the watched and the watcher (Foucault 1977) to create fear. So when activists get around legal and political constraints or make light of surveillance, they weaken the effect that such power is supposed to have over them and enable resistance to take place or continue. Joining the movement in the face of these obstacles thus constitutes the first acts of defiance and dissent and the first signs of social change.

In addition, acts of resistance inspire similar acts in the future. Newcomers' contact with the movement transforms their thinking as they begin to see their personal struggles as part of a collective and see sexuality as a basis for political claims. The social relations that newcomers and activists build over time influence the former into developing a sense of duty and necessity to "do something about it" by joining the movement. Whatever the flaws, missteps, quarrels, and resolutions, the narratives of these struggles—passed on through intramovement friendships, influential leaderships, education, and tutelage—preserve and perpetuate the practices and knowledge associated with challenging an authoritarian state and offer lessons and hope to the next generation of activists (Jasper and Poulsen 1993; Polletta 2002). The Coalition's registration attempts, the Repeal 377A campaign, and Pink Dot show what can be done and, more important, what *more* needs to be done. As the movement grows, activists will have to address criticisms that their work is privileging middle-class constituents at the expense of the working classes.[21] In addition, they need to pay more attention to the interests of women and previously neglected racial and religious minorities. But whatever opinions are held regarding previous tactics, it is important to remember that one generation of gay activists "stood on [the] shoulders" (interview with Devi) of the one before them, and it started with the first few who dared to reimagine the possible.

Second, the use of run-of-the-mill tactics creates "free spaces" (Evans and Boyte 1986; Polletta 1999a) that contribute to the milestones and exceptional accomplishments. Away from the direct control of the state and dominant culture, gays and lesbians and future activists acquire new self-respect, cultivate stronger group identities, and learn to work together (also see Adam, Duyvendak, and Krouwel. 1999; Armstrong 2002). Many of these spaces appear to be primarily social; some of the Internet portals are even commercial. But such demarcations of gay spaces are not always clear (Armstrong 2002; Plummer 1999). What is cultural is also political, and changing one has implications for the other (Bernstein 1997, 2003; Taylor et al. 2009). All of them help to cultivate a movement base of grassroots supporters who became crucial to escalations in mobilization (McAdam 2003), such as Repeal 377A and Pink Dot. In spite of the rise of Christian Right opponents, their groundwork is making a difference. Activists start to sense this with the relatively growing ease of obtaining signatures for petitions and other forms of publicly visible support.

> Once you give us the space to do this, you cannot take it back. So this process of establishing a beachhead, it's like once we entrench our position, then we stretch the boundaries and push, push, push. (Tai)

Of course, what Tai said is not entirely true. The government can pull back the boundaries, as they did with the circuit parties. Cynics may also question the sincerity and practical impact of political statements that suggest a more "balanced" approach toward homosexuality. Perhaps they are driven by nothing more than the motivations of turning Singapore into a more "creative" and "culturally vibrant" city to attract international talent and investment. After all, no formal legal change ever followed.

Third, what is consistent, however, is that gay activists do not stay complacent; they do not let sociopolitical conditions determine the course of their movement, but engage in continuous strategic adaptation, thus improving their skills and sustaining interactions that help to open up political and media space. The movement's emergence, development, and three patterns of change turn on how activists make sense of their conditions (McAdam 1996, 1999), and adjust to shifting signals. They take advantage of what they perceive to be opportunities to push boundaries, for example, regardless of the sincerity of political statements and the intentions of licensing exemptions, which clearly do not have gay activism in mind. Out of containment and tokenism, they fashion resistance. Even though the boundaries fluctuate, by putting up a constant fight, these activists make reversals of political and media space much harder as time goes by. Through persistence, activists build up sustained interactions with the state and media over the years. Living to tell the tale boosts confidence for subsequent encounters. These experiences hone their skills in reading signals and determining boundaries.

The constitutional challenges of *Tan Eng Hong* 2013 and *Lim Meng Suang* build on the persistent survival, constant fight, and cumulative gains of the movement. When I conducted fieldwork in 2006 and 2009, almost no activist could imagine such a development. Most of them looked at the judiciary's lack of record in upholding constitutional rights in the face of governmental arguments that they ought to be restricted in the "public interest" and dismissed litigation as a viable tactic. Besides, it would be too confrontational, many of them said: It would amount to shaming the government openly. Yet, by 2010, at least a few activists seized the opportunity presented by the arrest and prosecution of Tan Eng Hong. Lim and Chee, the gay couple in the second lawsuit, run an informal group that organizes social events and supports various movement activities. The activists who support their legal campaign come from various movement organizations discussed in Chapters 3–7. Some help the couple to handle public relations; others assist with fundraising. A key member of their legal team at the lower court is a young activist who started out in one of the lesbian organizations. The case also involves testimonies from gay activists. Such confidence, courage, and resources are the results of the labors of a movement that has, for twenty years, plodded along, building confidence and efficacy, honing and refining tactical skills, cultivating grassroots and ally support, and creating space for progress. The lawsuits are just one part of the movement's history. Gay activists, regardless of their involvement in the constitutional challenges, understand that social change for them neither began nor will end with a lawsuit. The judicial outcomes will simply contribute to the movement's cumulative gains from which current and future generations of gay activists draw for inspiration and lessons.

From timorous beginnings to contemporary times, activists deployed pragmatic resistance to shape three patterns of incremental changes. Since most of these changes are informal, they may lack predictability and accountability and have limited impact. However, social change means more than formal legal changes for Singapore's gay movement. This type of change encompasses growing efficacy, free spaces to build collective identities, and the strengthening of grassroots and amassing of ally support as well as skills to implement and sustain tactics that help to open up political and media space. My analysis of the movement's development since its inception and the implications of pragmatic resistance suggests that the proverbial glass can be seen as both half empty and half full. How we make sense of pragmatic resistance raises important issues that relate to the book's theoretical framing in Chapter 1. In the final chapter, I examine the place of pragmatic resistance in the study of social movements, how and where law matters to social movements, the meanings of rights for law and society scholarship, and what a politics of gay rights entails under authoritarian conditions.

8

Pragmatic Resistance, Law, and Social Movements

Throughout this book, I followed a group of activists and their movement to examine how they organized and pursued social change in Singapore, a state known to restrict civil-political liberties and collective mobilization. Whereas the strategy and tactics of Stonewall and gay liberation drew from a decade of civil rights protests, black militancy, campus demonstrations, and the rise of the New Left in the United States, the pragmatic resistance of Singapore's gay movement was born of strategic adaption to almost fifty years of single-party, authoritarian rule in the postcolonial state. Deploying pragmatic resistance to advance their movement without jeopardizing its survival, gay activists interact with formal law, political norms and shifts in these forces to push the boundaries of political norms at the same time that they toe the line. Over the course of twenty years, they produced three patterns of change—coming out of the movement, tactical escalation and movement expansion and diversification, and opening up of political and media space—that have complicated consequences.

In this concluding chapter, I make further sense of pragmatic resistance by returning to the book's theoretical motivations and elaborating on its contributions. Unpacking the processes of pragmatic resistance enriches the study of social movements in two ways. Because this central theme emphasizes activists' perceptions of survival and opportunity, the book's analysis centered not only on context-specific conditions but also on social actors' interactions with them; thus, it returned the attention of social movements to an interaction-driven, meaning making–centered approach. Placing pragmatic resistance tactics along a scalable spectrum of covert-overt action and expanding the scope to include covert tactics that activists sometimes adopt to avoid retaliation by an authoritarian state, the book informs the understanding of social movements and the relationship between repression and mobilization.

Close examination of the processes of pragmatic resistance also advances law and society's understanding of the multiple roles and sites of law for social movements situated in authoritarian contexts. For Singapore's gay activists, law on the books and law in action are obvious sources of suppression for homosexuality and collective mobilization. Through the collective strategy of pragmatic resistance, however, it is also a source and site of contestation. Gay activists resist at and through repressive law. In the process, they treat legality as a means of survival and opportunity and thus treat law as a pragmatic concern rather than an ideological dilemma between empowerment and co-optation.

Furthermore, examining the processes of pragmatic resistance refines the meanings of rights in law and society scholarship. According to the polyvocal and contextual meanings of the rights of Singapore's gay activists, rights embody their movement objectives but the effectiveness of rights-based tactics are questionable because civil-political rights are traded off to maintain political hegemony. Yet, the activists are able to make "rights work" by wielding their influence quietly and generating a cumulative effect that has collective consequences.

The result is a politics of gay rights under authoritarian conditions. Gay activists in Singapore dispute with the state and with movement opponents over not only the meanings that rights have for gay equality but also civil-political freedoms that enable them to mount these contestations. Because rights are deeply imbricated in social relations, rights-based tactics and claims are considered nonconformist in Singapore, where formal laws and political norms are unfriendly to rights. The politics of gay rights, therefore, are unusual politics for Singapore compared with the politics of rights in societies where rights are normalized.

Drawing from analysis of original data, I developed the idea of pragmatic resistance from the ground up to capture the resilient and creative human agency of Singapore's gay activists and through their subjective experiences understand how they make sense of social problems and take action collectively. The choice of the word *pragmatic* was inspired by the ways in which these actors simultaneously drew lessons from their individual biographies and collective history; attended to their interpretations of current constraints, opportunities, and risks; and looked toward the future, a clear vision that their movement needs to survive to thrive. From these processes, in which the past, present, and future inform and shape one another, emerged a tale about human agents who collectively pursue the promise of social change, but stay realistically and firmly rooted in their social circumstances.

Consequently, I found inspiration for this grounded concept in American pragmatism (Dewey 1922; Joas 1997; Frye 2012) and contemporary sociological theories on culture that have pragmatist influences.[1] Consistent with these schools of thought, gay activists in Singapore interpret and draw from their existing cultural schemas made up of shared experiences and resources, their cultural toolkit (Swidler 1986; Becker 1998), to respond to problems and changes in their environment—in this case, discrimination against homosexuality and the legal restrictions, political norms, and their shifts that affect collective organizing. Although cultural schemas involve habits or acquired predispositions to certain modes of responses (Dewey 1922), they do not predetermine actions (Whitford 2002) and so do not perpetually lead to social reproduction without change (Gross 2009). Rather, as Singapore's gay activists demonstrated throughout this book with social movements' notion of strategic adaptation, when social actors encounter emerging exigencies that cannot be solved with habitual responses, they "continuously engage patterns and repertoires from the past, project hypothetical pathways forward in time, and adjust their actions" (Emirbayer and Mische 1998, 1012). Hence, cultural schemas and the institutions with which they interact are reconstituted through the creativity of human agency (Joas 1997), whereas the new response is integrated into the cultural schemas drawn on for future exigencies (Gross 2009).

Like these theories concerned with action and social problems, I emphasized human agency in "pragmatic resistance." However, I did so with empirical analysis of an understudied case and used it to refine sociological understandings of social movements[2] and law and society scholarship, which form the book's theoretical motivations. I centered meaning making by locating Singapore's gay movement in relation to other societies' and engaged contemporary law and society studies (see Chapter 1). My approaches to both types of scholarship draw influences from the sociological study of culture, which has roots in American pragmatism. Hence, through strategic adaptation of pragmatic resistance, activists collectively participate in mutually constitutive, constructed processes with state actors, other social actors such as their opponents, formal institutions such as law, and informal norms such as the political boundaries that appeared in preceding chapters. In these processes, because law forms part of the cultural schemas on which activists and other social actors draw, the interactions produce multiple meanings of rights and law.

Bearing in mind these theoretical influences, I elaborate on the theoretical contributions of this book, first to the study of social movements, followed by law and society.

Pragmatic Resistance and Social Movements

With the central theme of pragmatic resistance, I provided a more complete and nuanced analysis on how a gay movement emerged and how its strategy and tactics developed under authoritarian conditions. As discussed in Chapter 1 although social movement studies acknowledge that gay activists under authoritarian conditions leverage politically palatable or resonant norms, they seldom unpack the complex movement processes involved. Hence, this book advances social movement scholarship in two ways.

First, it refocuses attention on an interaction-driven, meaning making–centered approach in social movements and extends it to the empirical study of gay organizing under authoritarian conditions. Motivated by the social and relational nature of human agency (Emirbayer and Mische 1998), I examined collective action along a spectrum of covert-overt forms of resistance that make up pragmatic resistance. This approach allows for activists' tactical choices to scale up or down, depending on their interpretations of signals. Of course, the specific tactics of pragmatic resistance used by Singapore's gay activists may not be effective elsewhere. For example, tactics that rely on legal legitimacy may attract brutal repression if attempted in other regimes that have little regard for formal law. Whereas rights litigation has cultural resonance or legitimacy in the United States (Meyer and Boutcher 2007; Gamson 1995; but see Lovell 2012), it may attract backlash or even state retaliation in another place. Rather than privileging forms of contention that are safer or popular in liberal democratic societies (Scott 1990), my approach with pragmatic resistance considers the authoritarian conditions under which activists mobilize and the covert tactics that they sometimes choose for a better chance at survival and success. Hence, focusing on context and actors' perceptions of risks and opportunities in the face of repression, I explicated how a gay movement—comprising organized and sustained collective action over time (Tilly and Tarrow 2007)—could and did emerge under authoritarian conditions.

Second, using grounded analysis of an understudied movement in an understudied context, this book refines the understanding of the dynamics between mobilization and repression (Davenport, Mueller, and Johnston 2005). In particular, I built on research that takes an expansive view of movement processes. Johnston (2006), for example, examines how oppositional speech acts that are smaller in scale and earlier in time can escalate to more public forms of contention in Eastern European regimes. Even liberal democracies have both eras of oppression and greater freedom and correspondingly a range of covert and overt forms of collective action over time. Activists of the homophile movement in the United States deployed a conformist and nonconfrontational strategy, in contrast to gay liberationists who succeeded them armed with different political experiences and visions of achieving social change. With a longer view of the development of gay organizing in the United States, D'Emilio's (1998) study of the homophile movement offered a counterpoint to the common myth of Stonewall as its genesis. Community organizing by the Student Non-violent Coordinating Committee (Payne 1996) before the rise of black insurgency was also less confrontational and threatening to formal institutions at the time. In earlier works on movement abeyance, the incremental, intermittent, and less visible work of social movements (Sawyers and Meyer 1999; Taylor 1989) highlights the ways in which the outcomes of one struggle turn into resources for future challenges. By extending the social movement concept of strategic adaptation to pragmatic resistance to articulate its dynamics, I accounted for changing empirical realities under authoritarian conditions—rather than treating them as monolithic and static—and the waxing and waning of a gay movement over time, rather than analyzing it as "birth" or "immaculate conception" (Taylor 1989) at particular moments.

As a result, I illuminated the circumstances under which activists ratchet up tactics to make demands of an authoritarian state (or vice versa): It is not when "objective" conditions turn favorable. Rather the decision to escalate tactics is intertwined with whether and how activists interpret signals in ways that galvanize or discourage them. This, in turn, depends on cumulative movement processes that involve activists' perceptions of constraint, risk, and opportunity; confidence levels; perceptions of grassroots and ally support; and the collective experiences of social actors whose biographies intersect with the history of the movement and their society (Mills 2000).

The Multiple Sites and Roles of Law

As I unpacked the processes of pragmatic resistance, I uncovered their inescapability from law. From the movement's timorous beginnings to its coming out, activists continued to interact with formal law and the political norm of legal legitimacy as important factors that shape their tactics. Although I return to the meanings of rights later, unlike law and society studies that focus on individual social actors or privilege the examination of rights, I take this book further to an understudied area in the scholarship—where and how law matters to collective action under authoritarian conditions.

> I think it's very hard to run a place like this and not [think] about issues of law. After all, this is Singapore. (Lacey)

Law resides in multiple locales and plays numerous, seemingly contradictory, roles for Singapore's gay movement. Lacey is one of the few activists who astutely point out the ubiquity of law. During the fieldwork for this book, many other activists initially responded to requests for interviews by saying that they did not think their labors had much to do with law. As the fieldwork and data analysis progressed, however, it was evident that law is "all over" (Sarat 1990). It permeates the movement's strategy, tactics, and very existence, even when the activists do not directly challenge formal law or seek changes to it.

Law on the Books as a Source of Oppression

Assuming the form of formal restrictions found in statutes, subsidiary legislation, licensing conditions, and executive orders, law on the books suppresses both sexuality and collective mobilization around it. First (at press time), Section 377A of the Penal Code criminalizes same-sex sexual conduct between men. Although in most cases this has not been enforced in private, consensual situations, the prosecution enjoys constitutionally protected powers of discretion to do so (L. Chua 2012). Using Section 377A's existence as justification, other laws and regulations discriminate against gays and stifle expressions of homosexuality. Even if Section 377A is repealed, no law yet exists to protect gays from discrimination on the basis of sexuality or to provide people in same-sex relationships with access to government benefits and services that are available to those in opposite-sex marriages. Media content that "promotes," "justifies," or "glamorizes" homosexuality is prohibited, and the offending media company risks heavy penalties, even losing its operating license.

Second, a variety of formal laws impinge on civil-political liberties and thus constrain collective mobilization and expressions of dissent. Gay activists do not expect to receive permission under the Public Order Act to hold demonstrations on public streets. Even Hong Lim Park, where licenses for public assemblies and performances are exempted, requires preregistration with the police and adherence to preset conditions; its exemptions are tokenism that confines free speech and the right to assembly to an area the size of two American football fields, efforts that amount to pacification of growing demands for freedoms (see, e.g., Beirne and Quinney 1982; Collins 1982). The Societies Act requires groups with ten members or more organizing around "sexual orientation" to seek approval for registration, which no gay activist group has successfully obtained. Most groups remain unregistered and risk legal sanctions should the government choose to enforce the law strictly. Activists also have to make sure that their speech does not attract legal sanctions under such laws as the Sedition Act and must comply with legal conditions on speech content when holding public talks. Court rulings that found for defamation against PAP politicians, who were awarded large sums of damages, also serve as warning signals to activists who wish to criticize the government or ruling party.

Law in Action as a Source of Oppression

Law's oppressive power extends beyond formal sanctions on the books. It is further inflicted when law is put into action as part of cultural schemas. The restrictive regulations on various civil-political liberties replace physical violence as a means of controlling political dissent and collective mobilization in less perceptible ways that are nevertheless exertions of violence. Unlike physical violence, such force has legal authority. It becomes more easily accepted as legitimate and normal (Thompson 1975; Fernandez 2009), and control is thus subtler, taking the form of discipline (Foucault 1977) or channeling (Earl 2006). Always prepared for license denials, gay activists in Singapore organize their activities with contingency plans for such possibilities. When conceiving of Pink Dot, none of them—not even Nelson, who first suggested holding a pride parade—contemplated taking the event beyond the physical parameters of the exempted park, but worked with these restrictions in mind. The laws and regulations limiting the where, when, and how of mobilization become part of the landscape that activists negotiate, rather than arise as conflicts (Lukes 1974) or become part of the issues they challenge (Fernandez 2009).

As a cultural source of oppression, law interacts with political norms to constitute and reinforce each other. The state and the ruling party justify prohibitive laws by linking continued economic development to social stability, which in turn lends support to efforts to quell confrontation. Meanwhile, the norm against confrontation endorses the formal laws and sanctions prohibiting street protests, and these restrictions reciprocate with authority for the former. Furthermore, the threat of losing legal legitimacy deters the transgression of formal restrictions. The power of legal legitimacy is so strong that gay activists in Singapore consider it one of the political norms that they must heed in their actions. Staging a street protest without a legal permit not only attracts formal sanctions, such as fines or imprisonment, but also risks the loss of cultural legitimacy. Hence, gay activists avoid breaking the law for fear of being viewed as "troublemakers" and risking the loss of their cause's credibility with the state and people.

Law as a Source and Site of Contestation

Conversely, law also has the power to confer cultural legitimacy. The ruling party relies on winning legally mandated elections to claim authority over the population, and both party and state leverage adherence to laws to defend their legitimacy internationally and to promote Singapore as a "rule of law" society. Such cultural power of law is another important reason why gay activists, both men and women, continue to fight for the repeal of Section 377A, even though the provision specifically targets men only. They are not appeased by the nonenforcement policy not only because the prosecution has legal impunity to renege on a political compromise that lacks legal teeth but also because of the symbolic importance of the penal provision. By explaining its retention as a reflection of mainstream values, whether intentionally or not, Prime Minister Lee was implying that the law needed to make a statement because there was something unacceptable about homosexuality.

These phenomena further reveal the following about law: It also serves as a *source and site of contestation* (Thompson 1975; Benton 2002). While the state and ruling party undoubtedly deploy law as a tool of control and oppression, the struggles of Singapore's gay movement show that law also has relative autonomy. Both the authorities and Singapore's gay activists believe in legal legitimacy to at least some degree; consequently, it means that law mediates the power of the state and ruling party and sometimes its own logic and rules end up inhibiting their actions to the advantage of the movement. Hence, gay activists mount pragmatic resistance to contest repressive law, fighting with the state and others over its meanings, and use law to contest sexual and other forms of political oppression. Because formal law interacts with other formal institutions, the political norms, and social actors, including gay activists, the contestation occurs not only in the shadow of the law (Mnookin and Kornhauser 1979) but also in the collective shadow of these complex interactions. As elaborated in Chapter 1, law and society scholarship has a long tradition of studying such resistance by individuals. But what is significant about this study is that it concerns *collective* contestation, which, as a result of activists' efforts at reading political signals and strategically adapting their tactics to pragmatic resistance, has more commonly unfolded through the cultural powers of law than in the form of tactics directly challenging or seeking to change formal law.

First, the movement in itself contests laws and regulations that suppress sexuality. Activists' openness about their own sexuality (or the sexuality of their family members or friends) undermines the legal authority and heteronormativity in which it is embedded. By using pragmatic resistance to represent homosexuality positively through whatever cracks they can find or pry open in formal law and advocating for decriminalization and acceptance of homosexuality, they further defy the symbolism of Section 377A and regulations that inherently treat homosexuality as wrong or deviant. Such affirmations have important implications for the movement. Throughout the book, people took up gay activism after having come into contact with movement activities and activists who helped newcomers to accept their own sexuality, whose influence politicized their grievances into collective ones, and who inspired them to join. Gay activists' openness, public expressions and affirmations of homosexuality, and advocacy work dispute the meanings of sexuality that the state seeks to stabilize and preserve with formal law.

Second, gay activists mount resistance *through* repressive law that impinges on civil-political liberties. When gay activists mobilize against sexual control, they do so through such formal restrictions as the Societies Act, the Public Order Act, and subsidiary legislation. With pragmatic resistance, they circumvent, mitigate, or make use of them. By avoiding violation of these restrictions, they maintain cultural legitimacy and ensure the survival of the movement so that, in the words of one activist, it can "live to fight another day." Moreover, by resisting through formal restrictions, their tactics challenge and reshape the meanings of political norms with which law interacts. Most evidently in the case of Pink Dot and the Repeal 377A campaign, which gay activists made use of restrictions to carry out, the meaning of social stability was redefined to include the acceptance of diverse types of sexuality. Activists also argued that the color pink, found on national identity cards issued only to citizens, inherently embraces homosexuality among citizens, who are the electorate on which the PAP relies to stay in power, another important political norm in Singapore.

Third, as a result of pragmatic resistance, gay activists also challenge formal restrictions on civil-political liberties and subvert repressive law. The majority of their movement organizations are unregistered and non-legal. On one hand, activists take cues from precedents suggesting that registration applications for their groups will be rejected under the Societies Act. Still, they could have pursued registration under the Companies Act, which the Open Church and the Beacon did under Billy's leadership. On the other hand, staying unregistered frees activist groups from even more legal restrictions and regulations that are imposed on registered organizations. Their lack of legal status, the reality that gay activist groups have been denied such status, and the very requirement for registration expose the repressiveness of these laws and the Singaporean state. Every time gay activists stand up in front of an audience to explain how the licensing rules dictate what they can and cannot do at the event, they expose the repression. When they comply with restrictions but at the same time exploit them, they ridicule and mock these laws and the Singaporean state's rule-bound nature that give rise to the very political norm of legal legitimacy that compelled their adherence in the first place.

Law as a Pragmatic Concern

Despite the contestations, one may argue that Singapore's gay activists are co-opted. At the end of Chapter 7, I pointed out that pragmatic resistance could result in routinization if gay activists cannot or do not attempt other strategies either out of habit or out of fear of attracting nonroutine, heightened repression. Such a situation arguably can lead activists to reaffirm the power of formal law and legal legitimacy and participate in the dialectic construction of power, endlessly repeating their own oppression with active resignation (Mitchell 1990).

In response, I elaborate in the following paragraphs another perspective on the role of law: For activists in Singapore's gay movement, law matters as a pragmatic concern and not as an ideological dilemma. Going back to co-optation—the concern is that, because of the law-abiding nature of pragmatic resistance, the role of law as legal restriction and a source of cultural legitimacy is reinforced and remains as a source of power that is continually wielded to control civil-political liberties and their movement. In the interest of the survival of their movement, Singapore's gay activists place great emphasis on adherence to formal law, the enactment and enforcement of which lies with state authorities. They clearly recognize a line between the legal and illegal and adhere strategically to its demarcation.

However, a similar point about co-optation leading to reinforcement of the status quo can be made about romanticism with *illegality* or nonconformity to formal institutions more generally. Deliberately illegal—or nonconformist—tactics also imply acceptance of a dichotomy between the legal and illegal and hence a particular sociopolitical order (Lukács 1920). The point is that *both* following laws and breaking them can either promote or imperil the prospects for social change. The concern with co-optation then poses gay activists in Singapore and others in like situations with a conundrum—comply with the law or defy it? How should activists on the ground address this conundrum?

To answer this question, perhaps another question ought to be asked: Should they care about this conundrum? Or more precisely, should those outside the movement worry about this question for those inside it? On the basis of the empirical realities—how Singapore's gay activists think and what they do—perhaps one way forward and out of such a conundrum is to "slough off both the cretinism of legality and the romanticism of illegality" (Lukács 1920) by regarding the conformist-nonconformist nature of movement strategy and tactics as simply that—purely tactical. Gay activists in Singapore certainly are conscious of the workings of power. They strategically adapt to their sociopolitical conditions to use pragmatic resistance. When pushing boundaries, they appreciate the risks, and when toeing the line, they recognize when pushing can become crossing the line.

However, the fact that their actions may end up reifying power is not a good enough reason to dismiss their choices as stemming from false consciousness or a lack of awareness that they are under the influence of domination. While the Singaporean state, ruling party, gay activists, and countermovement actors mutually participate in the processes of pragmatic resistance, they contest over the meanings of rights and law. It is possible to think of gay activists' strategic choices as simultaneously reaffirming and seeking to undermine law and existing formal political structures (Benton 2002; Bourdieu 1977). These activists understand the dual effect, and some of them willingly accept it.

To them, however, their concern lies not with whether their strategy challenges the larger order of power—by transgressing its legal rules—for the sake of doing so. They make choices, not between subordination to and liberation from the existing order, but between tactics based on what they believe can best advance the movement and keep it alive. To them, law is a matter of survival and making gains. Perhaps then, law ultimately matters to Singapore's gay movement as a pragmatic concern and not an ideological dilemma. Legality is tactical, a pragmatic means to an end. Seen in this light, perhaps they are ironically decentering the power of law.

The Polyvocal and Contextual Meanings of Rights

The multiple sites and roles of law affect the ways in which gay activists in Singapore relate to rights—whether and how they think about rights and exercise or demand them. In Singapore, the state deploys formal law not only to control homosexuality but also to curtail civil-political rights and suppress collective mobilization. Meanwhile, legal legitimacy is an important political norm to delegitimize any exercise of rights that violates formal restrictions. In return, in their collective quest for justice and equal rights, gay activists navigate these signals and adapt strategically. Although the area of law and society is replete with studies about rights,[3] it has not paid much attention to their meanings situated in social movements that intersect with authoritarian contexts. Hence, this book reveals new ways of thinking about the meanings of rights.

> I think the discourse in Singapore has borrowed [the rights] language or that framing, though we have chosen to downplay it. But in our heart of hearts, that's how we see it. . . . That's how we think, and that's how we construct our identities and our mission. (Trey)

When gay activists in Singapore talk about rights, they have in mind a variety of meanings. Some of them refer to human rights, as associated with international human rights documents, such as the Universal Declaration of Human Rights. Some have in mind basic civil-political liberties that include speech, assembly, and association, while others include such socioeconomic rights as education, employment, housing, and physical safety. Most of the time, they elaborate on these in more concrete terms such as specific protections or entitlements enshrined in formal law, decriminalization, anti-discrimination laws, and the legal recognition of same-sex relationships. The reference points do not fall along any distinctive lines of organizational affiliation, gender, age, or activist generation.

What is important, however, is the nature of the relationship encapsulated in Trey's statement. On the surface, rights may seem to have little to do with Singapore's gay movement. After all, almost none of their accomplishments thus far have resulted in any greater entrenchment of rights in formal legal institutions. Yet, the relationship between gay activists in Singapore and rights is complex and polyvocal.

Rights as Embodiment of Movement Objectives

Rights are inherent to the *movement objectives* of Singapore's gay activists. In their interviews for this book and writings related to the movement, they speak about striving for rights to achieve greater dignity, freedom, and equality. Based on what they have done and said since the timorous beginnings of the early 1990s, such aspirational and instrumental regard for rights is also woven throughout the movement. When Keenan wrote to the police to object to their mistreatment of gay patrons at Rascals, even though he admitted that he deliberately avoided using the word *rights*, he was effectively demanding treatment that would be characterized as inherent qualities of rights in his interview—equality and human dignity. The Coalition further responded to this demand when they seized on the momentum of the Rascals letter campaign to hold community forums about "legal rights," educating people on how to handle police abuse of authority. Then, of course, one of the clearest articulations of rights as a movement objective took the form of the Repeal 377A petition campaign, which openly called for decriminalization on the basis that the provision violated the constitutional right to equality. These days, as gay activists strategize over their courtroom challenges against Section 377A's constitutionality, explicit references to rights are further amplified.

Like their peers who pursue rights as movement objectives in the United States, one aspect of the Singaporean activists' relationship to rights is instrumental. However, there is something different about how this part of the relationship looks as tactics: Their public form usually downplays the role and influence of rights or does not mention them explicitly. Only in recent years have the activists clearly associated their collective demands with rights in a public way. In their organizations' mission statements and most of their activist work, they seldom make such explicit articulations. As recently as the historic Pink Dot 2009, the organizers deliberately avoided making any official references to rights. More often than not, rights reside in their hidden transcripts of pragmatic resistance, manifest in pushing boundaries and toeing lines to exercise rights and achieve recognition without getting into trouble with the state for doing so. Whereas public transcripts are the openly observable speech and nonspeech interactions between the dominant and subordinated, hidden transcripts make up an offstage discourse of practices, speech, and claims that the subordinated do not openly declare to the power holders; they confirm, contradict, or vary from the public transcripts, thus revealing or even surreptitiously critiquing the power of the dominant (Scott 1990).[4]

Only occasionally do rights burst forth onto the open stage. In these rare moments, the divide between the two types of transcripts is ruptured as the oppressed utter the hidden in public. One such rare and poignant moment in Singapore's gay movement was the Repeal 377A campaign, when gay activists directed their claim at Parliament to opine that Section 377A impugned the constitutional right to equality. They identified an opportunity—a time when the Penal Code review was planned and public feedback was sought—and then made use of a little-known legal procedure to make their claims. By making sure that they also downplayed confrontation and played up the message of embracing diversity to promote social harmony, they crafted tactics of pragmatic resistance that adhered to political norms. In the process, they illuminated the possibility of resisting power and, conversely, the limits of doing so (Ewick and Silbey 2003), and their circumspection of rights was thus laid bare.

Rights as Trade-Offs and Circumspection

Singapore's gay activists for the most part have doubts about rights-based tactics. Their circumspection arises from their interpretation of rights as trade-offs. Around them, they detect a variety of signals suggesting that rights, particularly civil-political rights, are being traded off for the socially constructed goods of social stability and economic progress that help to reaffirm and maintain existing political hegemony. These signals include the lack of protection for constitutional rights, legal restrictions, prosecution of activists and opposition politicians who contravene those restrictions, and the state's constant defense against allegations of rights violations. Hence, they worry that rights, when exercised and claimed, may contradict the political norms surrounding collective mobilization in the Singaporean context. Such anxiety is consistent with the strategic character of pragmatic resistance of heeding survival. Most of Singapore's gay activist organizations are unregistered and exist without state retaliation because their strategies and tactics have balanced pushing boundaries and toeing the line; exercising or claiming rights without such balance and violating political norms could provoke the state to impose legal sanctions.

While law and society scholars already express wariness about the efficacy of rights, the circumspection and trade-off perspective of Singapore's gay activists refines these views. Law and society scholars have argued over whether rights vindication by the courts can indeed bring about social change and have questioned whether rights amount to nothing more than a "myth" (Scheingold 2004; Rosenberg 2008). After all, courtroom pronouncements do not automatically transform into legislative amendments or policy implementation, both of which take the cooperation of other branches of government, something that often does not materialize (Rosenberg 2008). The circumspection in the Singaporean story of gay activism suggests a variation of that myth—that the aspiration to attain rights may well remain just that because they may not even be attainable as legislative enactment or courtroom pronouncements, pushed back amid the interplay among political norms and laws and restrictions that seek to stifle them in the first place. This is a different take on the "myth of rights": The conventional version of the myth takes for granted the tactics and context in which rights vindication is first attained and instead focuses on their implementation thereafter. The version of the myth discussed here emphasizes the specific context in which rights are to be actualized, a consideration that affects not only rights in implementation but also rights as they are exercised and claimed collectively.

Making Rights Work: The Quiet, Everyday Snowballing Effects of Rights

Nevertheless, Singapore's gay activists still make rights work for them. They wield the influence of rights *quietly* and achieve *snowballing*, everyday effects that have collective consequences for their social movement. This perspective, therefore, refines existing views on the strategic and symbolic impact of rights on social movements.

Despite the circumspection and trade-off perspective, one activist describes rights as making up the "operating system" of Singapore's gay activists. When they organize and form groups, gather and meet, and hold talks or post commentaries on the Internet, they inherently exercise their rights to association, assembly, and speech. Even though they face tough legal restrictions and constraining political norms, they deploy pragmatic resistance against them. The extent to which they could have exercised those rights may have been greater without such restraints or may have taken different forms, but they have always acted as though they *were entitled* to organize, assemble, and speak out, and they have done this to an increasing extent over the last twenty years. Some of these activists have participated in protests and demonstrations in other countries; but when in Singapore, they shun street protests because they consider the unlikelihood of obtaining a permit—and thus staging a protest legally—the consequent difficulty of attracting participants, and the risk of delegitimization were they to hold an assembly illegally. The stringent laws, rules, and informal norms were roadblocks to be overcome, and the challenge, as they saw it, was to do so in ways that enabled their exercise of these basic civil-political liberties while simultaneously sustaining the movement. Their narratives demonstrated how rights latently shaped the ways in which they considered themselves inherently rights-bearing individuals, made sense of their grievances, found motivation to become activists, and collectively mobilized.

The allure of rights resonates with the perspectives of law and society scholars who take a more expansive view of the role of rights. Shifting the debate from questioning the efficacy of rights to examining *how* rights matter to social change, they argue that rights have far-reaching influence beyond their instrumental value of legal reform (Galanter 1983). They are also strategic and symbolic, serving as a "club" or bargaining chip used by activists against their opponents and as a "catalyst" (McCann 1994) to inspire and draw supporters to their movement's cause.

The conventional strategic and symbolic account, however, does not highlight the contextual nature of rights. It is usually assumed and left unquestioned. Rights as a "club" has leverage because the movement's opponents are embedded within a context where rights have amounted to a master frame (Snow and Benford 1992) so that formal institutions and social actors accept them and believe them to be legitimate claims and means of mobilization. Some degree of buy-in of rights exists within the given context, such that the recalcitrant party may fear formal legal consequences, moral sanctions for its rights violations, or pressure from transnational actors (Keck and Sikkink 1998; Bob 2005, 2009).

In contrast, the story in this book compels an emphasis on the contextual nature of rights to explicate the nuanced variations of how rights actually matter symbolically and strategically. Given the legal suppression of civil-political liberties, the lack of rights victories in the courtroom, and perceived incompatibilities with political norms, gay activists in Singapore do not brandish rights on the assumption that they form a master frame. They put rights to work by leveraging political norms to exert their effects quietly instead of relying on the existence of a buy-in of rights. For example, in the Repeal 377A campaign, they portray rights violations as tarnishes on the country's international legitimacy—instead of directly appealing to international human rights or transnational actors—and they portray recognition of rights as being conducive to a harmonious society where differences are accepted. Like the instrumental relationship with rights, this relationship with rights remains in hidden transcripts and publicly opaque, especially to the state: The public face of their tactics, the transcripts that are intended for the state to see, usually tempers rights language with familiar political norms.

> Within the community, we will say things like "you have a right" because sometimes when people come in they will be very depressed. When you say you have a right to be happy . . . it's more like you deserve better than this, they deserve better than the current situation that they're in. . . . For the public domain and the government—because the word "rights" has been too demonized by the government. . . . We don't really use rights. We don't really use the word "right." (Shelly)

Further, as in existing accounts about how rights give momentum and publicity to movements and change the ways people think about their social relationships, rights also serve as a catalyst for Singapore's gay activists. But again, they do so on a variation—the catalytic effect of rights takes the form of *quiet snowballing*. This is because the activists lack rights-affirmative laws and court cases, public events that can generate coalescence, and they believe that they cannot appear to be making a public call to arms to agitate for rights. However, when trying to attract supporters, conducting outreach work, raising political consciousness, and empowering gays and lesbians to believe in the efficacy of collective action, these activists speak quietly of dignity, the quest for justice and equal rights, and the right to live one's life as a gay person openly and happily. Whether such language is or can be legally recognized as rights, it is how they find words for their grievances, their prognosis and diagnosis, and use these words to motivate and recruit supporters and constituents, processes that some social movement scholars may identify as framing.[5] The impact of rights, therefore, is accumulated through the movement's outreach, consciousness-raising, and social events held by various groups over the past twenty years—the coffee hours in living rooms, the Coalition's Sunday forums, the dinners at hawker centers after swimming or a game of badminton, the chat room sessions and message postings on the Internet, the countless meetings to plan the next event, and the talks, exhibitions, poetry readings, film screenings, plays, and other events where old and new friends exchange ideas, catch up, and make or reforge alliances.

To be more precise, therefore, rights take on a quiet snowballing, *everyday* effect that leads to collective consequences for their movement. The movement activities provided an opportunity for rights to influence the ways in which participants thought about self-identity and their relationships with others. Eventually, some of these individuals became inspired to join the movement and in the process exercise basic civil-political liberties by resisting the laws and regulations that restrict them. These effects are thus reminiscent of the findings by law and society scholars interested in the influence of rights on people's everyday lives (see, e.g., Engel and Munger 1996, 2003) rather than their mobilization through formal institutions. Much of this work, however, has focused on individuals, not collective action. Singapore's gay movement shows that such effects have collective implications. People who came into contact with gay activists first became empowered by rights and began to question prevailing social institutions (see, e.g., Polletta 2000; Barclay, Bernstein, and Marshall 2009; Albiston 2010), not only those concerning sexuality but also repressive state-society relations more generally; some of them, such as Abby, Fiona, and Tai, eventually took up gay activism, succeeded earlier generations of activists, and contributed to the movement's gradual escalation and expansion.

Pragmatic Resistance and the Politics of Gay Rights

> Chua: Did you talk about gay rights?
> Kang: Oh, we certainly used that vocabulary . . . and we were completely aware that you can't use that vocabulary in Singapore.
> Chua: You used it only within the circle [gay community]?
> Kang: Yeah.
> Chua: Why not to the government?
> Kang: Well, because you have to speak multiple languages in Singapore, right?

I have explained the theoretical motivations behind the book's central theme of pragmatic resistance and considered its contributions to social movement studies and law and society scholarship on the meanings of law and rights. In this section, I bring them together to articulate a politics of gay rights under authoritarian conditions. I resume the discussion of the last point, the polyvocality and multiple meanings of rights, and build from there.

Kang aptly describes the multiple and contradictory ways in which Singapore's gay activists relate to rights. They pursue rights in the instrumental sense, as movement objectives. But they are also circumspect about the effectiveness of rights-based tactics, seeing civil-political rights as being traded off to maintain political hegemony. At the same time, they leverage the symbolic and strategic power of rights in quiet ways and create everyday snowballing effects for their movement. These different strands of their relationship with rights coexist within each activist, among them, and across the movement.

In this polyvocal relationship, in spite of Singapore's legal and political constraints, rights maintain an allure with gay activists. They themselves are unable to explain clearly how they are drawn to rights. Most of them cannot pinpoint a particular source of influence, whether it is books, the Internet, their families, or experiences abroad. The prevailing sense is that they became aware of rights at some point in their lives, and this awareness increased with their involvement with the movement. In *The Common Place of Law: Stories from Everyday Life,* Ewick and Silbey (1998) reconcile three seemingly contradictory schemas of legal consciousness—law as majestic, law as a game, and law as a source of power to be resisted—as law's hegemony at work (also see Silbey 2005). Although people in their study recognize law's oppression and resist it, they still hold it in awe and play along with its rules. That is how, the authors argue, law's domination is sustained, perpetuated, and propagated. With Singapore's gay activists, one can make an analogous attempt to reconcile the contradictory strands of rights: Even though rights' efficacy remains suspect when openly exercised or claimed in their context, people continue to be seduced by the promise, leverage, and empowerment of rights, precisely because rights have a powerful hold over people's imagination as to how to achieve social change and how it looks.

One response to such an understanding is to consider the hegemonic power of rights and question assumptions about their good. Critics of rights from a variety of backgrounds offer a long list of concerns: Rights are absolutist and individualistic (see, e.g., Glendon 1991) and neglect the complex social relationships within which individuals are embedded (Bumiller 1988; Goldberg-Hiller 2004; Merry 1999, 2006); they reinforce stigmatized identities (Goldberg-Hiller 2004) or revictimize people (Bumiller 1988); and because they are elitist (Hull 2001; Nielsen 2004), they reify existing political orders and assimilate the interests of marginalized groups, including gays and lesbians, rather than transform or reorganize social relations (see, e.g., Stein and Plummer 1994; W. Brown 1996).

Another type of response is to draw inspiration from E. P. Thompson (1975) and return to this book's theoretical motivations. From my study of Singapore's gay movement, the meanings of rights emerge as contextual and situational, shaped by the processes of pragmatic resistance involving interactions among formal law and other institutions, norms outside formal law, such as socially constructed political norms, and social actors, including activists, state agents, and movement opponents. In other words, to build on Thompson's (1975) conception of law's relationship to society, rights are deeply imbricated in social relations; they both produce and are produced by their complex interactions. Regardless of whether rights are made public in movement tactics or reside in their hidden transcripts, they are manifest in pragmatic resistance. Whenever gay activists deploy pragmatic resistance, they inherently struggle over the meanings of rights. Hence, they continue to argue that Singapore's constitutional right to equality includes nondiscrimination against gays and entails the repeal of Section 377A. Their actions of speaking out, collective organizing, and holding public gatherings inherently dispute the curtailment of their basic rights and thus contest their meanings vis-à-vis the state's vision. The reaction that questions the powerful influence of rights on Singapore's gay activists needs to take these contextualized struggles into consideration. In societies where rights are mainstream and normalized ways of doing politics (Gamson 1989), perhaps problems with reifying the hegemonic power of rights are more self-evident and immediate. For example, movement tactics surrounding same-sex marriage in the United States do not revolutionize society but "renew" the existing political culture (Cohen 1985) and reinforce institutions such as marriage and law. Under those circumstances, the politics of gay rights may well be politics as usual whereby activists, in their pursuit of rights as a politically efficacious and ethically sufficient principle of government, reaffirm the socially constructed acceptance of rights as political legitimacy (Scheingold 2004; but see Lovell 2012). In contrast, Singapore's gay activists are embedded in a society where the ideology of rights as political legitimacy is insecure. Even though rights are an imperfect means of redressing grievances, in an authoritarian context where they are severely curtailed and their claims discouraged, the politics of gay rights are unusual politics. The mere exercise of rights to make claims and the pursuit of rights are nonconformist acts.

So, to articulate a politics of gay rights under authoritarian conditions, I bring together two points. The first is that because the meanings of rights are polyvocal, contextual, and socially imbricated, the politics of gay rights in certain contexts are unusual. The second is what law and society scholars already know, that is, gay rights are social processes through which meanings are contested among gay activists, their constituents and supporters, the state, and such third parties as countermovement actors (Barclay, Bernstein, and Marshall 2009).

Building on these two points, the politics of gay rights in authoritarian contexts mean more than fighting for equality on the basis of sexuality, a meaning that opponents of homosexuality continue to deny and challenge.

In face of authoritarian restrictions on basic civil-political liberties and collective mobilization, these collective processes of gay rights also encompass activists' struggles and risk taking to exercise freedom of speech, assembly, and association to speak out, organize collectively, and make rights-based claims for equality. The struggles to exercise such freedoms, which are often taken for granted by gay activists in the United States and other democracies, make visible the sources of power—law and non-law—that seek to suppress dissent from being seen or heard.

To defy these powers is to push forward social change for gays and lesbians because seeking redress begins with airing and making known their grievances. So when a gay activist in Singapore starts an organization, holds a public talk or social event, helps to orchestrate Pink Dot, or launches a campaign to repeal Section 377A, that person gives life to gay rights. When someone attends an activist's public talk or joins a social gathering; brings a parent, sibling, or friend to form a human pink dot together at Hong Lim Park; or signs a repeal petition, he or she participates in the meaning making of gay rights.[6] When an opponent, such as a state authority or countermovement, attempts to block the actions of a gay activist or participant or prevent their quest to realize gay equality, it too partakes in gay rights. In these unusual politics, the meanings of gay rights are collectively shaped and reshaped through the contestations among various actors around equality for gays as well as the freedoms that enable the challenge for equality.

The next question is whether pragmatic resistance and the Singaporean brand of gay rights politics have any implications for social change more broadly. I discussed in Chapter 7 how the strategy has helped to achieve progress for their movement as well as gay and lesbian constituents, but I also highlighted the lack of changes to formal institutions and the danger of routinization. Furthermore, since these activists consider law as a pragmatic concern, a tactical means for survival and advancement, they may have no desire to take on a bigger fight beyond gay rights. After all, that may well contradict the spirit of pragmatic resistance.

One answer to the question on broader change is that it is hard to tell. My study respondents do not talk about the need to replace existing formal political structures entirely. Many of them acknowledge that they are ironically products of the current government's success (regardless of its flaws). One of them described the movement's actions as making improvements. The sobering reality is that the PAP offers the movement the greatest hope for achieving gay equality. Although the party is increasingly feeling pressure from opposition parties, which together won the unprecedented number of six Parliamentary seats out of eighty-seven in the 2011 elections—a momentous victory by Singaporean standards—the opposition is still not strong enough to win elections and form a new government. Politicians of one opposition party have also told my informants that they cannot publicly support gay activism for fear of losing support.[7] These findings are consistent with recent research on China—while social actors can make small changes here and there in specific areas, they may not desire to mount broader challenges, and so a one-party state can and does remain largely resilient in the face of political overhauls (Tsai 2007; Stern 2013).

Yet, Singapore's gay movement may inadvertently bring about broader changes with pragmatic resistance. Collective organizing was not within the "imagination of the possible" of its gays and lesbians in the 1970s (interview with Oliver). Just as gay activists interpret signals from around them, the confident existence of their movement today may serve as inspiration or send out signals that are interpreted favorably by others beyond the gay movement. Pink Dot 2009 was the first public rally ever held at Hong Lim Park after the new exemption was enacted. Since then, other groups have carried out similar tactics to hold rallies in the same park to protest government proposals on population planning and Internet regulation. Perhaps, at the very least, Pink Dot set a precedent and redefined what is possible for not only the movement but also their society, modifying the political norm of nonconfrontation just a little bit. The constitutional challenges against Section 377A may set another precedent for the unusual politics of rights. But, of course, whether Singapore's gay movement has any direct impact on other kinds of collective mobilization is difficult to measure.

Nevertheless, I want to suggest a takeaway beyond the particulars of this case study: What is true about Singapore's gay movement is that it is not the same twenty years after its start. What has endured but changed the movement is activists' resilient and creative human agency in preserving and advancing it with pragmatic resistance. If nothing else, pragmatic resistance keeps them fighting. With continuity of the movement, hope lives on and with it the possibility of change, both intended and unintended.

> We are in the middle of Stonewall. It's just that the way we are changing things is a little different from what has happened in the States and what has happened in Australia. (Stella)

I began this book with Keenan's story about the Rascals letter campaign of 1993, a moment sometimes described by activists as Singapore's Stonewall. At its conclusion, I turn to another Stonewall reference. Unlike Keenan, though, Stella was not specifically thinking of Rascals when she mentioned Stonewall. Rather, she had in mind broader but related points revealed through my chronological analysis of the movement—the belief and optimism that the movement is slowly but surely achieving change and an understanding and appreciation of the particulars of their context. Notice also that Stella did not speak of Stonewall as a moment of rupture, but used the phrase "in the middle" to describe Singapore's version. It emphasizes what this book has also highlighted, that is, the movement makes gains incrementally with pragmatic resistance and builds current efforts on the past, with an eye on future survival and progress.

At the center of it all, Stella stresses the social and relational nature of human agency, which is central to the book's theoretical motivations. It is in this tenor that I want to close. At their core, social movements under different legal, social, and political conditions share one common feature. Activists are social actors whose biographies intersect with their collective history (Mills 2000) and whose strategic and tactical choices arise from the social and relational agencies forged at that intersection. Piven and Cloward (1977) argue that poor people's movements emerge because the limitations of their formal political institutions prevent those with their marginalized status from gaining access and seeking change; instead, they see protests as the only possible recourse. Singapore's gay movement clearly did not mobilize the way the movements in Piven and Cloward did, but it still speaks to their point. It is quite simply this: Context matters, and so does the human agency with which it interacts. The marginalized do what *they* find to be strategically and tactically available and feasible within their reality. The choices of Singapore's gay activists remind us of how exercising human agency truly matters. It is not about making choices when they are easy or clear-cut, but when they are tough.

Appendix A: Research Design and Methods

Given the lack of both empirical and theoretical knowledge on the collective struggle for gay rights in Singapore and the role of law in these processes, I designed the research as an interpretive, qualitative project aimed at theory refinement (Snow, Morrill, and Anderson 2003) and generation (Glaser and Strauss 1967). In doing so, I followed an established tradition among law and society scholars in using interpretive and qualitative approaches to explore how people think of and use the law, including whether and how they come together to fight for their legal rights or use the law to fight for a collective cause (see, e.g., McCann 1994; H. Silverstein 1996; Kostiner 2003). With these aims, I designed the study to collect data from multiple sources using a variety of methods. Comprising a preliminary study conducted in 2006, fieldwork conducted between March and December 2009, and occasional returns to the field in 2010–2012, the study generated more than two hundred hours of semistructured, in-depth interviews with one hundred interviewees, more than 150 hours of field observations, and primary documents that span two decades of activist correspondence with the state, activist organizational materials such as publicity campaigns, announcements and press statements, local media reports, government statements, and local legislation and court cases. In the following sections, I elaborate on each data collection method, data analysis, and the writing process. In the Appendixes B and C, I include background information on the respondents and their movement organizations.

Interviews

I performed a preliminary study in the summer of 2006 to establish contact, initiate access, and refine the research design for the primary fieldwork, which began in 2009. I recruited informants who had been involved in the movement for at least several years, in order to gain a sense of how the movement had developed over the years and how gay activists in Singapore engaged the state and thought about their movement. Using my existing connections in Singapore and making direct contact with movement organizations, I successfully recruited three informants. With the help of two of them, I began to collect primary documents, particularly hard copies of the Coalition's newsletters printed in the early 1990s and unavailable in electronic form.

For the primary fieldwork, I recruited respondents using a theoretical, purposive sampling of "gay activists," chosen on the basis of the relevancy and potential of data to generate and refine theory (Glaser and Strauss 1967). In this work, *gay activists* are defined as founders, leaders, and active members involved in implementing tactics. Given the sociopolitical environment, any form of activism that involves association, assembly, and speech is a symbol of challenge to authority; these are people associated with not only the political aspects but also the social, cultural, or commercial aspects of the local gay community (Armstrong 2002). Because the preliminary study also showed an absence of gay politics explicitly in the form of rights, confining the movement to the "political" would limit theoretical opportunities for discovery and refinement. The word *gay* in *gay activists* refers to the nature of the issues that they address—of interest or concern to gay men, lesbians, and bisexuals—and the activists themselves need not identify as gay. Though the movement is sometimes referred to colloquially as *LGBT,* I excluded transsexual and transgender individuals from my study. They deal with different laws and issues in Singapore, and gay activists also do not address their concerns or do so more as an afterthought. Throughout the study, where relevant, I approach activists' sexuality on the basis of their self-identification, but I do so with an appreciation for various perspectives on the relationship between globalizing processes and sexuality—particularly what Tom Boellstorff (2005) calls *Gay Planet,* or the view that nonnormative sexuality and gender will converge on Western models of politics and identity, and *McGay,* the view that different indigenous sexual cultures will be negatively affected by globalization.

Recruitment and Access

I created three databases on the basis of the preliminary study and background research. The first identified movement organizations and their founders and leaders; the second set out the movement timeline and identified key personalities. Using these two databases, I generated a third database that listed potential respondents. By making use of contacts established since the preliminary study, I contacted potential respondents by e-mail and on the social media site Facebook. On entering the field in March 2009, I began to spend time at the physical spaces of activists' organizations, attended various events, and volunteered for Pink Dot 2009. In addition to carrying out field observations, I went to these places and activities to meet people. Sometimes a contact introduced me to other people or I went there with the hope of meeting and introducing myself to certain people on my list. Having profiled the potential respondents, I was able to predict who would show up at which events. After every interview, I also asked the respondent to recommend others I should interview; frequently, the respondent volunteered suggestions. These additional names were placed on my list as well.

I contacted a total of 114 potential respondents and successfully recruited one hundred of them. Thirty-four of the one hundred were no longer involved with the movement by the time of the interviews. They left the movement for reasons such as career, family, relationships, and school (see Appendix B for demographic information on the respondents). Because they make up one-third of the respondents, the study was able to account for differences between and similarities across generations of activists, thus giving nuance and texture to the analysis. Two of the fourteen nonrecruits clearly declined to participate. The remaining twelve did not reply to my e-mails, telephone calls, text messages, or Facebook messages. However, I did not find these fourteen absences to have affected the findings and analysis: Their roles and backgrounds were similar to those of recruited interviewees, and as I approached the last twenty to thirty interviews, I began to find similar perspectives over and over from people with different backgrounds, affiliations, past and current involvements, and demographic features. In other words, I no longer walked away from every interview having learned something new that could meaningfully modify the emerging patterns, and thus I was confident that the study had reached theoretical saturation (Luker 2008).

The interviewees were generous with their time and spoke candidly about their experiences. Before I entered the field, some mentors and peers expressed concern that the people I contacted might refuse to be interviewed out of fear. However, as the fieldwork progressed, I noticed that the occasional difficulties with access arose from reasons far more diverse and complex than a caricature about fear. Most of the interviewees were reluctant initially because they did not think that they had much to say about law or considered themselves unimportant, inexperienced, or irrelevant. These interviewees did not need much persuasion, once I reassured them that I was not looking for legal experts or that I was looking for a range of activists and they fit the profile, so all they had to do was to talk about themselves. Some potential recruits, I eventually realized, were simply not the "e-mail type"; in such cases, I found them at movement events or obtained their telephone numbers through informants.

Overall, I enjoyed generous access to the movement and activists. Before this study, I was already familiar with Singapore's culture and languages. Until I was eighteen years old, I lived in Malaysia, a country that neighbors Singapore and has strong cultural ties to it. I also lived and worked in Singapore for five years as an adult. Besides English, I am fluent in spoken and written Mandarin Chinese and have some fluency in Malay. These are three of the four official languages in Singapore (the fourth being Tamil). In addition, I know Singlish, which is a local variation of English mixed with Chinese dialects, Malay, and South Asian languages. Even though the interviews were conducted in English, my ability to use and understand Singlish helped me to establish rapport and trust. Because the interviewees identified with me as someone with a degree of shared cultural and political cues, they felt comfortable going into detail about local political intrigue and nuances rather than providing a simplified version, as they might have for someone they viewed as a foreigner. One respondent explained that he did not want to confuse a foreigner with too many details and subtleties that may elude him or her anyway.

Interviewing Process

I interviewed eighty-seven of the one hundred respondents face to face in Singapore. I usually let the respondent choose the interview location, but I drew the line at such places as hawker centers and *kopitiams*,[1] where the audio quality of the recordings would be severely compromised by the noise level. Most of the time, we ended up at cafés all around the island, at interviewees' offices, and at their homes or my apartment. The remaining thirteen interviewees were outside Singapore, so I conducted those interviews from Singapore through Skype-to-Skype or Skype-to-telephone connections (noted in Appendix B). I took contemporaneous notes during each interview and used them to construct a debrief as soon as I could, usually on the same day or the next day.

The semistructured interviews were conducted with a prepared guide of topics that included the key topics that were planned but left room for deviation to pursue unanticipated perspectives and leads. They usually started with "How did you become involved?" to warm up the interviewee by asking for a chronological narrative. The response also helped me to get to know the interviewee better—what makes the person tick and what may cause him or her to recoil. Often, the answer to this question organically addressed some of the following planned topics:

- How did you get involved?
- What did/do you want to achieve?
- How did you engage the government? Examples?
- How have things changed over time? Examples?
- What are your fears/concerns?
- What were the challenges? What did you do?
- What do rights mean to you?
- How would rights work here in Singapore?
- What do you think of litigation?
- What do you think the movement has achieved?

Consistent with the research design, I did not look for a rights-based strategy or focus on the issue of rights during the interviews. Instead, I asked open-ended questions about engagement with the state, strategy and tactics, involvement, and challenges. At the same time, from the preliminary interviews and as the fieldwork progressed, I noticed the emergence of rights as a potentially important theme, not necessarily taking center stage as a strategy or tactic, but in how they are truncated and perceived to be *in*effective. So I paid attention to whether respondents brought up rights, litigation, or both voluntarily. If not, I would then ask about these topics later in the interviews. In a similar vein, I asked interviewees to tell me what they thought the movement had achieved and whether anything had changed; I did not presume what social change or movement success meant, according to existing theoretical understandings in law and society or social movement studies.[2]

I tailored the wording of the questions to the rhythm and personality of each respondent. Sometimes, instead of asking a question, I deployed a technique known as *interview by comment* (Snow, Zurcher, and Sjoberg 1982), especially when asking the respondent about a controversy in which he or she was intimately involved, hence coming across as less threatening and demanding. I frequently repeated the interviewees' statements back to them, another "interview by comment" technique that often elicited more candid responses. The sequence of planned topics following the first question also was not fixed and depended on the ebb and flow of each conversation, but I usually eased toward the end by asking about the interviewee's personal life. There were a few exceptions, however, in which I decided to let the interviewee go on about personal stories right from the first question. In those instances, I sensed that the interviewees felt more at ease sharing personal life stories, so I allowed more time to establish rapport and build up toward talking about the movement.

After the initial interviews, I often followed up by e-mail or online chats. I also conducted informal, unrecorded interviews during my time in the field. I did not keep an exact count of the amount of time spent on this type of interview because they took place while "hanging out" in the field, during which impromptu conversations occurred. Around the sixtieth interviewee, I started to discern recurring patterns and important theoretical leads. While continuing to move ahead with new interviewees, I contacted earlier respondents for re-interviews, especially the first ten. Altogether, I conducted nine re-interviews. Unlike the initial interviews, however, the re-interviews were not accompanied by a guide. They were customized to the specific issues that needed further responses from individual interviewees.

Accuracy, Recall, and Bias

One common concern with interview data is reliability. Interviewees may have faulty or selective memories (Freeman, Romney, and Freeman 1987) or may succumb to human tendencies to lie, embellish, or "put it on" for the researcher (Douglas 1976). However, while recall-based data may suffer from factual accuracy, they also tend to bias long-term patterns—what *usually* happens in a particular context or situation (Freeman, Romney, and Freeman 1987). Therefore, they remain useful for studying practices and norms, such as movement strategy and tactics. In other words, the relevant degree of reliability depends on one's purpose for the data (Morrill 1995).

Nevertheless, I did address the issue of accuracy and recall. I used multiple sources within the same type of data, comparing the facts and descriptions of individual events among multiple respondents. Furthermore, I drew on multiple *types* of data to cross-examine the interview data—field observations and documents by or about activists, their organizations, the government, and the media. I adopted facts that appear to be consistent across these multiple data sources and types. When I had doubts about varying accounts, I made them known and factored the differences into my analysis.

In addition, I addressed the potential problem of "trouble cases" (Morrill 1995), the incidents that stand out in the interviews, thus causing the researcher to concentrate excessively on them and leading to bias. In this study, "trouble cases" would be analogous to the milestones, the moments of leaps and bounds (D'Emilio 1998) for the movement. On one hand, these momentous events are significant because activists regard them to have strongly shaped the movement's development and the persons involved to have influenced the ways in which they unfolded. From the perspective of theoretical sampling, giving these events more weight is justifiable. On the other hand, I supplemented the interview data with field observations and documents that reflect the mundane and ordinary details of what these activists did and said. This is to confirm that the patterns and themes informing the study's theoretical framework emerged not only from the data on milestones but also from data across the board, thus spanning both the extraordinary and the everyday aspects of activists' experiences.

Field Observations

Observations in the field took place primarily between March and December 2009 and then intermittently from 2010 onward. I selected events affiliated with organizations that were shortlisted in the databases generated from my preliminary study and background research. As the fieldwork progressed, I also observed events that had not been anticipated earlier. All together, I observed more than 150 hours of meetings, talks, exhibitions, religious services, plays, film screenings, and social gatherings. They included both run-of-the-mill events and milestones and major incidents.

With the exception of Women's World meetings, the other events and activities were open to anyone who was interested. However, I usually informed my informants in advance about my attendance. Being seen with other activists helped me to make connections and establish rapport more easily. The organizers of Women's World's monthly gatherings, which invites women at various stages of dealing with their sexuality to meet and socialize, expressed concerned that my constant presence might make participants uncomfortable. But they were kind enough to let me attend one meeting as long as I did not take notes or record the activities, conditions to which I agreed. It is because of similar concerns on my part that I did not attend support group meetings. However, I did collect interview and documentary data on such meetings—announcements and publicity materials—and these were included in the documentary analysis.

To minimize the effect of my presence, I did not make any audio or video recordings or take notes openly during observations. Like many other ethnographers, I snuck away at opportune moments to bathrooms and innocuous corners to scribble down notes while my memory was fresh. For the Women's World meeting, I honored the organizers' request, so the data from that meeting relied entirely on recollection. After the observations, as with the interviews, I wrote debriefs as soon as I could. They comprise a section of factual descriptions built on the field notes as well as a commentary section alongside the relevant descriptive material (Emerson, Fretz, and Shaw 1995).

Documentary Data

I organized the documentary data into four types: "event," "organizational," "government," and "media." Event data concentrated on the milestone events of the movement. They ameliorate concerns about the recall and accuracy of interview data because the documents were produced during or temporally much closer to the actual occurrence of the events. Organizational data pertained to the everyday operations of movement organizations and included their run-of-the-mill activities as opposed to the milestones. They address the concern with biasing "trouble cases." Government data focused on direct statements by and reactions of the state regarding homosexuality or gay activism. They reflect the state's positions on these issues that are not in direct response to specific incidents classified as event data. By not focusing on the extraordinary moments of the movement, government data also helped to address the potential bias of "trouble cases." "Media data" involved the local media's treatment of gay activism and homosexuality. Under this category, the media themselves are being analyzed. Such data are distinguished from the previous categories in which I drew on media reports as sources that provide data on activists, their organizations, and the state.

Event Data

I first determined what counted as a significant event or milestone for the movement, on the basis of my background research and databases, their consistent mentions by interviewees, and media or government attention. Afterward I purposively sampled for data on each event from three sources—activists, their organizations, and the state. Data in this category include blog entries, media statements, and letters to local newspapers by activists or their organizations. For the first two sources, I selected only materials by the activists or organizations that started the event or are directly connected to its organization or implementation. For example, I selected the statements by Morris and the Portal in connection with the circuit party bans because the Portal was the organizer. However, I excluded them as data sources for the creation of the pride festival because this event was planned and executed by the Coalition. On the government side, I located statements by officials and politicians from local newspapers and the *Hansard* records of parliamentary debates.

Organizational Data

The sampling of organizational documents included a combination of random and purposive sampling, depending on the nature of the documents and materials I could locate. The materials from certain organizations are more ephemeral than others. Some groups archive their publicity announcements on the Internet and update their websites and social media sites regularly, whereas the documents of defunct entities usually disappeared along with the groups. Hence, I was more likely to locate the data of organizations that still survive or that endured longer. This may appear to create a bias. However, because I was interested in strategy and tactics, the weaker presence of certain organizations also meant that they had less influence in shaping the movement under study.

The materials I purposively sampled were all of what I could find on the various groups' versions of their histories and origins, self-descriptions, mission statements, and objectives, the type of documents that do not pertain to a specific event or incident. My searches spanned both the physical world for hard copies and the virtual world, including websites, blog sites, mailing lists, and in recent years, social media sites. For Argot and the Harbor, organizations that existed and disappeared before 1997 and the emergence of the Internet as an organizing medium, I relied on their announcements and writings published in the Coalition's newsletter. The selections of these articles are distinguished from the process of sampling articles from the newsletter for analysis on the Coalition itself.

The materials I randomly sampled were those pertaining to events or incidents affiliated with an organization, but I excluded the major ones already covered by event data. First, I counted the number of entries for each type of document ("category") in a particular organization, such as publicity e-mails, blog postings, and press releases.[3] Then I labeled each entry in a category numerically in chronological order, from the earliest to the latest. Next, I created a random number table using a "virtual dice" program and sampled 25 percent of the total number of entries in each category.

I handled the Coalition's materials in the manner described earlier, but a note is warranted on its hard copy newsletter published before 1997 and its migration to the Internet. The entire newsletter collection consists of twenty-seven issues, from the first to the twenty-eighth (the sixteenth was missing), published between March 1993 and November 1996. I decided to sample 25 percent of them (seven issues) randomly as well. I decided against systematic sampling by the *kth* number (Krippendorf 2004) because the issues, though intended to be monthly, were not published regularly. Some of them did not even have publication dates. Within the seven, I then purposively sampled only from the relevant types of articles, such as announcements of Coalition activities or statements on local gay issues, while excluding articles that reviewed movies or reprinted foreign media reports on gay events elsewhere without reframing them for local relevance.

Government Data

I concentrated on two types of sources, *Hansard* records of parliamentary debates and local media reports that contain public statements by state officials or politicians. For *Hansard,* I used the search string *gay or lesbian or homosexual or bisexual* to search the database of parliamentary proceeding transcripts. I found that words such as *same sex* or *sodomy* did not yield productive results. The former term is still not commonly used in Singapore, and the latter is not a term used in relevant criminal provisions, such as Section 377A. Next, I sieved through the search results to discard those that did not use the term in a relevant context. Then I selected for analysis only those statements and reactions by significant politicians and state officials, excluding members of Parliament who held little political weight. The heavyweights, such as the three former and current prime ministers and deputy prime ministers, ministers, and other rising stars in the ruling party's ranks, are the people who gain the attention of the population and others in government. On the other hand, in a one-party-dominated system, the lesser known members of the ruling party are often elected to office by the sheer might of the party itself and tend to make up the numbers in Parliament without exhibiting much individual leadership or influence.

For government statements in media reports, I concentrated on the *Straits Times,* the mainstream English newspaper. Unlike its rival, *TODAY,* which was launched in November 2000, the *Straits Times'* coverage spans the entire movement period. My objective was to use local media to locate government statements and positions and not to analyze the media themselves. Either mainstream newspaper would have reported on speeches and interviews and even reproduced the transcripts. I used the search string *"homosexual* or gay* or lesbian* or bisexual*" AND "minister or ministry or BG."*[4] Articles that did not contain statements by politicians or officials who met the criteria discussed earlier were discarded. Also discarded were articles that responded to such statements and were not first-time reports.

In addition, I searched such legal documents as statutes, subsidiary legislation, rules and regulations, and court cases. However, few legal documents referred specifically to homosexuality, sexuality, or gay activism. The exceptions were the Penal Code provisions, the Societies Act of 2004, and censorship rules. Judicial decisions on sex crimes treated the acts clinically and did not situate them in the context of these social issues. Hence, other than rare, explicit references to homosexuality or gay activism, I took into account the reticence to mention homosexuality in these formal legal documents.

I also wrote directly to the police, the Attorney General's Chambers, the Ministry of Home Affairs, the Ministry of Defence, the Ministry of Manpower, the Ministry of Foreign Affairs, and the Ministry of Education to identify their policies and practices related to homosexuality or same-sex relations. As expected, these government agencies mostly did not reply or said that they could not disclose the information requested (Singapore has no right to freedom of information). The most substantial answer came from the Ministry of Manpower, which replied that the government does not discriminate against "homosexual foreigners" seeking employment, but does not issue dependent passes to same-sex spouses because such unions do not have legal recognition in Singapore. In response to my query about its policy toward openly gay teachers, the Ministry of Education asked me to submit an application to seek approval for conducting my research on the ministry. One of the conditions on the application stated that the researcher must "seek clearance from the Ministry before publishing any of the findings from this study." I decided not to pursue the inquiry.

Media Data

I used the search string *homosexual* [h] *or gay* [h] *or lesbian* [h] *or bisexual* [h] to search the *Straits Times* electronic database. Archiving articles from 1989 onward, about five years before the gay movement began in Singapore, it is the only local English newspaper that covers the entire period of the movement. Local newspapers in Malay, Mandarin Chinese, and Tamil languages, the other three official languages in Singapore, gave less attention to the debates surrounding Section 377A; Repeal 377A, the movement in general, and the countercampaign also targeted mainly local English-language media, an interesting phenomenon that lies outside the scope of this study.[5]

From the *Straits Times* search results, I excluded entire reprints of statements and transcripts by politicians or state officials because they are covered under government data. I selected only those that treated homosexuality or gay activism as more than a tangential, by-the-way issue, mentioned only in passing. For example, articles about HIV/AIDS did not meet this criterion, unless they specifically discussed the virus or disease in relation to the gay community.

Data Analysis and Writing

As is common practice for those who perform studies aimed at theory generation, expansion, or refinement, I began data analysis concurrently with the fieldwork, carrying out three phases of coding and memo writing. During the first phase, I wrote a debrief memo for each interview and observation based on contemporaneous field notes. Then I coded it manually for emergent key patterns and wrote memos on how they related to previously collected data and how they could be explored as I moved forward. At this time, key patterns such as "rights-seen-as-confrontational" and "focus-on-specifics" appeared, and I systematically kept track of their definitions and applications.

After verbatim interview transcripts became available, I launched the second round of coding. This time, I used a software program to code the interview transcripts, observation memos (again), and documentary sources. In addition to the analytic categories developed in the first phase for key patterns, I used open coding (Charmaz 2006), paying attention to details and nuances, thus working my way down to subthemes. Simultaneously with this round of coding, I developed the earlier set of code definitions and applications into a codebook on which I conducted two rounds of coding consistency tests with four local university students.

Alongside the second phase of coding, I wrote bimonthly research memos, during which I did not conduct any fieldwork. I carved out the time to step back into an intellectual space to reexamine the coded data. These memos eventually evolved into a new phase of analytic memos in which I integrated the codes with one another more cohesively and continuously refined the theoretical framework (Emerson, Fretz, and Shaw 1995). For example, I subsumed the code, "rights-seen-as-confrontational" under the theme of "rights don't work" and used the elements of confrontation to tease out the political norms. On the basis of codes such as "focus-on-specifics," I developed "toeing the line" and "pushing boundaries" and integrated them into the concept of pragmatic resistance. Through these analytic memos, the architecture of the thesis took shape. They were essentially the book's rough drafts. As I prepared them, I returned intermittently to the literature to refine how my thesis should be situated in relation to existing scholarship. The analytic memos also served as the foundation and focus for elaborating on the broader intellectual merits of my study and repeatedly ask myself the question "What is this a case of?" (Luker 2008).

When I started writing a more polished first draft, from time to time I returned to the data for a third round of coding. This phase of coding grew out of my scrutiny of the data as I outlined each chapter and made decisions about how to present the data. At that point, I did a "scrub through" of the coded data, re-coding or revising the codebook where necessary as I fleshed out the nuances of arguments from the overall architecture. Meanwhile, in the midst of writing, I met with four informants to share my core findings, get their feedback, and check on the accuracy of certain factual details. Around the time I started to prepare the manuscript for publication, I invited all of the respondents who were in Singapore to attend a discussion session, during which I shared my findings with them and asked them for their further views. Therefore, I continued to analyze and refine the study during the writing process.

Appendix B: Study Respondents: Singapore's Gay Activists

TABLE AB.1. BRIEF PROFILES OF SINGAPORE'S GAY ACTIVISTS[a]

Pseudonyms (real names)	Age	Gender	Race	Education[b]	Religion	Key Affiliations[c]	Joined Movement
Abby Events coordinator	35	F	Chinese	B	Christian	Queer Women's Alliance; The Coalition	Post-1997
Adalyn Civil servant	30	F	Chinese	B	None	Queer Women's Alliance; The Coalition	Post-2005
Aidan Artist	32	M	Chinese	M	Christian	Christian Fellowship; The Beacon	Post-1997
Ai-Mee (Joo Hymn) Stay-at-home mother	40	F	Chinese	LL.B.	None	Family and Friends Network; Repeal 377A	Post-2005
An-Dee Filmmaker	27	M	Chinese	B	None	Pink Dot; Film	Post-2001
Arun[d] *Freelance writer*	*36*	*M*	*South Asian*	*B*	*Hindu*	*The Coalition*	*Post-1997*
Becky Journalist	32	F	Chinese	M	None	Women's World	Post-2001
Billy Corporate executive	46	M	Chinese-South Asian	M	Christian	Christian Fellowship; The Beacon; Open Church; The Coalition	Post-1997
Bo-Liang Student	*32*	*M*	*Chinese*	*Ph.D. (ongoing)*	*Buddhist*	*None*	*Post-2001*
Brandon Corporate executive	34	M	Chinese	B	Agnostic	Biz Tribe	Post-2005
Brett Lawyer	*41*	*M*	*Chinese*	*LL.B.*	*Christian*	*The Coalition*	*Pre-1997*
Bryce Corporate executive	*39*	*M*	*Chinese*	*M*	*Christ believer*	*The Umbrella*	*Post-2001*
Burton Civil servant	37	M	Chinese	Ph.D.	Christian	Open Church	Post-1997

TABLE AB.1. BRIEF PROFILES OF SINGAPORE'S GAY ACTIVISTS[a] *(continued)*

Pseudonyms (real names)	Age	Gender	Race	Education[b]	Religion	Key Affiliations[c]	Joined Movement
Camille*[e] Lawyer	27	F	Chinese	LL.M.	Atheist	Friendship League	Post-2005
Chan Corporate executive	38	M	Chinese	B	Buddhist	Resource Central; Sutra Fellowship	Post-2001
Cheryl IT professional	*38*	*F*	*Chinese*	*M*	*Christian*	*The Coalition; Argot*	*Pre-1997*
Chloe Civil servant	27	F	Chinese	M	Christian	Queer Women's Alliance	Post-2005
Colin* Corporate executive	25	M	Eurasian	B	Catholic	Voicestream	Post-2001
Damien Family counselor	*33*	*M*	*Chinese*	*M*	*Christian*	*Open Church*	*Post-2001*
Devi Spiritual counselor	*36*	*F*	*South Asian*	*B*	*Hindu*	*None*	*Pre-1997*
Doris Teacher	39	F	Chinese	B	Christian	Open Church	Post-2005
Edgar Professor	*61*	*M*	*White*	*Ph.D.*	*Unitarian*	*Christian Fellowship*	*Post-1997*
Ernest Civil servant	*44*	*M*	*Chinese*	*M*	*Christian*	*The Sporting Club; Christian Fellowship*	*Post-1997*
Eu-Jin Journalist	40	M	Chinese	B	Free thinker	The Portal; Pink Dot	Post-2001
Fabian Doctor	*32*	*M*	*Chinese*	*M.D.*	*Free thinker*	*The Sporting Club*	*Post-1997*
Fiona Corporate executive	23	F	Chinese	M	Christian	Youth Support	Post-2005
Frances Teacher*	*47*	*F*	*White*	*M*	*None*	*Women's World*	*Post-2001*
Frank Corporate executive	*45*	*M*	*Chinese*	*M*	*Buddhist*	*Christian Fellowship*	*Pre-1997*
Gail Professor	48	F	Chinese	LL.M.	Buddhist	Theater	Pre-1997
Gillian Artist	42	F	Chinese	"A" levels	Christian	Argot	Pre-1997
Gina Corporate executive	48	F	Chinese	"O" levels	Catholic	Queer Women's Alliance	Post-2005
Li-Ling Artist	*41*	*F*	*Chinese*	*LL.B., M*	*None*	*The Coalition*	*Pre-1997*
Haley Corporate executive	25	F	Chinese	B	Christian	Open Church	Post-2001
Han Writer	30	M	Chinese	B	Daoist/Buddhist	Theater	Post-2001
Harriet Student	36	F	Eurasian	Ph.D. (ongoing)	Agnostic	Virtual Sister; Pink Dot	Post-1997

TABLE AB.1. BRIEF PROFILES OF SINGAPORE'S GAY ACTIVISTS[a]

Pseudonyms (real names)	Age	Gender	Race	Education[b]	Religion	Key Affiliations[c]	Joined Movement
Henry University administrator	34	M	Chinese	B	Atheist	Chalkboard Caucus; Pink Dot	Post-2005
Hsin Dentist	50	M	Chinese	M	Vedic traditions	AIDS Initiative	Pre-1997
Imran IT professional	34	M	Malay	High school	Muslim	The Beacon; Muslim Fellowship	Post-2005
Irwin Commercial artist	42	M	Chinese	M	Buddhist	Brotherhood	Post-2005
Jared IT professional	49	M	Chinese	M	Buddhist	The Coalition	Pre-1997
Jerome* Professor	32	M	Chinese	Ph.D.	Agnostic	Connection Hub	Post-1997
Jian Teacher	35	M	Chinese	M	Christian	Christian Fellowship	Pre-1997
Kai Peng Construction safety officer	45	M	Chinese	B	Unidentified	The Coalition	Post-1997
Kaleb (Otto) Artist	42	M	Chinese	B	Buddhist	None	Post-2005
Kang Corporate trainer	46	M	Chinese	M	Christian	The Coalition; The Harbor	Pre-1997
Karl Entrepreneur	49	M	White	M	Christian	Open Church	Post-2001
Keith Social worker	36	M	Chinese	B	None	AIDS Initiative	Post-2005
Keenan Lawyer	47	M	Chinese	LL.B.	Catholic	AIDS Initiative	Pre-1997
Khalid Playwright	33	M	Malay	B	Muslim	Theater; Pink Dot	Post-1997
Kurt University administrator	30	M	Chinese	B	None	Pink Dot	Post-2005
Kwan* Entrepreneur	48	M	Chinese	Ph.D.	Was Christian	The Beacon; Theater	Pre-1997
Lacey Corporate executive	34	F	Chinese	M	Christian	Singapore Lesbians Online; Resource Central; Women's World	Post-1997
Lewis Corporate executive	34	M	Chinese	M	Christian	Open Church	Post-2001
Liam Scientist	33	M	Chinese	Ph.D.	New age	The Beacon	Post-1997
Li-na Corporate executive	45	F	Chinese	M	Free thinker	The Beacon	Post-2001

TABLE AB.1. BRIEF PROFILES OF SINGAPORE'S GAY ACTIVISTS[a] *(continued)*

Pseudonyms (real names)	Age	Gender	Race	Education[b]	Religion	Key Affiliations[c]	Joined Movement
Liz Journalist	34	F	Chinese	B	Christian	The Portal; Women's World; Pink Dot	Post-2001
Mabel Theater director	34	F	Chinese	Ph.D.	Daoist/Buddhist	Theater	Post-2005
Manisha Lawyer	22	F	South Asian	LL.B.	None	Queer Women's Alliance	Post-2005
Meihua Social worker	36	F	Chinese	M	Christian	Open Church	Post-1997
*Ming Choo** Professor*	59	*F*	*Chinese*	*Ph.D.*	*Atheist*	*Family and Friends Network*	*Post-2005*
*Mitchell** Public relations officer*	42	*M*	*South Asian*	*B*	*Christian*	*The Coalition*	*Pre-1997*
Morris (Stuart) Entrepreneur	37	M	Chinese	Ph.D.	Agnostic	The Portal; Repeal 377A	Post-2001
Nelson Doctor	52	M	Chinese	Ph.D.	Daoist	Pink Dot	Post-2001
Nina University administrator	54	F	Chinese	B	Christian	Open Church	Post-2001
Norm Corporate executive	27	M	Chinese	"A" levels	Free thinker	Youth Support	Post-2001
Oliver Retired professor	59	M	Chinese	Ph.D.	Agnostic	The Coalition	Pre-1997
Owen Lawyer	39	M	Chinese	LL.B.	Catholic	The Coalition	Pre-1997
Parker (George) Lawyer	47	M	Chinese	LL.M.	Catholic	Repeal 377A	Post-2005
Percy Corporate executive	25	M	Chinese	B	Christian	Voicestream	Post-2001
Loke Pastor	81	M	Chinese	Ph.D.	Christian	Open Church	Post-2001
*Quentin** Doctoral student*	45	*M*	*Chinese*	*Ph.D.*	*Was Catholic*	*The Coalition*	*Pre-1997*
Rahim Student	23	*M*	*Malay*	*B*	*Muslim*	*Youth Planet*	*Post-2005*
Rani Doctoral student	38	*F*	*Chinese-South Asian*	*Ph.D. (ongoing)*	*Hindu (non-practicing)*	*Virtual Sister*	*Post-1997*
Reid Corporate executive	31	M	Chinese	B	Catholic	Voicestream	Post-2005
Ricky Public relations executive	47	*M*	*South Asian*	*"O" levels*	*Was Christian*	*AIDS Initiative*	*Pre-1997*
Robbie Social worker	33	M	Chinese	B	Agnostic	The Beacon	Post-2001

TABLE AB.1. BRIEF PROFILES OF SINGAPORE'S GAY ACTIVISTS[a]

Pseudonyms (real names)	Age	Gender	Race	Education[b]	Religion	Key Affiliations[c]	Joined Movement
Shelly Engineer	27	F	Chinese	B	Free thinker	Queer Women's Alliance; The Coalition	Post-2005
Siew (Kum Hong) Lawyer	35	M	Chinese	LL.B.	Atheist	Repeal 377A	Post-2001
Sirius Lecturer	*43*	*M*	*Eurasian*	*M*	*Catholic*	*AIDS Initiative*	*Pre-1997*
Si-Yuan Professor	*41*	*M*	*Chinese*	*Ph.D.*	*Free thinker*	*The Coalition*	*Pre-1997*
Stella (Eileena) Massage therapist	39	F	Chinese	"O" levels	Buddhist	Singapore Lesbians Online; Resource Central; Women's World	Post-1997
Tai* Pastor	35	M	Chinese	M	Christian	The Coalition; Open Church	Post-1997
Taariq Civil servant	*39*	*M*	*Malay*	*M*	*Muslim*	*Muslim Fellowship; AIDS Initiative*	*Pre-1997*
Tony IT professional*	*44*	*M*	*Chinese*	*M*	*Atheist*	*The Coalition*	*Pre-1997*
Trey (Alex) Entrepreneur	*58*	*M*	*Chinese*	*B*	*None*	*The Coalition*	*Pre-1997*
Valerie Civil servant*	*26*	*F*	*Chinese*	*B*	*Unidentified*	*Women's World*	*Post-2001*
Vincent Corporate executive	41	M	Chinese	B	Buddhist	The Coalition; Sutra Fellowship	Post-1997
Viraj Journalist	*45*	*M*	*South Asian*	*M*	*Catholic*	*The Coalition*	*Pre-1997*
Walter Theater director	48	M	Chinese	M	Catholic	Theater	Pre-1997
Warren Civil servant	33	M	Chinese	M	None	Friendship League	Post-2005
Wei Entrepreneur	31	M	Chinese	B	Buddhist	Biz Tribe	Post-2001
Winston Public school administrator	35	M	Chinese	B	Was Catholic	Pink Dot; Chalkboard Caucus; The Coalition	Post-2005
Wong IT professional*	*40*	*M*	*Chinese*	*B*	*Buddhist*	*The Coalition*	*Pre-1997*
Xavier Social worker*	*35*	*M*	*Chinese*	*B*	*Christian*	*Christian Fellowship; The Beacon*	*Post-2001*
Yen Fang Corporate executive	27	F	Chinese	B	None	Women's World	Post-2005
Yi-Feng Social worker	*32*	*M*	*Chinese*	*M*	*Buddhist*	*The Beacon*	*Post-2005*

TABLE AB.1. BRIEF PROFILES OF SINGAPORE'S GAY ACTIVISTS[a] *(continued)*

Pseudonyms (real names)	Age	Gender	Race	Education[b]	Religion	Key Affiliations[c]	Joined Movement
Yusuf Teacher	20	M	Malay	Diploma	Muslim	Youth Society	Post-2005
Yvette Art space executive	35	F	Chinese	Diploma	Unitarian	Friendship League	Post-2005
Zac Public relations executive	47	M	Chinese	B	Atheist	Repeal 377A; Pink Dot	Post-1997
Zhou Social worker	35	M	Chinese	M	Free thinker	AIDS Initiative	Post-2001

a. Based on information in 2009.
b. "A" levels = pre-university; B = bachelor's; diploma = beyond high school "ordinary" level but not university level; M = master's; "O" levels = high school "ordinary" level.
c. "None" indicates that the activist was not affiliated with any organization or major campaign.
d. Italics denote those who are no longer involved in the movement.
e. *Indicates interviews via Skype.

TABLE AB.2. BRIEF BREAKDOWN OF SINGAPORE'S GAY ACTIVISTS BY GENDER, ETHNICITY, RELIGION, AND EDUCATION

Oldest (as of 2009)	81
Youngest	21
Average age	37.3
Women	31
Men	69
Ethnic Chinese	81
Malays	5
South Asian	6
Other ethnicities	8
Buddhists/Daoists	15
Christians	40
Muslims	5
Hindus	3
Other religious affiliations	4
No religious affiliations	33
Holding at least a bachelor's degree (or pursuing one)	93

The approximate ratio of women to men among the respondents is 1:2, so the thirty-one women make up almost one-third of the total number of interviewees. My initial shortlist database had a 1:4 ratio, which meant that I began with a significantly smaller pool of women and did not inadvertently underrecruit women. I made an effort to oversample women to make sure that their voices were represented as much as possible within the theoretical sampling. The conditions that give rise to the disparity between men and women in the movement and perhaps the question of whether they should even be considered as one single movement are beyond the scope of this study. Anecdotally, both men and women informants recall few women at activist gatherings of the early 1990s. Some confided that the lesbians they knew, especially those older than forty years old, preferred to socialize privately and were less interested in movement organizing; those who initially did often dropped out after settling down with their partners. Throughout Chapters 3–7, where relevant, I also analyzed the relationship between lesbians and gay men in the movement.

The categories of race and religion are based on respondents' self-identification. Some respondents are more specific than others, so someone who claims to have South Asian ethnicity may actually be multiracial but neglected to make it clear. The category of *ethnic Chinese* includes people who simply identified as *Chinese*, and those who emphasized being *Peranakan Chinese*, that is, Straits-born or native-born Chinese.[1] The dominance of Christians, only 18 percent of Singapore's general population, clearly stands out among gay activists. In contrast, despite being the most popular religions among 44 percent of Singapore's general population, Buddhism and Daoism are not so among my respondents.[2] The influence of different religions on gay activism lies beyond the scope of this study. Religious faith may well bear only a corelationship and not a causal relationship to gay activism, and other factors such as education may need to be examined more closely in such a study. For instance, 58 percent of the respondents have at least a basic university education, far higher than the 23 percent among the general population (Census 2010).

Appendix C: Singapore's Gay Movement Organizations and Major Events

TABLE AC.1. SINGAPORE'S GAY MOVEMENT ORGANIZATIONS AND MAJOR EVENTS[a]

AIDS Initiative	HIV/AIDS outreach organization with a men-who-have-sex-with-men (MSM) program
Annual Gay Pride Festival	Annual community showcase of talks, exhibitions, and performances held during August
Argot*[b]	Support and social group for women
The Beacon	Counseling service
Biz Tribe	Business networking group for local gay-owned and gay-friendly businesses
Brotherhood	Social group for men
Chalkboard Caucus*	Support and social group for teachers
The Coalition	The first group open about its gay advocacy agenda
Connection Hub	For-profit Internet website providing online space for the local gay community, especially men
Christian Fellowship*	Support group for Christians (succeeded by Open Church)
Family and Friends Network	Support group, operating mainly online, for family and friends of gay persons
The Friendship League	Gay-straight alliance
The Harbor*	Support group for Christians
Muslim Fellowship	Support and social group for Muslims
The Open Church	Church that supports and provides outreach to gay Christians
Pink Dot	Annual public gay rally
The Portal	For-profit Internet website that covers news of interest to gay communities in Singapore and other parts of Asia and provides online social space
Queer Women's Alliance	Advocacy group for queer women in Singapore
Rascals	Letter campaign conducted in 1993 against police raids of gay clubs
Repeal 377A	Parliamentary petition campaign conducted in 2007 for the repeal of Section 377A of the Penal Code
Resource Central	Library and community center
Singapore Lesbians Online	Online discussion group for women
Sports Club	Group that organizes social and sports activities
Sutra Fellowship	Support and social group for Buddhists
Talklist	Online discussion group
The Umbrella*	Group that organizes volunteer work and charity events
Virtual Sister*	Online support service for women
Voicestream*	Podcast on local gay issues
Women's World	Support and social group providing alcohol-free space for women
Youth Planet*	Online blog that provides support for gay youths
Youth Society	Social group for gay youths
Youth Support	Peer support group for youths in their late teens and early twenties

a. This list of organizations is not exhaustive, as it only captures the affiliations of study respondents during the time fieldwork was conducted.
b. *Denotes defunct groups.

Notes

Preface and Acknowledgments

1. A milk or fruit-flavored tea drink with small chewy tapioca balls, known as "pearls," that are usually consumed using oversized straws.

2. *Tan Eng Hong* 2013 and *Lim Meng Suang* are two similar constitutional cases heard three weeks apart between February and March 2012 by the same judge, who subsequently dismissed both claims. At press time, the two cases are scheduled to be heard in a joint appeal to the Court of Appeal, Singapore's highest court, in April 2014. See Chapter 7 for more details.

Chapter 1

1. See Appendix B for information about the interviewees.

2. In characterizing Singapore as "authoritarian," I recognize that there are different shades of authoritarian rule and that the lines dividing modern political regimes into such types as democractic, authoritarian, and totalitarian governments (see, e.g., Friedrich and Brzezinski 1956; Linz 1975; Perlmutter 1981) are not necessarily clear, on the basis of the extent of pluralism and participation (Brooker 2000; Linz 2000; Munck 1998).

3. I use the term *gay* or *gays and lesbians* when referring to the movement and activists who strive for social change for lesbians, gay men, and bisexuals. I also use one of these three terms to describe a person who identifies as such. Please refer to Appendix A for my research design and methods.

4. In fact, some scholars argue that the Stonewall raid was perhaps anomalous by the end of the 1960s because the existing movement had managed to curb widespread abuse through courtroom victories and political mobilization (D'Emilio 1992; Duberman 1993; Chauncey 2004).

5. Sexual conduct between adult, consenting women is not explicitly criminalized.

6. The Heritage Foundation produces its index by measuring ten components of "economic freedom." These include property rights, freedom from corruption, fiscal freedom, government spending, business freedom, labor freedom, monetary freedom, trade freedom, investment freedom, and financial freedom.

7. Throughout this book, I use *law* to refer to state, official, or formal law to distinguish it from other normative orders with which such "law" co-exists and highlight the coercive power of the state through its use of law (Merry 1988). I take the position that the plurality of normative orders, be they state or nonstate law, rather than being a point of contention over legal centralism, should be one of departure for empirical research (Benda-Beckmann 1988), so long as one makes clear the level of analysis and approach (Benda-Beckmann 2002). Hence, I treat law as the self-regulation of a semiautonomous field (S. Moore 1973) that is porous and susceptible to influences by rules and elements external to that field (Griffiths 1986). For debates in sociolegal scholarship over the definition of *law*—whether the term should be exclusive to state law or encompass other normative orders, see Griffiths 1986; Merry 1988; and Benda-Beckmann 1988, 2002.

8. They include framing (see, e.g., Snow and Benford 1988, 1992, 2000), new social movements (see, e.g., Melucci 1985; Laraña, Johnston, and Gusfield 1994; Kriesi et al. 1995), consciousness and movement culture (see, e.g., Fantasia 1989; Johnston and Klandersman 1995; Mansbridge and Morris 2001), emotions and moral outrage (see, e.g., Jasper 1997; Goodwin, Jasper, and Polletta 2001), collective identities (see, e.g., Taylor and Whittier 1992; Polletta and Jasper 2001; Polletta 2004; Meyer, Whittier, and Robnett 2002), fields (Ray 1999), and cultural-institutional approaches (Armstrong 2002; Armstrong and Bernstein 2008). Take framing, for example. Based on Erving Goffman's work on *frames*—defined as schemata of interpretation used by individuals "to locate, perceive, identify, and label occurrences within their life space and the world at large" (Goffman 1974, 21)—collective *framing processes* are interactive processes through which activists "assign meaning to, and interpret relevant events and conditions" (Snow and Benford 1988, 198) to take up collective action, motivate others to participate, and seek support from, challenge, or communicate with third parties. These processes, nevertheless, are only relatively agentic, as it is relatively constrained; activists are limited to drawing from existing meanings and ideologies. Sometimes, however, they are also able to build on these existing meanings and ideologies to modify or construct new meanings. Some frames, because of their cultural resonance, inclusivity, and broad interpretive value, can become master frames for collective action (Snow and Benford 1992). The civil rights frame of the civil rights movement arguably has evolved into a master frame for later movements, such as the women's and gay rights movements (McAdam 1994). Critics of framing, however, argue that it has become static (Benford 1997) and neglected issues that inherently involve centering interaction, such as its relationship with political conditions (Buechler 2000), power relations (Steinberg 1999; Ferree 2003), and ideology (Oliver and Johnston 2000).

9. Although the United States has not necessarily been at the forefront of gay rights, when other countries in Europe and Canada already recognize same-sex marriage nationwide, the voluminous scholarship on the United States and its contentious and complicated nature offer rich theoretical fodder that helps to illuminate the characteristics of the alternative story in Singapore.

10. The Mattachine Society was emboldened momentarily by small gains, for example, when one of its founders successfully fought off charges stemming from police entrapment. However, those founders were eventually ousted because of members' fear of their ties to communism (D'Emilio 1998).

11. The issue of same-sex marriage is also contentious among those on the left, who have heatedly debated for and against marriage (see, e.g., Polikoff 1993; Epstein 1999; Ettelbrick 2001).

12. But see Lovell (2012), who questions the claim that Americans have rights consciousness that is deeply entrenched.

13. Exceptions such as Weiss (2006, 2013) consider specific issues or episodes within the Singapore gay movement's twenty-year trajectory.

14. These theories include Berger and Luckmann 1967; Bourdieu 1977; Foucault 1977; Giddens 1984; and Sewell 1992.

15. For examples of such law and society scholarship, see Bumiller 1988; Sarat 1990; Merry 1990; Greenhouse, Yngvesson, and Engel 1994; Morrill 1995; Ewick and Silbey 1998; Engel and Munger 2003; Nielsen 2004; Albiston 2010; and Boittin 2013.

16. The debates over rule of law are numerous and complicated. The Singaporean state-championed version of rule of law can be described as authoritarian (Rajah 2012) or as a thin notion, as opposed to thick versions that embrace certain fundamental values, such as liberalism (Peerenboom 2004).

17. See Meyer and Boutcher 2007 on reading signals in the context of American civil rights litigation and Stern 2013 on interpreting signals in authoritarian China.

18. In the mid-2000s, this was a popular pink-dollar argument linked to Richard Florida's (2002) creative classes, a book that attracted the PAP's attention too.

19. At press time, the Court of Appeal of Singapore is scheduled to hear the cases of *Tan Eng Hong* 2013 and *Lim Meng Suang,* which argue that Section 377A of the Penal Code contravenes the constitutional right to equality. See Chapter 7 for details.

Chapter 2

1. Singapore first became part of the British Straits Settlements, along with Malacca and Penang, in today's Malaysia. During World War II, Singapore was occupied by the Japanese, but returned to British control thereafter. It then became a separate Crown Colony in 1946.

2. In 1969, riots between ethnic Chinese and Malay erupted on Peninsular Malaysia and spilled over into Singapore. Also see Aljunied 2009 on the Nadra/Maria Hertogh riots, which occurred in 1950 after a colonial court in Singapore ruled in favor of Nadra/Maria's biological Catholic Dutch parents over the Muslim Javanese woman who had raised the girl as her own daughter.

3. The British colonial administration gave both men and women the right to vote for local legislative council representatives in 1948. Women ran for and were elected to office as early as the 1959 legislative assembly elections (Wang and Teo 1993).

4. The Women's Charter outlaws polygamous, non-Muslim marriages, whereas Muslim marriages remain separately regulated in Singapore under the Administration of Muslim Law Act.

5. See note 6 in Chapter 1.

6. On the PAP's rule more generally, see, e.g., Rajah 2012, Rodan 2004; Bell et al. 1995.

7. The statute was inherited from the British. It was intended originally to control Chinese triads and then communist organizations posing as social organizations (Mauzy and Milne 2002).

8. Before the Public Order Act, a gathering of five or more persons constituted unlawful assembly if they intended to commit an offense or resisted the execution of any law or legal process. Chapter 7 details how gay activists circumvent these broad restrictions to stage annual gay rallies.

9. For critical views of state control over the Singaporean media, see *The Media Enthralled: Singapore Revisited* (1998) by Singapore's former solicitor-general, Francis Seow, and *Freedom from the Press: Journalism and State Power in Singapore* (2012) by Cherian George.

10. The government launched Operation Coldstore in February 1963 to detain at least 111 left-wing activists without trial (also see Hong and Huang 2008; Turnbull 2009; Rajah 2012).

11. When the PAP lost six out of eighty-seven seats to the opposition in the 2011 elections, the outcome was considered a major and unprecedented defeat to the party. See Chapter 8 on the future of gay rights politics in Singapore.

12. But see Singapore's former chief justice's commentary on judicial review of administrative and executive actions (Chan 2010).

13. Strictly speaking, the government did accept the narrow ruling of the case *Chng Suan Tze v. Ministry of Home Affairs* (1989) on the grounds of procedural defect. But on release, the detainees were immediately rearrested and detained with the proper paperwork. Their subsequent challenge for judicial review failed because the courts upheld the new constitutional and legislative amendments (see also G. Silverstein 2003).

14. Stern's (2013) study of environmental litigation in China examines how people try to "suss out" political attitudes with imperfect information and interpret conflicting signals.

15. On the relationship between the Singaporean state and race, see, e.g., Vasil 1995; Heng and Devan 1992; Puru Shotam 2000.

16. While civil-political liberties are also curtailed by legislation in liberal democracies, such as by the American PATRIOT Act, constitutional challenges against such curtailments are more commonly successful.

17. On Singapore's international status concerning gay rights, see Obendorf 2013.

18. On the relationship between the Singaporean state and homosexuality, see, e.g., Bong 2011; B. Chua 2008; Debbie Goh 2008; Heng and Devan 1992; Leong 2008, 2010; Lyons 2004; Oswin 2010; Tan 2009; and Tan and Jin 2007.

19. Section 377, repealed in 2007, read, "Whoever has carnal intercourse against the order of nature with any man, woman or animal, shall be punished with imprisonment for life, or with imprisonment for a term which may extend to 10 years, and shall also be liable to fine. Explanation—Penetration is sufficient to constitute the carnal intercourse necessary to the offence described in this section." Section 377A reads, "Any male person who, in public or private, commits, or abets the commission of, or procures or attempts to procure the commission by any male person of, any act of gross indecency with another male person, shall be punished with imprisonment for a term which may extend to 2 years." Unlike Section 377, which is more commonly found among former British colonies that derived penal statutes from the Indian Penal Code, Section 377A was inherited by only some of its former colonies (Sanders 2009). The colonial government introduced the provision into Singapore in 1938, basing it on Section 11 of the United Kingdom Criminal Law Amendment Act of 1885, the "gross indecency" law used to prosecute Oscar Wilde in the 1890s. For analyses on the types of cases prosecuted under the former Section 377 and Section 377A of the Penal Code in Singapore, see L. Chua 2003. Also see Amirthalingam 2008 and Hor 2012 on the prosecution's use of Section 377A.

20. See Chua B. 1997 and Sun 2011 on Singapore's housing and population policies.

21. The study in this book does not extend to activism on transgender issues because they are distinct from those of the gay community. See Appendix A on the research design and sampling of subjects.

22. See Tan 2012 for an analysis on homosexuality in the Singaporean military.

23. On the relationship between Singaporean media and the portrayal of homosexuality, see, e.g., Detenber et al. 2007, 2012; and Leong 2005.

24. I hesitate to use the term *come out* in every instance of making known one's sexuality and reserve the use of this term for cases in which the persons in question identify with the concept. This is because some gays and lesbians, including activists, in Singapore do not embrace the term. Among interviewees, some prefer the concept of "coming home." Propounded by Chinese scholar Chou Wah-Shan (2000), the concept rejects what it sees as emphasis on acceptance of differences in "coming out" and advocates focusing on the integration of oneself and one's partner into the family. "Coming out" in the United States

also bears different meanings in different eras (Chauncey 1994). For autobiographical accounts of gays and lesbians in Singapore, see, e.g., Y. Ng 2006 and Leow 2013. For discussions about gay life or culture in Singapore more generally, see, e.g., Offord 2000; R. H. K. Heng 2001; Yue 2007; Bong 2011; Maulod and Jamil 2012; and Yue and Zubillaga-Pow 2012.

25. It is still common for adult children in Singapore to live with their parents.

26. *English-speaking* and *Chinese-speaking* refer to the default language of communication at home. It does not mean that the Chinese speakers cannot or do not speak English; however, the English speakers may not be as fluent in Mandarin Chinese as the Chinese speakers.

27. A *hawker* is someone who sells inexpensive cooked food at stalls in "hawker centers" or on the side of the street.

28. However, this does not mean that religious and racial prejudices do not exist within the gay community in Singapore.

Chapter 3

1. Seow later published a critical account of his experiences in the book, *To Catch A Tartar: A Dissident in Lee Kuan Yew's Prison* (1994).

2. The International Commission of Jurists (1987) criticized the Singapore government's allegations as baseless and the crackdown as a violation of human rights. For accounts by former detainees and their close friends and family, see Teo 2010 and Fong 2012. For the impact of the alleged Marxist conspiracy and its crackdown on Christianity and liberal churches in Singapore, see Daniel Goh 2010.

3. For a detailed analysis of the development of Christianity in Singapore, see Daniel Goh 2010.

4. Besides documenting such reports, Heng (2001) also discusses the visible transgender scene in the Bugis Street area in the 1950s–1960s.

5. One of the earliest reports on lesbians in Singapore appeared in the now defunct, *The New Nation,* an afternoon daily newspaper.

6. For critical discussions on Singaporean theater, see, e.g., Lo 2004 and Chong 2010.

7. After some revisions, Chay Yew and Eleanor Wong were allowed to stage their plays in 1989.

8. On the relationship between Singaporean theater and gay activism, see, e.g., Lim 2005, 2013.

9. See Lyons 2004 and Chong 2012 for discussions on AWARE's engagement with issues of sexuality. The roles of lesbians in relation to the American movement have been considered in a wider array of literature. See, e.g., D'Emilio 1998; Winnow 1992; Whittier 1995; Patton 1990; Epstein 1996; and Stockdill 2003.

10. In 1989, state authorities withdrew the liquor license of the gay disco, Niche, and without providing any reason gave the business only a week to close down. According to Heng (2001), an informant personally involved with Niche's operations believed that it was in reaction to the HIV/AIDS-related death.

11. To protest the arrests and homophobic media coverage, two performance artists created events in December 1993. One of them ended his act by snipping off his pubic hair on stage. The other swallowed burnt ashes of the newspaper that sensationally reported the case and then vomited on stage. Their performances outraged the authorities and resulted in a ban on unscripted art forms. The ban was not lifted until 2003.

12. Also see Chong 2010 for analysis of the relationship between Singaporean theater and the state.

13. Of course, though the decrease in media coverage of entrapment may suggest actual reduction in entrapment, it can also simply mean the diminishment of newsworthiness. Searches of available databases for reported and unreported Singaporean judgments did not turn up cases that explicitly or implicitly involved entrapment after 1994, the year of the *Tan Boon Hock* decision, except for two dubious incidents in 1998: In one, the police officer acted on a complaint, but the judge found his evidence unreliable and hinted at suspicions of fabrication; in another, the complainant was identified as a police officer, but it was unclear whether he was acting on official entrapment duty while at the public pool. We also cannot know of plea bargains that have taken place because the prosecution does not divulge such information.

14. Months after the last correspondence, the Coalition wrote another letter to the Ministry of Home Affairs with the endorsement of a sympathetic NMP. The letter reiterated the request for an explanation of the grounds of rejection. The ministry replied within a month with the same nonanswer that again cited the Societies Act provisions.

Chapter 4

1. On Internet regulation and the Singaporean state, see, e.g., Keshishoglou and Aquilia 2004; Rodan 2003; and George 2006. In May 2013, the Singaporean government announced new rules requiring online news sites that report regularly on Singapore to obtain a license. The proposed rules attracted criticism from Singapore-based bloggers and other online commentators, who worried that the rules would extend to them as well. The ostensible reason for the new rules was to bring the news sites in line with the licensing rules on newspapers and television news stations and thus hold them accountable according to the same restrictions.

2. For a study on the Internet's effect on local gay men in Singapore, see K. Ng 1999.

3. According to the Singaporean government, the country's household wired broadband penetration rate has reached more than 100 percent.

4. Other online groups for women existed before Singapore Lesbians Online, such as one for Singaporean and Malaysian lesbian and bisexual women that was cofounded by a Singaporean based in North America.

5. The person who posted the first message went by pseudonyms even in real life. According to several informants, he retains conservative Christian affiliations and keeps quiet about his sexuality. They are still not sure what his actual name is! One informant contacted him on my behalf and told me that he was open to an interview. When I followed up on numerous occasions, however, he did not respond.

6. See note 27 in Chapter 2.

7. To be more accurate, Quentin participated only in the second session, having contracted chickenpox just before the first one. Select papers presented at the events were published in 2003 as an edited book volume.

8. Singapore's age of sexual consent is sixteen years old (though this is, of course, set with heterosexual relations in mind). Statutory rape applies to having sex with a girl younger than fourteen years old. The age for marriage without parental consent is twenty-one years.

Chapter 5

1. Chee was a local university lecturer in neuropsychology until the university fired him in 1992 for allegedly misappropriating funds. This coincided with his contestation in general elections as an opposition candidate. Due to his legal battles, particularly over defamation suits filed against him by PAP leaders, Chee carried a bankrupt legal status for years and consequently was barred from running for office or leaving Singapore without the permission of the Official Assignee.

2. After stepping down as prime minister, Lee continued to run for and was elected to the office of MP, for which he was then appointed senior minister in Goh's cabinet.

3. For works on Singapore's theater and gay activism, see note 8 in Chapter 3.

4. The ban on unscripted art forms was also lifted in 2003. See note 11 in Chapter 3.

5. The Coalition's survey results showed that 46 percent of respondents on the street and 74 percent on the Internet would be able to accept a gay sibling, while 41 percent and 66 percent, respectively, could accept a gay child. However, the local university's survey found that that 90 percent of seventeen- to thirty-five-year-olds would be disappointed if they found out that their child was gay and 80 percent would be "upset" to know that a sibling was gay. In the latter survey, respondents were asked whether they agreed with the statement "I would be upset if I learned that my brother or sister was homosexual." This is a problematic question because the word "upset" could convey meanings other than being intolerant, such as empathizing with the personal struggles that one's sibling may face. For more recent academic surveys, see Detenber et al. 2012.

6. See Chua and Hildebrandt (forthcoming) on the influence of Chinese and Singaporean governments' HIV/AIDS funding on gay activism.

7. At press time, the church is making plans to purchase its own premises.

8. However, it is important to note that allies from theater and other arts circles predate such involvement and that at least two people who signed the Coalition's first registration application are non-gay friends of the Coalition signatories.

9. Sadasivan died of colon cancer at the age of 55 years in 2010.

10. According to official figures in 2012, 47 percent of those who became infected reported they were heterosexual, 45 percent reported that they were homosexual, 6 percent reported that they were bisexual, and 0.4 percent reported that they were intravenous drug users.

11. Some informants surmised that authorities could have been pressured to withdraw the license after receiving complaints from people affiliated with the Christian Right countermovement, but this cannot be independently verified.

Chapter 6

1. Singapore's Supreme Court consists of the High Court and the Court of Appeal, which is the final court of resort.

2. The use of the term *queer* to describe or name gay activist organizations appeared more frequently after 2005. Founders of these organizations believe that *queer* has less baggage in Singapore compared with the United States and therefore see an opportunity to claim (or reclaim) the term positively for the movement.

3. They could also simply opt for the tactic that harks back to the days of Quentin's closed-door forum—by changing the public event into a private affair using invitations and RSVPs and avoiding the licensing rules altogether.

4. In 2009, the new Public Order Act was passed and defined public assemblies to include demonstrations by lone individuals, so the legality of the Pink Run tactic may not be as secure under the new rules. Passage of the Public Order Act occurred after opposition politician Chee Soon Juan and his supporters tried to circumvent the old laws against public assemblies by arguing that they were demonstrating in groups of fewer than five and therefore the restrictions did not apply.

5. For further analysis on the relationship between HIV/AIDS activism and the gay movement in Singapore, see Chua and Hildebrandt (forthcoming).

6. For the full text of these two provisions, see note 19 in Chapter 2.

7. The website team submitted the open letter to the prime minister on the first day of the Section 377A debates in Parliament. It was meant to complement the petition, but

it confused some people, who thought that the letter and the petition referred to the same document.

8. There were, however, people who refused to sign the petition because they worked for the government or held prominent professional positions.

9. The official count was 2,341, which may have been a result of disqualifying illegible entries.

10. On how the use of legal procedures reshaped and transformed collective grievances, see, e.g., Mather 1998, Hagan 2000, and Hoffman 2008.

11. Although Siew submitted the petition before the amendment bill would be read for the second time, the petition actually had not been reviewed by the Public Petitions Committee by the time the second reading was scheduled for October 22, 2007, which fell on a Monday. Usually, the contents of petitions are not disclosed to MPs until the committee has presented its report, but the Repeal 377A petition had already been circulated on the Internet and reported in the media. On the preceding Saturday, Siew had a conversation with the house leader, who agreed that the petition and the bill should be debated together because separate debates about each of them without consideration of the other would be artificial.

12. See Chen (2013) for a public choice theory explanation of the state's position.

13. See Hoffman (2008) for an example of how birth activists in the United States used legislative committee hearings to obtain legal legitimacy and earn procedural justice.

14. See Chapter 2 for a discussion of Singapore's population demographics.

15. In the same speech, Thio said that she received an e-mail in August 2007 from a stranger who said that he would defile her grave on the day Section 377A was repealed and that she was so upset that she reported the incident to the police. The writer of the e-mail later apologized and admitted that he had sent the message after a night of drinking. He was questioned by the police, but no further legal action was taken by the authorities or Thio against him.

Chapter 7

1. Gay activists in Anchorage, Alaska, Salt Lake City, New York City, Montreal, Hong Kong, Taiwan, and Okinawa, Japan, have held Pink Dot events.

2. For more details about the incident, see Leong 2012 and Chong 2012.

3. Three different motions for votes of no confidence were tabled, and the vote counts were 1414:761, 1412:762, and 1419:755 against the new Exco. Not all votes cast against the new Exco were triggered by its anti-gay stance. Women who were incensed by the new Exco's takeover of AWARE cited a variety of other reasons, such as the new Exco's alleged lack of experience in activism, ignorance of feminism, and takeover tactics.

4. Also see Chapter 3 on the relationship between mainstream women's groups and the gay movement.

5. Nevertheless, PAP leaders expressed unhappiness with the nature of the campaign on both sides, alluding to the heated exchanges in letters to newspaper editors and during the seven-hour-long extraordinary general meeting.

6. It also coincided with the eve of the International Day Against Homophobia, or IDAHO, which is usually commemorated on May 17.

7. Pink Dot 2013, held on June 29, 2013, attracted more than 21,000 people.

8. After 2010, the concerts during Pink Dot were held on the stage immediately adjacent to and overlooking the park and fell outside of Hong Lim Park's boundaries (though they look connected). For those concerts, Pink Dot organizers separately obtained entertainment licenses from the censorship authority and permission from the community club to use the stage (the community club is a "grassroots organisation" under the People's Association, set up by the government as a statutory body—i.e., a government agency).

9. Pink Dot organizers have been questioned by police about the possible inadvertent participation of foreigners in the Pink Dot formation. To "cover our behinds," one informant said that they started putting up clearer signage in subsequent years.

10. The event also includes transgender communities, which are not within the scope of my study. See Appendix A.

11. Local gay and lesbian culture more broadly interacts with that of both Western and non-Western societies. Singaporean gays and lesbians also pay attention to pop stars and other media celebrities who are known to be gay from places such as Taiwan, Hong Kong, Korea, Japan, and China. See note 24 in Chapter 2 for more references to studies on Singaporean gay and lesbian culture.

12. The others are the Convention on the Rights of the Child and the Convention on the Rights of Persons with Disabilities.

13. The Indian provision in question was Section 377 of the Indian Penal Code, which resembles Singapore's former Section 377 that was removed as part of the Penal Code amendments in 2007. Singapore's Penal Code, as is the case with the penal codes of other former British colonies, is a progeny of the Indian Penal Code. Hence, decisions on the latter are often seen as important and persuasive, though not by any means binding on local courts. At press time, however, the Indian decision in question has just been overturned by the Indian Supreme Court.

14. The charge in relation to Tan's co-accused was similarly substituted, and the co-accused also pleaded guilty under Section 294(a).

15. At press time, a segment of the local gay community has started to question whether the activists who organize and support *Lim Meng Suang* are trying to whitewash their community by presenting litigants who are perceived to be more palatable to the rest of Singaporean society. Lim and Chee are corporate executives in a long-term, stable relationship, whereas Tan Eng Hong is publicly associated with having sex in a public toilet. The decision to organize *Lim Meng Suang* is actually complex, and the interactions involving the judicial process, the litigants, the activists who support them, and their lawyers form a separate and ongoing study that I am conducting.

16. Because Singapore's lower courts are bound by previous decisions that narrowly applied the legal test on whether ordinary legislation violated the right to equality, Justice Loh's judgments are probably unsurprising to Singaporean constitutional law experts. However, the Court of Appeal is not bound by any other court or its own prior decisions. In any case, the lawyers and activists supporting *Tan Eng Hong* 2013 and *Lim Meng Suang* have always set their eyes on the apex of the judiciary, regardless of the outcome at the lower court.

17. See Appendix A on my attempts to find out information about the hiring policies of government agencies. Shortly after Goh's announcement about gays in civil service, one activist who was a civil servant told his human resources director that he was gay and asked about his agency's "official policy." He was told, "'Oh, there is no formal policy. We have not heard anything.' And [the human resources director] said, 'But rest assured, you will not be prejudiced in any way now that you have told me.'"

18. In 2008, a man called Chan Mun Chiong had consensual oral sex with a sixteen-year-old in the toilet cubicle of a shopping mall without disclosing that he was HIV positive. Chan's sex partner later filed a complaint about Chan's failure to disclose his HIV status. Besides being charged under the Infectious Diseases Act, Chan was charged under Section 377A. Even though the sex was consensual and the sixteen-year-old complainant was not underage according to law, the government said that it took into consideration his age and the location where the sex took place (see Hor 2012).

19. The police refused to grant Pink Dot 2013 organizers permission to close off a road next to Hong Lim Park partially so that they could open up more standing room for

the swelling number of participants (not for marching). They also denied their license application to move the event to a larger venue that, unlike Hong Lim Park, is not automatically exempted from the license application process.

20. Of course, this is a question of degree because Western democracies also have the element of personal rule. The ways in which state agents implement rules on the ground are shaped by who they are and the people with whom they interact (Gilliom 2001; Maynard-Moody and Musheno 2003).

21. For example, see note 15 in this chapter on the intramovement tensions related to the two Section 377A constitutional cases *Tan Eng Hong* 2013 and *Lim Meng Suang*.

Chapter 8

1. I am grateful to Calvin Morrill for drawing my attention to American pragmatism.

2. Mische (1997, cited in Emirbayer and Mische 1998) extended a particular aspect of human agency to her analysis of Brazilian youth mobilization.

3. See Chapter 1 for a discussion of the literature in this area.

4. The powerful also have hidden transcripts, practices, and claims of their rule that cannot be openly avowed (Scott 1990), as in the case of the Singaporean state and ruling party.

5. See note 8 in Chapter 1 on framing.

6. I thank George Chauncey for pointing this out during one of our many conversations on Singapore's gay movement.

7. There are other opposition parties that have publicly supported the repeal of Section 377A. In June 2013, a politician from one of these parties for the first time in Singaporean party politics announced publicly that he was gay.

Appendix A

1. A traditional type of coffee shop and eating place, usually without air conditioning, found in Singapore and other parts of Southeast Asia. *Kopi* is the word for *coffee* in Malay, and *tiam* means *shop* in the Chinese dialect of Hokkien.

2. In her study of education activists, Kostiner (2003) asked interviewees what *social change* meant to them, rather than imposed theoretical understandings of the term, a critique she made of McCann 1994 and H. Silverstein 1996.

3. Facebook postings and "tweets" on Twitter were left out. These were often repetitious of the content in the other media.

4. "*" indicates "wild card"—whatever permutation that comes after the word. *BG* stands for Brigadier General, another title held by Prime Minister Lee Hsien Loong.

5. See Chen (2013), which provides a content analysis of Malay- and Chinese-language newspapers.

Appendix B

1. *Straits* refers to the Malacca Straits between the Malaysian Peninsula and the Indonesian island of Sumatra. Peranakan Chinese identify with a specific culture that is a melting pot of Chinese, Malay, and Western heritage.

2. The two, of course, are distinct religious faiths, and a small number of the activists exclusively identify with one or the other. However, they are lumped together (and often with traditional Chinese forms of ancestral worship) in the Singaporean census, and this reflects how they are commonly practiced and professed in a conflated fashion among local, non-Christian Chinese.

References

Adam, Barry D. 1995. *The Rise of a Gay and Lesbian Movement*. New York: Simon and Schuster Macmillan.
Adam, Barry D., Jan Willem Duyvendak, and André Krouwell eds. 1999. *The Global Emergence of Gay and Lesbian Politics: National Imprints of a Worldwide Movement*. Philadelphia: Temple University Press.
Albiston, Catherine R. 2006. "Legal Consciousness and Workplace Rights." In *New Civil Rights Research: A Constitutive Approach*, ed. B. Steiner and L. B. Nielsen. Dartmouth, UK: Ashgate Press.
———. 2010. *Institutional Inequality and the Mobilization of the Family and Medical Leave Act: Rights on Leave*. New York: Cambridge University Press.
Aljunied, Syed Muhammad Khairudin. 2009. *Colonialism, Violence and Muslims in Southeast Asia: The Maria Hertogh Controversy and Its Aftermath*. London: Routledge.
Altman, Dennis. 2001. *Global Sex*. Chicago: University of Chicago Press.
Amirthalingam, Kumaralingam. 2008. "Criminal Law and Private Spaces: The Regulation of Homosexual Acts in Singapore." In *Regulating Deviance: The Redirection of Criminalisation and the Futures of Criminal Law*, ed. S. Bronitt, B. McSherry. and A. Norrie. Oxford: Hart Publishing.
Andersen, Ellen Ann. 2006. *Out of the Closets and into the Courts: Legal Opportunity Structure and Gay Rights Litigation*. Ann Arbor: University of Michigan Press.
Armstrong, Elizabeth A. 2002. *Forging Gay Identities: Organizing Sexuality in San Francisco, 1950–1994*. Chicago: University of Chicago Press.
Armstrong, Elizabeth A., and Mary Bernstein. 2008. "Culture, Power, and Institutions: A Multi-institutional Politics Approach to Social Movements." *Sociological Theory* 26:75–99.
Barclay, Scott, Mary Bernstein, and Anna-Maria Marshall, eds. 2009. *Queer Mobilizations: LGBT Activists Confront the Law*. New York: New York University Press.
Barkan, Steven. 1977. "Political Trials and the Pro Se Defendant in the Adversary System." *Social Problems* 24:324–336.

―――. 1980. "Political Trials and Resource Mobilization: Towards an Understanding of Social Movement Litigation." *Social Forces* 58:944–961.

―――. 1984. "Legal Control of the Southern Civil Rights Movement." *American Sociological Review* 49:552–565.

―――. 1985. *Protestors on Trial: Criminal Prosecutions in the Southern Civil Rights and Vietnam Antiwar Movements.* New Brunswick, NJ: Rutgers University Press.

―――. 2006. "Criminal Prosecution and the Legal Control of Protest," *Mobilization* 11:181–195.

Becker, Penny E. 1998. "Making Inclusive Communities: Congregations and the 'Problem' of Race." *Social Problems* 45:451–472.

Beirne, Piers, and Richard Quinney. 1982. "Marxist Theories of Law: An Introduction." In *Marxism and Law,* ed. P. Beirne and R. Quinney. New York: John Wiley and Sons.

Bell, Daniel, D. Brown, K. Jayasuriya, and D. M. Jones. 1995. *Towards Illiberal Democracy in Pacific Asia.* New York: St. Martin's Press.

Benda-Beckmann, Franz von. 1988. "Comment on Merry." *Law and Society Review* 22:897–902.

―――. 2002. "Who's Afraid of Legal Pluralism?" *Journal of Legal Pluralism and Unofficial Law* 47:37–82.

Benford, Robert D. 1997. "An Insider's Critique of the Social Movement Framing Perspective." *Sociological Inquiry* 67:409–430.

Benton, Lauren. 2002. *Law and Colonial Cultures: Legal Regimes in World History, 1400–1900.* London: Cambridge University Press.

Berger, Peter L., and Thomas Luckmann. 1967. *The Social Construction of Reality.* New York: Anchor Books.

Bernstein, Mary. 1997. "Celebration and Suppression: The Strategic Uses of Identity by the Lesbian and Gay Movement." *American Journal of Sociology* 103:531–565.

―――. 2002. "Identities and Politics: Toward a Historical Understanding of the Lesbian and Gay Movement." *Social Science History* 26:531–581.

―――. 2003. "Nothing Ventured, Nothing Gained? Conceptualizing Social Movement 'Success' in the Lesbian and Gay Movement." *Sociological Perspectives* 46:353–379.

Blackwood, Evelyn. 2007. "Regulation of Sexuality in Indonesian Discourse: Normative Gender, Criminal Law and Shifting Strategies of Control." *Culture, Health and Sexuality* 9:293–307.

Bob, Clifford. 2005. *The Marketing of Rebellion: Insurgents, Media, and International Activism.* New York: Cambridge University Press.

―――, ed. 2009. *The International Struggle for New Human Rights.* Philadelphia: University of Pennsylvania Press.

Boellstorff, Tom. 2005. *The Gay Archipelago.* Princeton, NJ: Princeton University Press.

Boittin, Margaret L. 2013. "New Perspectives from the Oldest Profession: Abuse and the Legal Consciousness of Sex Workers in China." *Law and Society Review* 47:245–278.

Bokhorst-Heng, Wendy. 2002. "Newspapers in Singapore: A Mass Ceremony in the Imagining of the Nation." *Media, Culture and Society* 24:559–569.

Bong, Sharon A. 2011. "Negotiating Resistance/Resilience through the Nexus of Spirituality-sexuality of Same-sex Partnerships in Malaysia and Singapore." *Marriage and Family Review* 47:648–665.

Boudreau, Vince. 2005. "Precarious Regimes and Matchup Problems in the Explanation of Repressive Policy." In *Repression and Mobilization,* ed. C. Davenport, C. Mueller, and H. Johnston. Minneapolis: University of Minnesota Press.

Bourdieu, Pierre. 1977. *Outline of a Theory of Practice.* Trans. Richard Nice. Cambridge: Cambridge University Press.

Brooker, Paul. 2000. *Non-Democratic Regimes.* London: McMillan.

Brown, Stephen. 1999. "Democracy and Sexual Difference: The Lesbian and Gay Movement in Argentina." In *The Global Emergence of Gay and Lesbian Politics: National Imprints of a Worldwide Movement*, ed. B. Adam, J. W. Duyvendak, and A. Krouwel. Philadelphia: Temple University Press.

Brown, Wendy. 1996. *States of Injury: Power and Freedom in Late Modernity*. Princeton, NJ: Princeton University Press.

Buechler, Steven M. 2000. *Social Movements in Advanced Capitalism: The Political Economy and Cultural Construction of Social Activism*. New York: Oxford University Press.

Bumiller, Kristin. 1988. *The Civil Rights Society: The Social Construction of Victims*. Baltimore: Johns Hopkins University Press.

Cain, Patricia A. 1993. "Litigating for Lesbian and Gay Rights: A Legal History." *Virginia Law Review* 79:1551–1641.

Census of Population. 2010. Singapore: Republic of Singapore.

Central Intelligence Agency. 2010. *World Factbook*. Washington, DC: Central Intelligence Agency.

Chan, Sek Keong. 2010. "Judicial Review—From Angst to Empathy." *Singapore Academy of Law Journal* 22:469–489.

Charmaz, Kathy. 2006. *Constructing Grounded Theory: A Practical Guide through Qualitative Analysis*. London: Sage Publications.

Chauncey, George. 1994. *Gay New York: Gender, Urban Culture, and the Making of the Gay Male World, 1890–1940*. New York: Basic Books.

———. 2004. *Why Marriage? The History Shaping Today's Debate over Gay Equality*. New York: Basic Books.

Chen, Jianlin. 2013. "Singapore's Culture War over Section 377A: Through the Lens of Public Choice and Multilingual Research." *Law and Social Inquiry* 38:106–137.

Chng Suan Tze v. Minister of Home Affairs. 1989. (Singapore Court of Appeal.) *Malayan Law Journal* 1:69.

Chong, Terence. 2010. *The Theatre and the State in Singapore: Orthodoxy and Resistance*. London: Routledge.

———. 2012. *The Aware Saga: Civil Society and Public Morality in Singapore*. Honolulu: University of Hawaii Press.

Chou, Wah-Shan. 2000. *Tongzhi: Politics of Same-sex Eroticism in Chinese Societies*. London: Haworth Press.

Chua Beng-Huat. 1997. *Political Legitimacy and Housing: Stakeholding in Singapore*. London: Routledge.

———. 2008. "Singapore in 2007: High Wage Ministers and the Management of Gays and Elderly." *Asian Survey* 48:55–61.

Chua, Lynette J. 2003. "Saying No: Sections 377 and 377A of the Penal Code." *Singapore Journal of Legal Studies* 209–261.

———. 2012. "The Power of Legal Processes and Section 377A of the Penal Code: Tan Eng Hong v. Attorney General." *Singapore Journal of Legal Studies* 457–466.

Chua, Lynette J., and Timothy Hildebrandt. Forthcoming. "From Health Crisis to Rights Advocacy? HIV/AIDS and Gay Activism in China and Singapore." *Voluntas: International Journal of Voluntary and Nonprofit Organizations*.

Cohen, Jean L. 1985. "Strategy or Identity: New Theoretical Paradigms and Contemporary Social Movements." *Social Research* 52:663–716.

Collins, Hugh. 1982. *Marxism and Law*. Oxford: Oxford University Press.

Comaroff, Jean, and John L. Comaroff, eds. 2006. *Law and Disorder in the Postcolony*. Chicago: University of Chicago Press.

Cress, Daniel M., and David Snow. 2000. "The Outcomes of Homeless Mobilization: The Influence of Organization, Disruption, Political Mediation, and Framing." *American Journal of Sociology* 105:1063–1104.

Currier, Ashley. 2009. "Deferral of Legal Tactics: A Global LGBT Social Movement Organization's Perspective." In *Queer Mobilizations: LGBT Activists Confront the Law*, ed. S. Barclay, M. Bernstein, and A. Marshall. New York: New York University Press.
———. 2012. *Out in Africa: LGBT Organizing in Namibia and South Africa*. Minneapolis: University of Minnesota Press.
Davenport, Christian, Carol Mueller, and Hank Johnston, eds. 2005. *Repression and Mobilization*. Minneapolis: University of Minnesota Press.
della Porta, Donatella. 1988. "Recruitment Processes in Clandestine Political Organizations: Italian Left-wing Terrorism." *International Social Movement Research* 1:155–169.
D'Emilio, John. 1992. *Making Trouble: Essays on Gay History, Politics, and the University*. New York: Routledge.
———. 1998. *Sexual Politics, Sexual Communities,* 2nd ed. Chicago: University of Chicago Press.
———. 2002. *The World Turned: Essays on Gay History, Politics, and Culture*. Durham, NC: Duke University Press.
Detenber, Benjamin H., Mark Cenite, Moses K. Y. Ku, Carol P. L. Long, Hazel Y. Tong, and Magdalene L. H. Yeow. 2007. "Singaporeans' Attitudes toward Lesbians and Gay Men and Their Tolerance of Media Portrayals of Homosexuality." *International Journal of Public Opinion Research* 19:367–379.
Detenber, Benjamin H., Shirley S. Ho, Rachel L. Neo, Shelly Malik, and Mark Cenite. 2012. "Influence of Value Predispositions, Interpersonal Contact, and Mediated Exposure on Public Attitudes toward Homosexuals in Singapore." *Asian Journal of Social Psychology* 15:1–16.
Dewey, John. 1922. *Human Nature and Conduct: An Introduction to Social Psychology*. New York: Holt.
Douglas, Jack D. 1976. *Investigative Social Research: Individual and Team Field Research*. Beverly Hills: Sage Publications.
Drucker, Peter, ed. 2000. *Different Rainbows*. London: Millivers.
Duberman, Martin. 1993. *Stonewall*. New York: Dutton.
Dudas, Jeffrey R. 2008. *The Cultivation of Resentment: Treaty Rights and the New Right*. Palo Alto, CA: Stanford University Press.
Earl, Jennifer. 2000. "Methods, Movements, and Outcomes: Methodological Difficulties in the Study of Extra-movement Outcomes." *Research in Social Movements, Conflicts and Change* 22:3–25.
———. 2003. "Tanks, Tear Gas, and Taxes: Toward a Theory of Movement Repression." *Sociological Theory* 21:44–68.
———. 2004. "The Cultural Consequences of Social Movements." In *Blackwell Companion to Social Movements,* ed. D. A. Snow, S. A. Soule, and H. Kriesi. Oxford: Blackwell.
———. 2005. "'You Can Beat the Rap, But You Can't Beat the Ride:' Bringing Arrests Back into Research on Repression." *Research in Social Movements, Conflicts and Change* 26:101–139.
———. 2006. "Introduction: Repression and the Social Control of Protest." *Mobilization* 11:129–143.
———. 2011. "Political Repression: Iron Fists, Velvet Gloves, and Diffuse Control." *Annual Review of Sociology* 37:261–284.
Elegant, Simon. 2003. "The Lion in Winter." *Time* (Asian edition) 161, no. 26 (July 7): 32–36.
Emerson, Robert M., Rachel I. Fretz, and Linda L. Shaw. eds. 1995. *Writing Ethnographic Fieldnotes*. Chicago: University of Chicago Press.
Emirbayer, Mustafa, and Jeff Goodwin. 1994. "Network Analysis, Culture, and the Problem of Agency." *American Journal of Sociology* 99:1411–1454.

Emirbayer, Mustafa, and Ann Mische. 1998. "What Is Agency?" *American Journal of Sociology* 103:962–1023.

Engel, David M., and Frank W. Munger. 1996. "Rights, Remembrance, and the Reconciliation of Difference." *Law and Society Review* 30:7–54.

———. 2003. *Rights of Inclusion: Law and Identity in the Life Stories of Americans with Disabilities.* Chicago: University of Chicago Press.

Epstein, Steven. 1996. *Impure Science: AIDS, Activism, and the Politics of Knowledge.* Berkeley: University of California Press.

———. 1999. "Gay and Lesbian Movements in the United States: Dilemmas of Identity, Diversity, and Political Strategy." In *The Global Emergence of Gay and Lesbian Politics: National Imprints of a Worldwide Movement,* ed. B. Adam, J. W. Duyvendak, and A. Krouwel. Philadelphia: Temple University Press.

Essig, Laurie. 1999. *Queer in Russia.* Durham, NC: Duke University Press.

Ettelbrick, Paula L. 2001. "Domestic Partnership, Civil Unions, or Marriage: One Size Does Not Fit All." *Albany Law Review* 64:905–914.

Evans, Sara, and Harry C. Boyte. 1986. *Free Spaces: The Sources of Democratic Change in America.* New York: Harper and Row.

Ewick, Patricia, and Susan S. Silbey. 1998. *The Common Place of Law: Stories from Everyday Life.* Chicago: University of Chicago Press.

———. 2003. "Narrating Social Structures: Stories of Resistance to Legal Authority." *American Journal of Sociology* 108:1328–1372.

Fantasia, Rick. 1989. *Cultures of Solidarity: Consciousness, Action, and Contemporary American Workers.* Berkeley: University of California Press.

Feeley, Malcolm. 1979. *The Process Is the Punishment: Handling Cases in a Lower Criminal Court.* New York: Russell Sage Foundation.

Felstiner, William L. F., Rick Abel, and Austin Sarat. 1981. "The Emergence and Transformation of Disputes: Naming, Blaming, Claiming . . ." *Law and Society Review* 15:631–654.

Fernandez, Luis A. 2009. *Policing Dissent: Social Control and the Anti-globalization Movement.* New Brunswick, NJ: Rutgers University Press.

Ferree, Myra Marx. 2003. "Resonance and Radicalism: Feminist Framing in the Abortion Debates of the United States and Germany." *American Journal of Sociology* 109:304–344.

Fetner, Tina. 2008. *How the Religious Right Shaped Lesbian and Gay Activism.* Minneapolis: University of Minnesota Press.

Florida, Richard. 2002. *The Rise of the Creative Class: And How It's Transforming Work, Leisure, Community and Everyday Life.* New York: Basic Books.

Fong Hoe Fang, ed. 2012. *That We May Dream Again.* Singapore: Select Books.

Foucault, Michel. 1977. *Discipline and Punish: The Birth of the Prison.* Trans. Alan Sheridan. New York: Vintage Books.

Freeman, Linton C., A. Kimball Romney, and Sue C. Freeman. 1987. "Cognitive Structure and Informant Accuracy." *American Anthropologist* 89:310–325.

Friedrich, Carl, and Zbiegniew Brzezinski. 1956. *Totalitarian Dictatorship and Autocracy.* New York: Praeger.

Frye, Margaret. 2012. "Bright Futures in Malawi's New Dawn: Educational Aspirations as Assertions of Identity." *American Journal of Sociology* 117:1565–1624.

Galanter, Marc. 1974. "Why the Haves Come out Ahead: Speculations on the Limits of Legal Change." *Law and Society Review* 9:95–160.

———. 1983. "The Radiating Effects of Courts." In *Empirical Theories about Courts,* ed. K. Boyum and L. Mather. New York: Longmans.

Gamson, Josh. 1989. "Silence, Death, and the Invisible Enemy: AIDS Activism and Social Movement 'Newness.'" *Social Problems* 37:351–367.

———. 1995. "Must Identity Movements Self-Destruct? A Queer Dilemma." *Social Problems* 42:390–407.
Gamson, William, and David Meyer. 1996. "Framing Political Opportunity." In *Comparative Perspectives on Social Movements: Political Opportunities, Mobilizing Structures, and Cultural Framings*, ed. D. McAdam, J. D. McCarthy, and M. N. Zald. New York: Cambridge University Press.
George, Cherian. 2006. *Contentious Journalism and the Internet: Towards Democratic Discourse in Malaysia and Singapore*. Seattle: University of Washington Press.
———. 2012. *Freedom from the Press: Journalism and State Power in Singapore*. Singapore: National University of Singapore Press.
Gevisser, Mark. 1995. "A Different Fight for Freedom: A History of South African Lesbian and Gay Organisation from the 1950s to the 1990s." In *Defiant Desire: Gay and Lesbian Lives in South Africa*, ed. M. Gevisser and E. Cameron. New York: Routledge.
Giddens, Anthony. 1984. *The Constitution of Society*. Berkeley: University of California Press.
Gilliom, John. 2001. *Overseers of the Poor: Surveillance, Resistance, and the Limits of Privacy*. Chicago: University of Chicago Press.
Ginsburg, Tom, and Tamir Moustafa, eds. 2008. *Rule by Law: The Politics of Courts in Authoritarian Regimes*. Cambridge: Cambridge University Press.
Glaser, Barney G., and Anselm L. Strauss. 1967. *The Discovery of Grounded Theory: Strategies for Qualitative Research*. New Brunswick, NJ: AldineTransaction.
Glendon, Mary Ann. 1991. *Rights Talk: The Impoverishment of Political Discourse*. New York: Free Press.
Goffman, Erving. 1974. *Frame Analysis: An Essay on the Organization of the Experience*. New York: Harper and Row.
Goh, Daniel P. S. 2010. "State and Social Christianity in Post-colonial Singapore." *Journal of Social Issues in Southeast Asia* 25:54–89.
Goh, Debbie. 2008. "It's the Gays' Fault: News and HIV as Weapons against Homosexuality in Singapore." *Journal of Communication Inquiry* 32:383–399.
Goldberg-Hiller, Jon. 2004. *The Limits to Union: Same-sex Marriage and the Politics of Civil Rights*. Ann Arbor: University of Michigan Press.
Goldberg-Hiller, Jonathan, and Neal Milner. 2003. "Rights as Excess: Understanding the Politics of Special Rights." *Law and Social Inquiry* 28:1075–1118.
Goodwin, Jeff, James M. Jasper, and Francesca Polletta. 2001. *Passionate Politics: Emotions and Social Movements*. Chicago: University of Chicago Press.
Gould, Deborah. 2009. *Moving Politics*. Chicago: University of Chicago Press.
Gould, Roger V. 1991. "Multiple Networks and Mobilization in the Paris Commune, 1871." *American Sociological Review* 56:716–729.
Graff, Agnieszka. 2006. "We Are (Not All) Homophobes: A Report from Poland." *Feminist Studies* 32:434–449.
Green, James N. 2000. "Desire and Militancy: Lesbians, Gays, and the Brazilian Workers Party." In *Different Rainbows*, ed. P. Drucker. London: Millivers.
Greenhouse, Carol J., Barbara Yngvesson, and David Engel. 1994. *Law and Community in Three American Towns*. Ithaca, NY: Cornell University Press.
Griffiths, John. 1986. "What is Legal Pluralism?" *Journal of Legal Pluralism and Unofficial Law* 24:1–55.
Gross, Neil. 2009. "A Pragmatist Theory of Social Mechanisms." *American Sociological Review* 74:358–379.
Gruszczynska, Anna. 2009. "Sowing the Seeds of Solidarity in Public Space: Case Study of the Poznan March of Equality." *Sexualities* 12:312–333.
Habermas, Jürgen. 1984. *Theory of Communicative Action*. Trans. Thomas McCarthy. Boston: Beacon Press.

Hagan, John. 2000. "Narrowing the Gap by Widening the Conflict: Power Politics, Symbols of Sovereignty, and the American Vietnam War Resisters' Migration to Canada." *Law and Society Review* 34:607–650.
Handler, Joel. 1992. "Postmodernism, Protest and the New Social Movements." *Law and Society Review* 26:697–732.
Heng, Geraldine. 1997. "A Great Way to Fly: Nationalism, the State and Varieties of Third World Feminism." In *Feminist Genealogies, Colonial Legacies, Democratic Futures*, ed. M. Alexander and C. T. Mohanty. New York: Routledge.
Heng, Geraldine, and Janadas Devan. 1992. "State Fatherhood: The Politics of Nationalism, Sexuality, and Race in Singapore." In *Nationalism and Sexualities,* ed. A. Parker, M. Russo, D. Sommer, and P. Yaeger. New York: Routledge.
Heng, Russell Hiang Khng. 2001. "Tiptoe out of the Closet: The before and after of the Increasingly Visible Gay Community in Singapore." In *Gay and Lesbian Asia: Culture, Identity, Community,* ed. G. Sullivan and P. A. Jackson. New York: Harrington Park Press.
Heritage Foundation. 2011. *Economic Freedom Index.* Washington, DC: Heritage Foundation.
Hewitt, Lyndi, and Holly J. McCammon. 2004. "Explaining Suffrage Mobilization: Balance, Neutralization, and Range in Collective Action Frames, 1892–1919." *Mobilization* 9:149–166.
Hildebrandt, Timothy. 2013. *Social Organizations and the Authoritarian State in China.* New York: Cambridge University Press.
Hill, Michael, and Kwen Fee Lian. 1995. *The Politics of Nation Building and Citizenship in Singapore.* New York: Routledge.
Hirshman, Linda. 2012. *Victory: The Triumphant Gay Revolution.* New York: Harper.
Hoad, Neville. 1999. "Between the White Man's Burden and the White Man's Disease." *GLQ: A Journal of Lesbian and Gay Studies* 5:559–584.
Hoffman, Bruce. 2008. "Minding the Gap: Legal Ideals and Strategic Action in State Legislative Hearings." *Law and Social Inquiry* 33:89–126.
Hoffmann, Elizabeth. 2005. "Dispute Resolution in a Worker Cooperative: Formal Procedures and Procedural Justice." *Law and Society Review* 39:51–82.
Hong, Lysa, and Jianli Huang. 2008. *The Scripting of a National History: Singapore and Its Pasts.* Hong Kong: Hong Kong University Press.
Hor, Michael. 2012. "Enforcement of 377A: Entering the Twilight Zone." In *Queer Singapore: Illiberal Citizenship and Mediated Culture,* ed. A. Yue and J. Zubillaga-Pow. Hong Kong: Hong Kong University Press.
Hull, Kathleen E. 2001. "The Political Limits of the Rights Frame: The Case of Same-sex Marriage in Hawaii." *Sociological Perspectives* 44:207–232.
International Commission of Jurists. 1987. "Singapore—International Mission of Jurists to Singapore Dismisses Allegations of 'Marxist Conspiracy.'" Available at http://www.icj.org. (Search in "ICJ Legal Resource Center" for "Singapore" under "Administration of Justice.") Accessed October 10, 2013.
Jasper, James M. 1997. *The Art of Moral Protest.* Chicago: University of Chicago Press.
Jasper, James M., and Jane Poulsen. 1993. "Fighting Back: Vulnerabilities, Blunders, and Countermobilization by the Targets in Three Animal Rights Campaigns." *Sociological Forum* 8:639–657.
Joas, Hans. 1997. *The Creativity of Action.* Chicago: University of Chicago Press.
Johnston, Hank. 2005. "Talking the Walk: Speech Acts and Resistance in Authoritarian Regimes." In *Repression and Mobilization,* ed. C. Davenport, C. Mueller, and H. Johnston. Minneapolis: University of Minnesota Press.
———. 2006. "'Let's Get Small': The Dynamics of (Small) Contention in Repressive States." *Mobilization* 11:195–212.

Johnston, Hank, and Bert Klandersman, eds. 1995. *Social Movements and Culture.* Minneapolis: University of Minnesota Press.
Keck, Margaret E., and Kathryn Sikkink. 1998. *Activists beyond Borders: Advocacy Networks in International Politics.* Ithaca, NY: Cornell University Press.
Keshishoglou, John, and Pieter Aquilia. 2004. *Electronic Broadcast Media in Singapore and the Region.* Singapore: Nanyang Technological University.
Kirchheimer, Otto. 1961. *Political Justice: The Use of Legal Procedure for Political Ends.* Princeton. NJ: Princeton University Press.
Kostiner, Idit. 2003. "Evaluating Legality: Toward a Cultural Approach to the Study of Law and Social Change." *Law and Society Review* 37:323–368.
Kriesi, Hanspeter, Ruud Koopmans, Jan Willem Duyvendak, and Marco G. Giugni. 1995. *The Politics of New Social Movements in Western Europe.* Minneapolis: Minnesota University Press.
Krippendorff, Klaus. 2004. *Content Analysis: An Introduction to Its Methodology.* Thousand Oaks, CA: Sage Publications.
Kurzman, Charles. 1996. "Structural Opportunity and Perceived Opportunity in Social-Movement Theory: The Iranian Revolution of 1979." *American Sociological Review* 61:153–170.
Laraña, Enrique, Hank Johnston, and Joseph R. Gusfield, eds. 1994. *New Social Movements: From Ideology to Identity.* Philadelphia: Temple University Press.
Lee Kuan Yew. 1998. *The Singapore Story: Memoirs of Lee Kuan Yew.* Singapore: Times Editions.
Leifer, Michael. 1964. "Communal Violence in Singapore." *Asian Survey* 4:1115–1121.
Leong, Laurence Wai-Teng. 2005. "The 'Straight' Times: News Media and Sexual Citizenship in Singapore." In *Journalism and Democracy in Asia,* ed. A. Romano and M. Bromley. Abingdon, UK: Routledge.
———. 2008. "Decoding Sexual Policy in Singapore." In *Social Policy in Post-Industrial Singapore,* ed. K. F. Lian Kwen Fee and C. K. Tong. Boston: Brill.
———. 2010. "Sexual Governance and the Politics of Sex in Singapore." In *Management of Success: Singapore Revisited,* ed. T. Chong. Singapore: Institute of Southeast Asian Studies.
———. 2012. "Sexual Vigilantes Invade Gender Spaces: Religion and Sexuality in the AWARE Saga." In *Queer Singapore: Illiberal Citizenship and Mediated Culture,* ed. A. Yue and J. Zubillaga-Pow. Hong Kong: Hong Kong University Press.
Leow, Yangfa. 2013. *I Will Survive: Personal Gay, Lesbian, Bisexual, and Transgender Stories in Singapore.* Singapore: Monsoon Books.
Lim, Eng Beng. 2005. "Glocalqueering in New Asia: The Politics of Performing Gay in Singapore." *Theatre Journal* 57:383–405.
———. 2013. "'Glocalqueer Pink Activism,' Scales of Production: Public Activism and the Performing Arts." In *Performance, Politics and Activism,* ed. P. Lichtenfels and J. Rouse. New York: Palgrave Macmillan.
Lim Meng Suang and Kenneth Chee Mun-Leon v. Attorney-General. 2013. Singapore High Court 73.
Linz, Juan. 1975. "Totalitarian and Authoritarian Regimes." In *Macropolitical Theory,* ed. F. Greenstein and N. Polsby. Boston: Addison-Wesley.
———. 2000. *Totalitarian and Authoritarian Regime.* London: Lynne Rienner.
Lo, Jacqueline. 2004. *Staging Nation: English Language Theatre in Malaysia and Singapore.* Hong Kong: Hong Kong University Press.
Lofland, John, and Rodney Stark. 1965. "Becoming A World-saver: A Theory of Religious Conversion." *American Sociological Review* 30:862–874.
Long, Scott. 1999. "Gay and Lesbian Movements in Eastern Europe: Romania, Hungary, and the Czech Republic." In *The Global Emergence of Gay and Lesbian Politics: National*

Imprints of a Worldwide Movement, ed. B. Adam, J. W. Duyvendak, and A. Krouwel. Philadelphia: Temple University Press.

Lovell, George I. 2012. "The Myth of the Myth of Rights." *Special Issue: The Legacy of Stuart Scheingold (Studies in Law, Politics, and Society)* 59:1–30.

Loveman, Mara. 1998. "High-risk Collective Action: Defending Human Rights in Chile, Uruguay, and Argentina." *American Journal of Sociology* 104:477–525.

Lukács, Georg. 1920. "Legality and Illegality." In *History and Class Consciousness,* ed. G. Lukács. Available at http://www.marxists.org/archive/lukacs/works/history/ch06.htm. Accessed March 2012.

Luker, Kristin. 2008. *Salsa-dancing into the Social Sciences: Research in an Age of Info-glut.* Cambridge, MA: Harvard University Press.

Lukes, Steven. 1974. *Power: A Radical View.* New York: Palgrave Macmillan.

Lyons, Lenore. 2004. *A State of Ambivalence: The Feminist Movement in Singapore.* Leiden, The Netherlands: Brill.

Mansbridge, Jane, and Aldon Morris, eds. 2001. *Oppositional Consciousness: The Subjective Roots of Social Protest.* Chicago: University of Chicago Press.

Marotta, Toby. 1981. *The Politics of Homosexuality.* Boston: Houghton Mifflin.

Massad, Joseph A. 2007. *Desiring Arabs.* Chicago: University of Chicago Press.

Massoud, Mark Fathi. 2011. "Do Victims of War Need International Law? Human Rights Education Programs in Authoritarian Sudan." *Law and Society Review* 45: 1–31.

Mather, Lynn. 1998. "Theorizing about Trial Courts: Lawyers, Policymaking, and Tobacco Litigation. *Law and Social Inquiry* 23:897–940.

Maulod, Nur'Adlina, and Nurhaizatul Jamila Jamil. 2010. "'Because Allah Says So': Faithful Bodies, Female Masculinities, and the Malay Muslim Community of Singapore." In *Islam and Homosexuality,* ed. S. Habib. Oxford: Praeger.

Mauzy, Diane K., and R. S. Milne. 2002. *Singapore Politics under the People's Action Party.* London: Routledge.

Maynard-Moody, Steven, and Michael Musheno. 2003. *Cops, Teachers, Counselors: Stories from the Front Lines of Public Service.* Ann Arbor: University of Michigan Press.

McAdam, Doug. 1983. "Tactical Innovation and the Pace of Insurgency." *American Sociological Review* 48:735–754.

———. 1986. "Recruitment to High-risk Activism: The Case of Freedom Summer." *American Journal of Sociology* 92:64–90.

———. 1994. "Culture and Social Movements." In *New Social Movements: From Ideology to Identity,* ed. E. Laraña, H. Johnston, and J. R. Gusfield. Philadelphia: Temple University Press.

———. 1996. "Conceptual Origins, Current Problems, Future Directions." In *Comparative Perspectives on Social Movements: Political Opportunities, Mobilizing Structures, and Cultural Framings,* ed. D. McAdam, J. D. McCarthy, and M. N. Zald. New York: Cambridge University Press.

———. 1999. *Political Process and the Development of Black Insurgency,* 1930–1950, 2nd ed. Chicago: University of Chicago Press.

———. 2003. "Beyond Structural Analysis: Toward a More Dynamic Understanding of Social Movements." In *Social Movements and Networks,* ed. M. Diani and D. McAdam. Oxford: Oxford University Press.

McAdam, Doug, John D. McCarthy, and Mayer N. Zald. eds. 1996. *Comparative Perspectives on Social Movements: Political Opportunities, Mobilizing Structures, and Cultural Framings.* New York: Cambridge University Press.

McCammon, Holly J., Soma Chaudhuri, Lyndi Hewitt, Courtney Sanders Muse, Harmony D. Newman, Carrie Lee Smith, and Teresa M. Terrell. 2008. "Becoming

Full Citizens: The U.S. Women's Jury Rights Campaigns, the Pace of Reform, and Strategic Adaptation." *American Journal of Sociology* 113:1104–1147.
McCann, Michael. 1994. *Rights at Work: Pay Equity Reform and the Politics of Legal Mobilization.* Chicago: University of Chicago Press.
Melucci, Alberto. 1985. "The Symbolic Challenge of Contemporary Movements." *Social Research* 52:789–816.
Merry, Sally E. 1988. "Legal Pluralism." *Law and Society Review* 22:869–896.
———. 1990. *Getting Justice and Getting Even: Legal Consciousness among Working-Class Americans.* Chicago: University of Chicago Press.
———. 1995. "Resistance and the Cultural Power of Law." *Law and Society Review* 29:11–26.
———. 1999. *Colonizing Hawai'i: The Cultural Power of Law.* Princeton, NJ: Princeton University Press.
———. 2006. *Human Rights and Gender Violence: Translating International Law into Local Justice.* Chicago: University of Chicago Press.
Meyer, David S. 2004. "Protest and Political Opportunities." *Annual Review of Sociology* 30:125–145.
Meyer, David S., and Steven A. Boutcher. 2007. "Signals and Spillover: Brown v. Board of Education and Other Social Movements." *Perspectives on Politics* 5:81–93.
Meyer, David S., and Suzanne Staggenborg. 1996. "Movements, Countermovements, and the Structure of Political Opportunity." *American Journal of Sociology* 101:1628–1660.
Meyer, David S., Nancy Whittier, and Belinda Robnett. eds. 2002. *Social Movements: Identity, Culture, and the State.* New York: Oxford University Press.
Mills, C. Wright. 2000. *The Sociological Imagination.* New York: Oxford University Press.
Mische, Ann. 1997. "Projects, Identities, and Social Networks: Brazilian Youth Mobilization and the Making of Civic Culture." Paper presented at the annual meeting of the American Sociological Association, Toronto, Ontario, Canada.
Mitchell, Timothy. 1990. "Everyday Metaphors of Power." *Theory and Society* 19:545–577.
Mnookin, Robert, and L. Kornhauser. 1979. "Bargaining in the Shadow of the Law: The Case of Divorce." *Yale Law Journal* 88:950–997.
Mogrovejo, Norma. 2000. "Lesbian Visibility in Latin America: Reclaiming Our History." In *Different Rainbows*, ed. P. Drucker. London: Millivers.
Moore, Barrington, Jr. 1966. *Social Origins of Dictatorship and Democracy: Lord and Peasant in the Making of the Modern World.* Boston: Beacon Press.
Moore, Sally Falk. 1973. "Law and Social Change: The Semi-autonomous Social Field as an Appropriate Subject of Study." *Law and Society Review* 7:719–746.
Morrill, Calvin. 1995. *The Executive Way: Conflict Management in Corporations.* Chicago: University of Chicago Press.
Morris, Aldon. 1984. *The Origins of the Civil Rights Movement.* New York: Free Press.
Moustafa, Tamir. 2007. *The Struggle for Constitutional Power: Law, Politics, and Economic Reform in Egypt.* New York: Cambridge University Press.
Munck, Gerardo. 1998. *Authoritarianism and Democratization.* University Park, PA: Penn State University Press.
Naz Foundation v. Govt. of NCT of Delhi. 2009. (Indian Delhi High Court.) *Delhi Law Times* 160:277.
Nemtsev, Mikhail. 2008. "How Did a Sexual Minorities Movement Emerge in Post-Soviet Russia?" Unpublished paper, Central European University.
Ng, King Kang. 1999. *The Rainbow Connection: The Internet and the Singapore Gay Community.* Singapore: KangCuBine Publishing.
Ng, Yi-Sheng. 2006. *SQ21: Singapore Queers in the 21st Century.* Singapore: Oogachaga.
Nielsen, Laura Beth. 2004. *License to Harass: Law, Hierarchy, and Offensive Public Speech.* Princeton, NJ: Princeton University Press.

Obendorf, Simon. 2013. "A Few Respectable Steps behind the World? Gay and Lesbian Rights in Contemporary Singapore." In *Orientation, Gender Identity and Human Rights in the Commonwealth: Struggles for Decriminalisation and Change*, ed. C. Lennox and M. Waites. London: School of Advanced Study, University of London.

Oberschall, Anthony. 1978. "The Decline of the 1960s Social Movements." *Research in Social Movements, Conflicts and Change* 1:257–289.

O'Brien, Kevin J., and Lianjiang Li. 2006. *Rightful Resistance in Rural China*. New York: Cambridge University Press.

Offord, Baden. 2000. "Singapore." In *Gay Histories and Cultures: An Encyclopedia*, Vol. 2, ed. G. E. Haggerty. New York: Garland.

Oliver, Pamela E., and Hank Johnston. 2000. "What a Good Idea: Frames and Ideology in Social Movement Research." *Mobilization* 5:37–54.

Oswin, Natalie. 2010. "The Modern Model Family at Home in Singapore: A Queer Geography." *Transactions of the Institute of British Geographers* 35:256–268.

Palmberg, Mai. 1999. "Emerging Visibility of Gays and Lesbians in Southern Africa: Contrasting Contexts." In *The Global Emergence of Gay and Lesbian Politics: National Imprints of a Worldwide Movement*, ed. B. Adam, J. W. Duyvendak, and A. Krouwel. Philadelphia: Temple University Press.

Patton, Cindy. 1990. *Inventing AIDS*. New York: Routledge.

Payne, Charles. 1996. *I've Got the Light of Freedom: The Organizing Tradition and the Mississippi Freedom Struggle*. Berkeley: University of California Press.

Peerenboom, Randall P. 2004. "Varieties of Rule of Law: An Introduction and Provisional Conclusion." In *Asian Discourses of Rule of Law*, ed. R. P. Peerenboom. London: Routledge.

Perlmutter, Amos. 1981. *Modern Authoritarianism*. New Haven, CT: Yale University Press.

Piven, Frances Fox, and Richard A. Cloward. 1977. *Poor People's Movements: Why They Succeed, How They Fail*. New York: Pantheon Books.

Plummer, Ken. 1999. "The Lesbian and Gay Movement in Britain: Schisms, Solidarities, and Social Worlds." In *The Global Emergence of Gay and Lesbian Politics: National Imprints of a Worldwide Movement*, ed. B. Adam, J. W. Duyvendak, and A. Krouwel. Philadelphia: Temple University Press.

Polikoff, Nancy D. 1993. "We Will Get What We Ask for: Why Legalizing Gay and Lesbian Marriage Will Not 'Dismantle the Legal Structure of Gender in Every Marriage.'" *Virginia Law Review* 79:1535–1550.

Polletta, Francesca. 1999a. "'Free Spaces' in Collective Action." *Theory and Society* 28:1–38.

———. 1999b. "Snarls, Quacks, and Quarrels: Culture and Structure in Political Process Theory." *Sociological Forum* 14:63–70.

———. 2000. "The Structural Context of Novel Rights Claims: Southern Civil Rights Organizing, 1961–1966." *Law and Society Review* 34:367–406.

———. 2002. *Freedom Is an Endless Meeting: Democracy in American Social Movements*. Chicago: University of Chicago Press.

———. 2004. "Culture Is Not Just in Your Head." In *Rethinking Social Movements: Structure, Meaning, and Emotion*, ed. J. Goodwin and J. M. Jasper. Lanham, MD: Rowman and Littlefield.

Polletta, Francesca, and James M. Jasper. 2001. "Collective Identity and Social Movements." *Annual Review of Sociology* 27:283–305.

Puru Shotam, Nirmala. 2000. *Negotiating Multiculturalism: Disciplining Difference in Singapore*. New York: Mouton de Gruyter.

Rajah, Jothie. 2012. *Authoritarian Rule of Law: Legislation, Discourse and Legitimacy in Singapore*. New York: Cambridge University Press.

Ray, Raka. 1999. *Fields of Protest: Women's Movements in India*. Berkeley: University of California Press.

Reger, Jo. 2002. "More than One Feminism: Organizational Structure and the Construction of Collective Identity." In *Social Movements: Identity, Culture, and the State,* ed. D. S. Meyer, N. Whittier, and B. Robnett. New York: Oxford University Press.

Report of the Censorship Review Committee. 1992. Singapore: Republic of Singapore.

Report of the Censorship Review Committee. 2003. Singapore: Republic of Singapore.

Rodan, Garry. 2003. "Embracing Electronic Media but Suppressing Civil Society: Authoritarian Consolidation in Singapore." *Pacific Review* 16:503–524.

———. 2004. *Transparency and Authoritarian Rule in Southeast Asia: Singapore and Malaysia.* London: Routledge.

Rosenberg, Gerald. 2008. *The Hollow Hope: Can Courts Bring about Social Change?* 2nd ed. Chicago: University of Chicago Press.

Rupp, Leila, and Verta Taylor. 1987. *Survival in the Doldrums: The American Women's Rights Movement: 1945–1960.* New York: Oxford University Press.

Sanders, Douglas E. 2009. "377 and the Unnatural Afterlife of British Colonialism in Asia." *Asian Journal of Comparative Law* 4:1–49.

Sarat, Austin. 1990. "'. . . The Law Is All Over': Power, Resistance and the Legal Consciousness of the Welfare Poor." *Yale Journal of Law and the Humanities* 2:343–379.

Sawyers, Traci M., and David S. Meyer. 1999. "Missed Opportunities: Social Movement Abeyance and Public Policy." *Social Problems* 46:187–206.

Scheingold, Stuart A. 2004. *The Politics of Rights: Lawyers, Public Policy, and Political Change,* 2nd ed. Ann Arbor: University of Michigan Press.

Schwartz, Mildred A. 2002. "Factions and the Continuity of Political Challengers." In *Social Movements: Identity, Culture, and the State,* ed. D. S. Meyer, N. Whittier, and B. Robnett. New York: Oxford University Press.

Scott, James C. 1985. *Weapons of the Weak: Everyday Forms of Resistance.* New Haven, CT: Yale University Press.

———. 1990. *Domination and the Arts of Resistance: Hidden Transcripts.* New Haven, CT: Yale University Press.

Seidman, S. 1993. "Identity Politics in a 'Postmodern' Gay Culture: Some Historical and Conceptual Notes." In *Fear of a Queer Planet: Queer Politics and Social Theory,* ed. M. Warner. Minneapolis: University of Minnesota Press.

Seow, Francis. 1994. *To Catch A Tartar: A Dissident in Lee Kuan Yew's Prison.* New Haven, CT: Yale University Press.

———. 1998. *The Media Enthralled: Singapore Revisited.* Boulder, CO: Lynne Rienner Publishers.

Sewell, William H., Jr. 1992. "A Theory of Structure: Duality, Agency, and Transformation." *American Journal of Sociology* 98:1–29.

Silbey, Susan. 2005. "After Legal Consciousness." *Annual Review of Law and Social Science* 1:323–368.

Silverstein, Gordon. 2003. "Globalization and the Rule of Law: 'A Machine that Runs of Itself?'" *International Journal of Constitutional Law* 1:427–445.

Silverstein, Helena. 1996. *Unleashing Rights: Law, Meaning, and the Animal Rights Movement.* Ann Arbor: University of Michigan Press.

Snow, David, and Robert Benford. 1988. "Ideology, Frame Resonance, and Participant Mobilization." *International Social Movement Research* 1:197–218.

———. 1992. "Master Frames and Cycles of Protest." In *Frontiers in Social Movement Theory,* ed. A. D. Morris and C. M. Mueller. New Haven, CT: Yale University Press.

———. 2000. "Framing Processes and Social Movements: An Overview and Assessment." *Annual Review of Sociology* 26:611–639.

Snow, David A., and Richard Machalek. 1984. "The Sociology of Conversion." *Annual Review of Sociology* 10:167–190.

Snow, David A., Calvin Morrill, and Leon Anderson. 2003. "Elaborating Analytic Ethnography: Linking Fieldwork and Theory." *Ethnography* 4:182–200.
Snow, David A., E. Burke Rochford, Jr., Steven K. Worden, and Robert D. Benford. 1986. "Frame Alignment Processes, Micromobilization, and Movement Participation." *American Sociological Review* 51 (4): 464–481.
Snow, David A., Louis A. Zurcher, Jr., and Sheldon Ekland-Olson. 1980. "Social Networks and Social Movements: A Microstructural Approach to Differential Recruitment." *American Sociological Review* 45:787–801.
Snow, David A., Louis A. Zurcher, Jr., and Gideon Sjoberg. 1982. "Interviewing by Comment: An Adjunct to the Direct Question." *Qualitative Sociology* 5:462–476.
Spires, Anthony J. 2011. "Contingent Symbiosis and Civil Society in an Authoritarian State: Understanding the Survival of China's Grassroots NGOs." *American Journal of Sociology* 117:1–45.
Stein, Arlene, and Ken Plummer. 1994. "I Can't Even Think Straight: 'Queer' Theory and the Missing Sexual Revolution in Sociology." *Sociological Theory* 12:178–187.
Steinberg, Marc W. 1999. "The Talk and Back Talk of Collective Action: A Dialogic Analysis of Repertoires of Discourse among Nineteenth-century English Cotton Spinners." *American Journal of Sociology* 105:736–780.
Stern, Rachel E. 2013. *Environmental Litigation in China: A Study in Political Ambivalence.* New York: Cambridge University Press.
Stockdill, Brett C. 2003. *Activism against AIDS: At the Intersections of Sexuality, Race, Gender, and Class.* Boulder, CO: Lynne Rienner Publishers.
Sun, Shirley Hsiao-Li. 2011. *Population Policy and Reproduction in Singapore: Making Future Citizens.* London: Routledge.
Swidler, Ann. 1986. "Culture in Action: Symbols and Strategies." *American Sociological Review* 51:273–286.
Tan Boon Hock v. Public Prosecutor. 1994. (Singapore High Court.) *Singapore Law Reports* 2:150.
Tan, Chris K. K. 2009. "'But They Are Like You and Me': Gay Civil Servants and Citizenship in a Cosmopolitanizing Singapore." *City and Society* 21:133–154.
———. 2012. "Oi, Recruit! Wake up Your Idea!': Homosexuality and Cultural Citizenship in the Singaporean Military." In *Queer Singapore: Illiberal Citizenship and Mediated Culture,* ed. A. Yue and J. Zubillaga-Pow. Hong Kong: Hong Kong University Press.
Tan Eng Hong v. Attorney-General. 2011. (Singapore High Court.) Unreported judgment.
Tan Eng Hong v. Attorney-General. 2012. Singapore Court of Appeal 45.
Tan Eng Hong v. Attorney-General. 2013. Singapore High Court 199.
Tan, Kenneth Paul, and Gary Lee Jack Jin. 2007. "Imaging the Gay Community in Singapore." *Critical Asian Studies* 39:179–204.
Tate, C. Neal. 1995. "Why the Expansion of Judicial Power?" In *The Global Expansion of Judicial Power,* ed. C. N. Tate and T. Vallinder. New York: New York University Press.
Taylor, Verta. 1989. "Social Movement Continuity: The Women's Movement in Abeyance." *American Sociological Review* 54:761–775.
Taylor, Verta, Katrina Kimport, and Nella Van Dyke. 2009. "Culture and Mobilization: Tactical Repertoires, Same-sex Weddings, and the Impact on Gay Activism." *American Sociological Review* 74:865–890.
Taylor, Verta, and Nancy Whittier. 1992. "Collective Identity in Social Movement Communities: Lesbian Feminist Mobilization." In *Frontiers in Social Movement Theory,* ed. A. D. Morris and C. M. Mueller. New Haven, CT: Yale University Press.
———. 1995. "Analytical Approaches to Social Movement Culture: The Culture of the Women's Movement." In *Social Movements and Culture,* ed. H. Johnston and B. Klandersman. Minneapolis: University of Minnesota Press.

Teo, Soh Lung. 2010. *Beyond the Blue Gate: Recollections of a Political Prisoner.* Singapore: Ethos Books.

Thayer, Millie. 1997. "Identity, Revolution, and Democracy: Lesbian Movements in Central America." *Social Problems* 44:386–407.

Thio Li-Ann. 2004. "'Pragmatism and Realism Do Not Mean Abdication': A Critical and Empirical Inquiry into Singapore's Engagement with International Human Rights Law." *Singapore Yearbook of International Law* 8:41–91.

Thio Su Mien. 2003. "No to Homosexuality." *Streats,* July 29.

Thompson, E. P. 1975. *Whigs and Hunters: The Origin of the Black Act.* New York: Pantheon Books.

Tilly, Charles. 1978. *From Mobilization to Revolution.* Reading, MA: Addison-Wesley.

Tilly, Charles, and Sidney Tarrow. 2007. *Contentious Politics.* Boulder, CO: Paradigm Publishers.

Tsai, Kellee S. 2007. *Capitalism without Democracy: The Private Sector in Contemporary China.* Ithaca, NY: Cornell University Press.

Turnbull, C. M. 2009. *A History of Modern Singapore 1819-2005.* Singapore: National University of Singapore Press.

Vaid, Urvashi. 1995. *Virtual Equality: The Mainstreaming of Gay and Lesbian Liberation.* New York: Anchor Books.

Valocchi, Steve. 1999. "Riding the Crest of the Protest Wave? Collective Action Frames in the Gay Liberation Movement, 1969–1973." *Mobilization* 4:59–73.

Vasil, Raj. 1995. *Asianising Singapore—The PAP's Management of Ethnicity.* Singapore: Heineman Asia.

Wachter, Robert. 1992. "AIDS, Activism, and the Politics of Health." *New England Journal of Medicine* 326:128–133.

Wang, Look Fung, and Nancy Teo. 1993. "Public Life and Leadership." In *Singapore Women: Three Decades of Change,* ed. A. K. Wong and W. K. Leong. Singapore: Times Academic Press.

Weiss, Meredith. 2006. "Rejection as Freedom? HIV/AIDS Organizations and Identity." *Perspectives on Politics* 4:671–678.

———. 2013. "Prejudice before Pride: Rise of an Anticipatory Countermovement." In *Global Homophobia: States, Movements, and the Politics of Oppression,* ed. M. Weiss and M. Bosia. Champaign: University of Illinois Press.

Werum, Regina, and Bill Winders. 2001. "Who's 'in' and Who's 'out': State Fragmentation and the Struggle over Gay Rights, 1974–1999." *Social Problems* 48:386–410.

Whitford, Josh. 2002. "Pragmatism and the Untenable Dualism of Means and Ends: Why Rational Choice Theory Does Not Deserve Paradigmatic Privilege." *Theory and Society* 31:325–363.

Whittier, Nancy. 1995. *Feminist Generations: The Persistence of the Radical Women's Movement.* Philadelphia: Temple University Press.

Winnow, Jackie. 1992. "Lesbians Evolving Health Care: Cancer and AIDS." *Feminist Review* 41:68–76.

Wong, Tessa. 2007. "Homosexuality: Older Youth More Open and Better Informed." *Straits Times,* September 24, p. 31.

Yue, Audrey. 2007. "Creative Queer Singapore: The Illiberal Pragmatics of Cultural Production." *Gay and Lesbian Issues and Psychology Review* 3:149–160.

Yue, Audrey, and Jun Zubillaga-Pow, eds. 2012. *Queer Singapore: Illiberal Citizenship and Mediated Culture.* Hong Kong: Hong Kong University Press.

Zemans, Frances. 1983. "Legal Mobilization: The Neglected Role of the Law in the Political System." *American Political Science Review* 77:690–703.

Index

Abby (interviewee), 55, 66–67, 87–88, 94, 103, 104, 105, 123, 132, 163
Abuse Suxx (play), 81
Adalyn (interviewee), 103, 139
Aidan (interviewee), 68, 74, 76
Ai-Mee (interviewee), 104–105, 113–115
Al Qaeda, 31
Ang Siang Hill, 48
Another Tribe (play), 54. *See also* Fong, Otto
Argot, 52, 62, 175
Asian Boys (play). *See* Sa'at, Alfian
AWARE (Association of Women for Action and Research), 46, 49, 122–125, 126, 129, 132, 138, 194n3

Beach Road, 1, 2
Beacon, 68–69, 71, 104, 122, 127; counseling service of, 88–89; formal development of, 86–90; neglect of women by, 72
Bedok Stadium, 48
Billy (interviewee), 67–69, 76, 88–91 passim, 122, 123, 155
Bistro, Le (gay club), 47
Black, Dustin Lance (director), 39
Bowers v. Hardwick reversal (U.S. Supreme Court, 2003), 8, 9
Brandon (interviewee), 71
Brett (activist), 59, 67, 123

Broadcasting Act, 31
Buddhism, 42, 70, 185

Censorship, 39, 48, 83; of the Internet, 63–64; through licensing, 31, 95–96; policy reviews of (1992, 2003), 54, 81; resistance to, 6; in theater, 80–81; in the United States, 6, 8, 12
Chan (interviewee), 16
Chan Mun Chiong, 195n18
Chay Yew (playwright), 48
Chee Soon Juan, 80, 193n4 (chap. 6)
Cheryl (interviewee), 52, 53, 62, 66, 100
Chew, Paddy, 80–81
Christian Fellowship, 67–70, 71, 76, 88, 122
Christianity: demise of liberal form of, 47, 90; role of, 42–43, 49, 52, 67–69, 185. *See also* Christian Fellowship; Christian Right; Harbor; "Reparative therapy," Christian
Christian Right, 9, 24, 107, 115–116, 138
Christians in Singapore, 28, 42
Civil rights movement, influence of, 188n8
Coalition (gay organization), 49–62, 64–65, 74, 104; newsletter by, 51, 52, 56, 59, 64, 170; registration attempts by, 81–83, 84, 85–94, 112
Cognitive liberation, 142
Collective mobilization, 5, 6, 30–33, 147, 152–153

Coming out: as individuals, 42, 104; meanings of, 190–191n24; as a movement, 23, 51, 95, 101, 105; reaction to, 115–117
Common Place of Law, The (Ewick and Silbey), 164
Communism, 29, 31, 46–47, 188n10, 189n7
Company organization tactic, 59, 88–90
Completely With/Out Character (play), 80
Constitution, 31–33, 38
Contempt of court laws, 31
Convention for the Elimination of All Forms of Discrimination against Women (CEDAW), 131–132
Counseling services, 72, 88; online, 71
Court of Appeal, 32–33, 135
Covert resistance, 15, 17, 138, 147
Criminalization of homosexuality, ix, 37–39, 109–110, 134, 151, 187n5; efforts to decriminalize homosexuality, 54, 154; impact of, on behavior, 89. *See also* Repeal 377A
Cruising grounds, 37, 48, 53, 136. *See also* Hong Lim Park
Cultural resonance, 10–11
Cyber organizing: as tactical adjustment, 64–65, 76–77; as tool for expansion and diversification, 65–70

Daughters of Bilitis, 8
DeGeneres, Ellen, 39
Development of gay movement. *See* Gay movement in Singapore, development of
Devi (interviewee), 134, 142

Entrapment by police, 8, 53–54, 55, 104, 192n13
Escalation of tactics, 52–53
Ethnicity, perceptions of within the movement, 43
Eu-Jin (interviewee), 121

Fabian (interviewee), 107–108
Facebook. *See* Social media
Family and Friends, 104–105
Fong, Otto, 41, 54
Frank (interviewee), 68
Free-to-Air Television Programme Code, 39
Fringe Center, 50, 51, 56, 73, 91–92

Gay activism, 154, 160; and AWARE, 132; growth of, 65, 66, 77, 124–125; public awareness of, 82, 97; and religion, 185; state attitudes toward, 89, 95–97

Gay Christians. *See* Christian Fellowship; Christianity, role of; Christian Right; Christians in Singapore
Gay culture, changes in, 47–48
Gay movement in Singapore, development of: early period, 47–52; and incremental change, 22–25; and tactical escalation, expansion, and diversification, 23–24, 52–53, 85, 103, 104–105, 118. *See also* Coming out; Internet; Opening of political and media spaces
Gay movements: in the United States, 8–9, 11; worldwide spread of, 9–10, 11
Gay organizing under authoritarian rule, 7–11, 15–16, 149–150. *See also* Political norms affecting gay organizing
Gay pride festival, 99–102
Gillian (interviewee), 52, 62, 64, 66, 100
Goh Chok Tong, 47, 90–91
Government agencies, attitudes of, 41
Guide to Your Legal Rights (pamphlet), 51

Harbor, 52, 62, 67
Harriet (interviewee), 72
HDB (Housing Development Board), 38
HIV/AIDs organizations, 46, 49, 50, 53, 86, 88
Hong Lim Park, 48; assembly restrictions in, 80, 99, 119, 128, 140, 152; and Pink Dot, 120–122, 128
Housing Development Board (HDB), 38

Ideological issues, 49
Internal Security Act (ISA), 28, 31
Internal Security Department, 55
International legitimacy, 21–22, 85–86
Internet: and expansion and diversification of the movement, 65–70; as tool of pragmatic resistance, 70–75
Intramovement relations, 18–19
ISA (Internal Security Act), 28, 31

Jackson on a Jaunt (play), 48
Jemaah Islamiyah, 31
Jointly and Severably (play), 81
Judiciary, 32–33

Kang (interviewee), 43–44, 52, 62, 67, 163
Keenan (interviewee), 1–3, 20, 32, 47, 48, 51, 54, 62
Kurt (interviewee), 125, 130

Lacey (interviewee), 66, 87, 92, 100, 151
Law and enforcement of political norms, 29

Law and legal procedures as tools of repression, 14–15, 31
Law and society, 15–16
Lawrence v. Texas (U.S. Supreme Court, 2003), 9
Law Society, 30, 46
Le Bistro (gay club), 47
Lee Hsien Loong, 34, 85, 99, 114, 117, 119
Lee Kuan Yew, 80
Legal conditions of gays and lesbians, 37–39, 57–58
Legalized discrimination, 37–39; using Section 354, 38; using Section 377A, 37
Legal legitimacy, 21, 35–36, 56–58
Legal Profession Act, 30
Lesbian activism, 8, 9, 10; in Singapore, 48, 49, 52–53, 62, 66–67
Lesbian response to male-centered movement, 18, 52–53, 66
Lesbian social spaces in Singapore, 40, 47, 48, 53
Liam (interviewee), 69
Li-Ling (artist/activist), 50, 53, 62, 66, 100
Lim Meng Suang and Kenneth Chee Mun-Leon v. Attorney-General, 135, 144, 189n19, 195n15
Loh, Justice Quentin, 135
Loke (interviewee), 16, 90, 91

Mabel (interviewee), 39, 42–43
Maintenance of Religious Harmony Act, 30, 47
Manisha (interviewee), 94
Mardi Gras (play), 81
Mattachine Society, 8, 188n10
Media (news and entertainment): managing exposure, 56–57; protest against, 191n11; reports by, on Repeal 377A, 113–114; representation of, 71–72, 96, 114, 136, 192n13; state control of, 31, 39, 56–57, 151; use of, 84, 93. *See also* Opening of political and media spaces; Social media
Mergers and Acquisitions (play), 54. *See also* Wong, Eleanor (playwright)
Ministry of Community Development, 48
Ministry of Education, 124–125
Ministry of Health, 109
Ministry of Home Affairs, 60, 109–110, 140
Mitchell (interviewee), 50, 51
Morris (interviewee), 20, 110, 113, 115, 120–121
Mother's Day forum 2006, 104, 123

Newsletters, 48, 51, 52. *See also* Coalition: newsletter by
Newspaper and Printing Presses Act, 31
Niche (gay disco), 48, 191n10
Nina (interviewee), 32, 90, 104–105
Nondiscrimination right, 151, 165

Oliver (interviewee), 47–59 passim, 74, 83, 84, 91, 102, 106, 108, 167
Open Church, 67, 69, 86–88, 95, 110; concerts organized by, 96, 109; and registration as a company, 89–90
Opening of political and media spaces, 24, 25, 79, 84–85
Opposition parties, 31

PAP. *See* People's Action Party (PAP)
Parker (interviewee), 110, 113, 115, 134
Parliament (Singapore), 31–32, 99, 159, 193–194n7; loss of seats in, 46; and Repeal 377A petition, 109–115, 116, 123
Party monopoly as a political norm, 29, 33, 31–32, 33–37
Pebble Bar (gay club), 47
People's Action Party (PAP), 4, 27–28, 45–46, 108, 109, 125, 135, 136, 139, 152, 154, 166, 189n18, 190n11, 194n5; attitudes of, 84; and informal tolerance versus intolerant policy, 24, 79, 95, 110, 113, 116–119 passim; response of, to activists, 136; self-image and legitimacy of, 21, 75, 85; and women's movement, 29. *See also* Party monopoly as a political norm; Rule of law
Perceptions of homosexuality: by ethnicity, 42, 43; in families, 42; by religion, 42, 43
Percy (interviewee), 40, 81, 86, 94, 104
Pink Dot, 118–130, 131, 139, 152, 154, 158, 166
Pink Picnic, 106–107
Pink Run, 106–107, 193n4 (chap. 6)
Playwrights, 48
Police raids, 1, 24, 48, 50, 53
Political norms affecting gay organizing, 33–37. *See also* Legal legitimacy; Party monopoly as a political norm; People's Action Party (PAP)
Portal, 70, 89, 90, 96–97, 110, 121
Pragmatic resistance: definition of, x; examples of, 49, 56, 57–58, 61, 81, 91, 105–106, 116, 119–122, 122–125; implications of, 136–144, 163–168; and the Internet, 65–66, 70–75; strategy of, 16–19; tactics of, 19–22, 57, 74, 103. *See also* Covert resistance

Press, role of. *See* Media (news and entertainment)
Prime minister, 47, 60, 61
"Privatizing" events as a tactic, 73
Public assemblies, 30, 99; definition of, 193n4 (chap. 6); public wariness of, 127–128
Public Order Act, 30, 140, 151, 154, 189n8, 193n4 (chap. 6)
Pushing boundaries versus toeing the line, 20–21, 138, 178

Queer Women's Alliance, 67, 88, 94, 124, 131
Quentin (interviewee), 46, 47, 49–59 passim, 73, 74, 81, 82

Race riots of the 1960s, 28, 189n2
Rahim (interviewee), 42, 138
Rani (interviewee), 72
Rascals (incident), 1–3; as analogous to Stonewall, 3, 20, 167–168; impact of, 50–51, 138
Registrar of Companies, 59, 89
Registrar of Societies, 30, 92, 93
"Reparative therapy," Christian, 43, 52, 60, 68, 115; influence of, on cell form of gay organization, 66, 69, 88
Repeal 377A, 105, 106, 111; debate about, in Parliament, 114
Repression by state: relaxation of, 47; renewal of, in 1980s, 46
Resource Central, 73, 86–87, 88, 92, 105, 127
Ricky (interviewee), 29, 34–35
"Rightful resistance," 16–19
Rights: meaning of, 6, 13; in scholarship, 12–14
Rights of access to courts and judicial review, 32–33
Rights of association and assembly, 30
Rights of life and liberty, 31
Rights of political access and representation, 31–32
Rights of speech and press, 30
Rigor Mortis (play), 48
Robbie (interviewee), 41–42
Rule of law: invoked in gay movement, 62; Singaporean interpretations of, 4, 14, 29, 35, 36, 135

Sa'at, Alfian (playwright), 81, 111
Sadasivan, Dr. Balaji, 95, 96, 109
Section 354, 38, 54
Section 377A of the Penal Code, ix, 2, 24, 32, 110, 135, 136, 140, 167, 190n19, 196, 199; definition of, 37; efforts to repeal, 4, 90, 119, 120, 153, 167, 189n19, 195n18; enforcement of, 139; and nondiscrimination right, 151, 165; in Penal Code revision debates, 114–115. *See also* Repeal 377A
Sedition Act, 30, 152
Seow, Francis, 31, 46
Shelly (interviewee), 56, 71, 162
Singapore Lesbians Online, 65–66, 77, 92
Singapore 21 Vision, 82
Si-Yuan (interviewee), 50, 51, 62
Social acceptance, 40–44; in families, 42–43; in government agencies, 41; in military, 41–42
Social conditions (for gays and lesbians), 37, 39; opening of, 24, 47
Social harmony. *See* Social stability
Social justice programs, 46, 50
Social media, 70–71, 75, 126
Social stability: as a movement political tactic or norm, 20–21, 34–35, 116, 118, 159; in PAP ideology, 29, 34, 35
Societies Act, 30, 61, 95, 152, 177
Speakers' Corner, 80
Speech, freedom of: in Hong Lim Park, 80, 99, 128, 140, 152; interpretations of, 157; legislation on, 99; and licensing, 73, 119, 139, 140; limitations to, in Singapore, 4, 29, 30–31, 32; movement subversion of speech laws, 70, 73–74, 81, 100; role of, in 2005 pride festival, 101–102. *See also* Media (news and entertainment)
Sports Club, 69, 91
State policy, 89–90
Stella (interviewee), ix, 32, 65–66, 72, 77, 87, 91, 100, 104, 105, 113–114, 123, 167–168
Stonewall uprising analogy, 1, 3, 8, 20, 146, 150
Straits Times, 84, 90, 93
Strategic adaptation, 4–5, 7–11, 16–19, 44, 143, 148
Street protests, 33
Supreme Court (Singapore), 99, 193n1
Surveillance by state, 41, 53–56, 76–77, 129, 141; impact of, 62, 76–77, 142; responses to, 57, 77, 102–109
Sutra Fellowship, 69

Taariq (interviewee), 77
Tai (interviewee), 69, 87–88, 107, 163
Talklist, 64–70, 74, 76
Tan Boon Hock (1994), 54–55
Tan Eng Hong v. Attorney-General (2013), 135, 144, 195n15

"Tanjung Rhu arrests," 53–54, 58, 103, 104
Tanjung Rhu-Fort Road, 48, 53
Ten Little Indians (play), 48
Theaters, role of, 39, 46; in gay activism, 48, 54, 80, 81, 126, 193n8
Thio Li-Ann, 115–116, 123
Thio Su-Mien, 91, 116, 123
Thompson, E. P., 164
"302 policy" in the military, 38–39; evaluation of status of, 39
Toeing the line, 20–21, 138, 178
Tony (interviewee), 59
Trade unions, 31
Treetops (gay club), 47
Trey (interviewee), 43, 52–64 passim, 75–84 passim, 91, 93, 106, 107, 122, 157; support groups of, 67, 68–69
Twitter. *See* Social media

United Nations, 86, 104, 131–132, 133

Vincent (interviewee), 77, 99–100
Violence, 40

Viraj (interviewee), 46, 47, 50, 54, 62
Virtual Sister, 71–72, 88

Warren (interviewee), 103, 105
Wills and Secessions (play), 54. *See also* Wong, Eleanor (playwright)
Winston (interviewee), 106, 120–121
Women's Charter, 29, 189n4
Women's movement in Singapore, 29. *See also* AWARE (Association of Women for Action and Research)
Women's World, 66, 68, 73, 92, 123
Wong, Eleanor (playwright), 48, 54, 81, 191n7
Workplace attitudes, 40

Xavier (interviewee), 68, 69, 87, 88, 123

Yen Fang (interviewee), 66, 68, 103
Yong, Chief Justice, 54–55
Youth Support, 105, 127
Yvette (interviewee), 15, 105

Zac (interviewee), 111, 115

Lynette J. Chua is Assistant Professor of Law at the National University of Singapore.